Presidential Leadership in Public Opinion
Causes and Consequences

Although presidents may have a difficult time actually leading the public and Congress, voters still desire strong leadership from their commander in chief. In *Presidential Leadership in Public Opinion,* Jeffrey E. Cohen argues that the perception of presidential leadership in American politics is affected not so much by what presidents accomplish but by whether voters think their president is a good leader. When assessing whether a president is a good leader, voters ask two questions: Does the president represent me and the nation? And, is the president strong? Cohen shows that presidential interactions with Congress affect voter perceptions of presidential representation and strength. These perceptions have important implications for public attitudes about American politics. They affect presidential approval ratings, the performance of candidates in presidential elections, attitudes toward Congress, and trust in government. Perceptions of presidential leadership qualities have implications not only for the presidency, but also for the larger political system.

Jeffrey E. Cohen is a professor of political science at Fordham University. Cohen is the author of thirteen other books. His book *Going Local: Presidential Leadership in the Post-Broadcast Age* (Cambridge University Press 2010) won both the 2011 Richard E. Neustadt Award from the Presidency Research Group of the American Political Science Association and the 2012 Goldsmith Award from the Joan Shorenstein Center on the Press, Politics, and Public Policy, John F. Kennedy School of Government, Harvard University. He is the author of more than fifty articles in academic journals such as the *American Political Science Review*, the *American Journal of Political Science*, and the *Journal of Politics*.

Presidential Leadership in Public Opinion

Causes and Consequences

JEFFREY E. COHEN
Fordham University

CAMBRIDGE
UNIVERSITY PRESS

CAMBRIDGE
UNIVERSITY PRESS

32 Avenue of the Americas, New York, NY 10013-2473, USA

Cambridge University Press is part of the University of Cambridge.

It furthers the University's mission by disseminating knowledge in the pursuit of education, learning, and research at the highest international levels of excellence.

www.cambridge.org
Information on this title: www.cambridge.org/9781107443693

© Jeffrey E. Cohen 2015

First published 2015

Printed in the United States of America

A catalog record for this publication is available from the British Library.

Library of Congress Cataloging in Publication Data

Cohen, Jeffrey E.
  Presidential leadership in public opinion : causes and consequences / Jeffrey E. Cohen.
     pages cm
  Includes bibliographical references and index.
  ISBN 978-1-107-08313-4 (hardback)–ISBN 978-1-107-44369-3 (pbk.)
  1. Presidents–United States–Public opinion. 2. United States. Congress–Public opinion. 3. Political leadership–United States. 4. Executive power–United States. 5. Public opinion–United States. I. Title.

  JK516.C52995 2015
  352.23'60973–dc23   2014031411

ISBN 978-1-107-08313-4 Hardback
ISBN 978-1-107-44369-3 Paperback

Contents

Figures

Tables

Acknowledgments

I incurred a large number of debts in writing this book. The idea for this book was planted in 2009, when Michael Hagen and Christopher Wlezien invited me to present some of my research at Temple University. Special thanks go to Chris, who took the extra time to talk to me about statistical methods and, more importantly, theory and encouraged me to continue the line of reasoning I was proposing. In 2012, I presented a more mature version of this research at Yale University, and again I received very helpful comments from the seminar attendees.

Closer to my academic home, my colleagues in the Political Science department at Fordham University provided me with support, encouragement, and, importantly, their ears and time. Three of those colleagues deserve a special thank you: Richard Fleisher, Costas Panagopoulos, and Robert Hume. Bob read several papers that became chapters of this text, providing me with insights on interpretation of the theory and findings. Also at Fordham, I want to thank the university, and its Faculty Fellowship program, which provided me with a semester's leave to finish writing this book. Dean Nancy Busch, Associate Vice President/Chief Research Officer at Fordham, also provided me with additional funding, which allowed me to buy some statistical software that helped me perform some of the analysis presented in these pages.

The anonymous readers of an early version of this manuscript provided me with a mass of useful comments and advice, much of which I followed, leading to an improved and more coherent piece of research and book. I also want to thank my editor at Cambridge University Press, Robert Dreesen. Robert is truly a scholar's editor, and, over the years, he has supported me through several projects, even at the early stages when my ideas were not fully formed or clear. His faith that I could produce worthy research provided important motivation to keep plugging away. I could not ask for better editorial and production staff than those at Cambridge University Press.

Finally, I want to thank my wife, Phyllis, who understands my irregular and at times annoying work habits, and puts up with me with grace and humor.

The Many Meanings of Presidential Leadership

THE UBIQUITY OF PRESIDENTIAL LEADERSHIP IN AMERICAN POLITICS

Leadership is an important standard by which presidents and presidential candidates are judged. For example, one voter had this to say about trying to decide whom to vote for in the 2012 presidential election: "What I look for in a candidate . . . Mostly, I want someone that I trust as a leader" (Appelbaum, March 17, 2012). Richard Wirthlin, who has conducted polls and provided advise for Republican presidential candidates, once asserted that "the single most important value of the American public is respect for strong presidential leadership" (Moore 1995, p. 205).

Candidates for the office recognize the importance of leadership to voters in selecting a president. The competing candidates routinely try to convince voters that they will do a better job of providing leadership than their opponent. A major theme of the challengers is that the incumbent does not provide strong leadership, that the incumbent is weak, and that they, the challengers, will do a better job of leading. For instance, during the 2012 presidential election campaign, Mitt Romney, the Republican nominee, continually criticized President Obama for his "appalling lack of leadership" (Memmott, April 4, 2012). On October 22, 2012, during the nationally televised presidential debate in Boca Raton, Florida, Romney stated that "what we need to do with respect to the Middle East is strong, steady leadership, not wrong and reckless leadership that is all over the map."[1] Although it may be uncomfortable for candidates to tout their leadership qualities, as opposed to attacking their opponents, their allies are often not so reticent in extolling those traits. Romney's vice presidential running mate, Paul Ryan, at the vice presidential

---

[1] The text of the debate can be found at the American Presidency Project site, http://www.presidency.ucsb.edu/ws/index.php?pid=102344, accessed January 4, 2014.

debate with Joseph Biden, illustrated Romney's ability to work with others and overcome the high level of partisanship in current politics by pointing to Romney's stint as governor. "Mitt Romney was governor of Massachusetts, where 87 percent of the legislators he served, which were Democrats. He didn't demonize them. He didn't demagogue them. He met with those party leaders every week. He reached across the aisle." And later, "Mitt Romney is uniquely qualified to fix these problems. His lifetime of experience, his proven track record of bipartisanship."[2]

In contrast, incumbents seeking reelection will tout their leadership bona fides. At the presidential debate in Boca Raton, President Obama offered several examples of his leadership, usually emphasizing policy accomplishment: "Under my leadership, what we've done is reformed education, working with Governors, 46 States. We've seen progress and gains in schools that were having a terrible time, and they're starting to finally make progress." In that same debate, the president defended his administration's actions in Libya, saying that, "Now, keep in mind that I and Americans took leadership in organizing an international coalition that made sure that we were able to – without putting troops on the ground, at the cost of less than what we spent in 2 weeks in Iraq." Presidential allies and supporters also praise the president's leadership. Secretary of State Hilary Clinton, for example, defended President Obama, claiming he demonstrated "smart leadership" on the Libyan crisis during fall 2011.[3] And these presidential allies will criticize opponents of the president, as Biden did at the vice presidential debate. Referring to Mitt Romney's actions with regard to the attack on the U.S. embassy in Libya, Biden criticized Romney, saying, "even before we knew what happened to the ambassador, the governor was holding a press conference – was holding a press conference. That's not presidential leadership."

John G. Geer's data on presidential election campaigns provide us with systematic evidence on the frequency that the competing candidates for the office talk about leadership. Of 732 criticisms by candidates of their opponents' traits in presidential contests from 1960–96, 45 percent (332) mention leadership, while candidates proclaimed their positive leadership traits in 17 percent of 1,345 mentions of their traits in television ads.[4] Leadership is a

---

2 American Presidency Project, http://www.presidency.ucsb.edu/ws/index.php?pid=102322, accessed January 4, 2014.

3 An NBC interview with Clinton, when she makes this claim, is posted on YouTube, http://www.youtube.com/watch?v=dwFmWAdTVBQ, October 24, 2011.

4 These data come from John G. Geer's data set on 757 TV ads in presidential campaigns. I thank him for making these data available. To calculate these figures, I coded positive leadership traits as "leadership" (code 29), "strong/forceful" (coded 35), and "strong/good leader" (code 36). Negative leadership traits are "old/bad/weak leadership" (code 129), "weak leader" (code 135), and "weak, not tough" (code 136). Overall, there are 99 positive trait codes and 99 negative ones. Each ad was coded for up to 20 trait mentions. See Geer (2006) for a full discussion of themes in presidential campaigns.

common theme in presidential election campaigns and is perhaps the dominant charge by candidates for the office against their opponents. Presumably,
candidates for the office would not raise the leadership theme if it did not
resonate with voters.

Like the candidates for office, journalists too commonly evaluate the quality of a president's leadership, both during election campaigns and while a
president is serving in office. Journalists and pundits often cite lack of leadership as a primary reason that a president failed. Consider these examples,
in which usually friendly journalists criticized Barack Obama for his lack of
leadership. In summer 2010, controversy erupted over building a Moslem
mosque in lower Manhattan, New York, just blocks away from Ground Zero,
the site of the September 11, 2001, terrorist attack. President Obama appeared
to waffle on the mosque controversy, backtracking from a statement made on
August 13, 2010, in which he supported building the mosque at that location
as an expression of freedom of religion. The president's position was criticized
in some circles, leading Obama to "clarify" his statements by saying that he
was not commenting on the wisdom of the proposed location for the mosque.
His clarification led the often-supportive *Washington Post* to title an editorial, "President Obama Needs to Show Strong Leadership on the Mosque
Debate."[5] Apparently to the *Post* editorial writers, presidential clarification
in this instance equaled backtracking and caving into critics. Strong leaders,
the editorial implied, should stand their ground in the face of public criticism,
especially when constitutional rights are at issue.

In a second incident, President Obama again was criticized from another
usually friendly source for failing to demonstrate strong leadership – this time
the issue concerned the federal budget deficit. *The New York Times* chided
the president on November 20, 2010, in an editorial concerning the release of
the Bowles Commission's report on the federal budget deficit. Notably in this
case, the Bowles Commission had been set up by the president, and there were
expectations that the president would follow its recommendations. Shortly after
the report was made public, members of Congress from both parties panned
aspects of the deficit reduction plan that the Commission recommended. The
Times editorial writers were troubled in particular by President Obama's "dis-
turbing silence on his commission's efforts," arguing that, "There is no way to
reduce the deficit without strong leadership from President Obama."[6]

Finally, as a third example, Maureen Dowd, *New York Times* columnist,
chided President Obama for not demonstrating enough leadership on the
gun control issue in the aftermath of the Newtown shootings. The Newtown
shootings, where 20 elementary school children and six school staffers were

---

5 http://www.washingtonpost.com/wp-dyn/content/article/2010/08/16/AR2010081604600.
   html accessed July 4, 2011.
6 http://www.nytimes.com/2010/11/21/opinion/21sun1.html?scp=1&sq=important%20presi
   dent%20strong%20leadership&st=cse, accessed July 4, 2011.

killed, occurred on December 14, 2012. In response to that tragedy, President Obama made gun control a signature issue in his State of the Union Address on February 13, 2013, and assigned Vice President Biden the task of lobbying Congress in the president's name for gun control legislation. But the administration's efforts failed on votes taken on April 17, 2013, because the Senate could not garner enough support to stop an eventual filibuster on gun control. Then columnist Dowd weighed in, blaming the president's lack of leadership for the failed Senate vote, even though strong public majorities supported increased gun regulations: "Unfortunately, he [President Obama] still has not learned how to govern . . . It's because he doesn't know how to work the system . . . Couldn't he [President Obama] have come to the Hill himself to lobby with the families [from Newtown] . . . Obama should have called Senator Heidi Heitkamp of North Dakota over to the Oval Office and put on the squeeze . . . Obama hates selling"(Dowd, April 20, 2013).

To give a more systematic sense of the importance of presidential leadership in the news, I conducted a search of the ProQuest National Newspaper Premier database and found "leadership w/5 Obama" mentioned 2,992 times from 2009 through 2013, about 1.5 times per day.[7] Presidential leadership is a major topic of news about the presidency. Academics, too, have invested considerable energy to the topic of presidential leadership. A search in JSTOR for the terms "presiden*"and "leadership" in the article's title or abstract for six journals from 1970–2010 recovered 131 article hits.[8]

Presidential leadership is thus a common topic for voters, candidates for the office, sitting presidents, journalists, and academics. Yet it is not clear what voters, candidates, journalists, and even academics mean when they use the term "presidential leadership." This is a book about *perceptions of presidential leadership*. I focus specifically on voters' perceptions of whether presidents in office offer good and/or effective leadership. This is a narrower take on presidential leadership than is often found in the literature. But this comparative narrowness has its virtues. It allows me to be more specific and precise about this one aspect of presidential leadership – voter perceptions – and, thus, to study these voter perceptions empirically. In this study, I ask three questions that are amenable to empirical scrutiny:

What do voters mean when they say a president is a good and/or effective leader?
What affects voters' assessment of the quality of presidential leadership?
What are the consequences for the president and the political system when voters think a president is a good leader or not a good leader?

---

7 The ProQuest National Newspaper Premier database consists of the largest 42 daily newspapers in the United States. One limitation of this search is that it cannot determine whether "leadership" refers to the president or not without reading the text of each article.

8 The *American Political Science Review*, the *Midwest/American Journal of Political Science*, the *Journal of Politics*, the *Western Political Quarterly/Political Research Quarterly*, *Polity*, and *Presidential Studies Quarterly*.

Furthermore, even though I have narrowed my empirical concerns to voters' perceptions of presidential leadership, these perceptions are quite important to both the presidency and American politics more generally.

Despite the volume of research on presidential leadership, we lack solid answers to the preceding questions. First there is considerable debate, confusion, and ambiguity over the definition of presidential leadership. This chapter reviews the literature on presidential leadership and tries to clarify the issues involved in conceptually defining presidential leadership. The intention here is not to settle on one definition of presidential leadership. Doing so is impossible because presidential leadership is a complex concept with several dimensions and levels (Goertz 2006). Yet by conceptually clarifying presidential leadership, it is easier to make sense of existing research on presidential leadership and provide a roadmap for future studies.

The conceptual clarification exercise enables us to address the first question: What is the basis of voter perceptions that a president is a good or bad leader? Briefly, voters perceive that a president is a good leader when that president is both strong and representative. With this definition in hand, we can then begin to address the second question: Where do these perceptions of presidential leadership come from; that is, what leads voters to view a president as strong and/or representative? News reporting on the president is the most important source of information for voters' perceptions of a president's leadership qualities.[9] As a research strategy, content analyzing news coverage on the president is overwhelming, due to the massive volume of such news. Thus, I take a different tack, looking at one type of presidential behavior that should be important to voter perceptions of presidential leadership and that the news media cover in enough quantity to inform those voter perceptions – presidential interactions with Congress.

Then I turn to the "so what" question: Does it matter for presidents and American politics whether voters think the president is a good leader or not? I show that voters' assessments or perceptions of presidential leadership affect presidential approval, presidential election outcomes, approval of Congress as an institution and its members, and, finally, trust in the political system. Public assessments of a president's leadership have rippling effects throughout the political system. Whether voters think the president is a good leader or not is consequential for American politics and policy making.

WHAT IS PRESIDENTIAL LEADERSHIP?

What is presidential leadership? No consensus currently exists on how best to define the term. With regard to presidency research in particular, Waterman and Rockman (2008), in a chapter titled, "What is presidential leadership?"

---

9 Not everyone attends to news about the president. These nonattentive individuals may learn about the president's leadership qualities through conversations with family members, friends, and co-workers, who may pay more attention to the news. On this indirect path of news coverage see Cohen (2010a, ch. 8).

say: "Before we can analyze the determinants of presidential leadership, it is . . . important to answer a basic question: what do we mean by the term presidential leadership?" (p. 1). But, they conclude, "a precise definition of the characteristics of presidential leadership has yet to emerge" (p. 8). In part, they arrive at this conclusion because presidential leadership is a complex concept, with several dimensions and levels.

Even the vast literature on leadership in general cannot agree on how to define *leadership*. For instance, Bass and Bass's (2008) comprehensive *Handbook of Leadership* lists 13 definitions of leadership used in the literature. Two of these are familiar to presidency scholars and political scientists: leadership as the exercise of influence and leadership as a form of persuasion, the latter most notably associated with Richard Neustadt (1960, 1991).[10] Leadership scholar Keith Grint, in reviewing the field, organizes leadership into four categories – position based, person based, results based, and process based (2010). According to Grint, there is no consensus on what leadership is, but he finds there is one crucial characteristic common to all leaders – one cannot be a leader without followers (p. 2).

THE MULTIDIMENSIONAL, MULTILEVEL NATURE
OF PRESIDENTIAL LEADERSHIP

Without an agreed-upon, or even clear, definition of presidential leadership, it is useful to spend some time developing and specifying a conceptual definition for presidential leadership. *Concepts* identify the essential elements and characteristics of phenomena (Goertz 2006, p. 5) and thus provide direction for specifying hypotheses, developing operational measures, and deciding where and how to study the concept. For instance, we study presidential leadership because we assume that it is intrinsically important, but we need to be able to specify when and why it is important, not merely assert or assume its importance. To specify when, why, and under what conditions presidential leadership is important, however, we must have some sense of what it is. This is no easy task because of the multidimensional, multilevel nature of presidential leadership. Scholars of presidential leadership may use the term "leadership" in different ways, with different meanings, and studies of presidential leadership are not always as conceptually clear as they might be. This may lead to studies talking past each other and, perhaps more

---

10 Ahlquist and Levi (2011) offer an extensive review of the political science, economics, and management literatures on leadership. Other than Canes-Wrone (2006) and Canes-Wrone and Shotts (2004), Ahlquist and Levi do not cite the voluminous literature on presidential leadership or even discuss presidential leadership as a topic. Their interest in leadership is more abstract and theoretical, dealing especially with problems of the relationship between leaders and followers, game theory explorations of that relationship, and whether leader emergence may be endogenous, for instance, when group members select their leader.

importantly, not recognizing the differences in what a particular study means by presidential leadership.

These issues in the concept of presidential leadership are not unusual for broad concepts in the social sciences. Gary Goertz (2006) provides a framework for dealing with broad concepts in the social sciences, such as democracy and leadership. There are three levels in Goertz's framework. The top, or basic level, provides the most general definition of a concept, identifying what it is and what it is not. In Goertz's formulation, there are three aspects of the basic level: a positive pole, a negative pole, and substantive content between the two poles (pp. 30–31). The positive pole tells us what the concept is, while the negative pole tells us what the concept is not. According to Goertz, the negative pole is the "negation of the positive: it has no theoretical existence" (p. 32). Once having identified the two poles, one can then specify the "gray zone" between and determine if that zone is continuous or dichotomous. For instance, with regard to leadership, it may be worthwhile to identify the positive pole with the "leader" and the negative pole with "follower." The multidimensional character of a concept appears at the second level, while the third level specifies indicators and operational measures. There may be several operational indicators for each secondary level dimension (Goertz, p. 7).

In conceptually defining *presidential leadership*, I draw on Bass and Bass's (2008) definition of leadership. As noted, in reviewing the literature on leadership, Bass and Bass identify a multitude of definitions used by leadership scholars. They partially bemoan this plethora of definitions, stating that, "Until an 'academy of leadership' establishes an accepted standard definition, we must continue to live with both broad and narrow definitions, making sure we understand which kind is used in any particular analysis" (p. 25). The "broad and narrow definitions" of leadership that Bass and Bass cite reflect Goertz's different conceptual levels. Some of the confusion and definitional contention among leadership scholars, including those who study presidential leadership, may be sorted out by applying Goertz's conceptual levels model. My aim is not to adjudicate or select the best definition of presidential leadership, but to demonstrate the multilevel and multidimensional nature of leadership – and presidential leadership – as concepts.

Despite calling the effort to define leadership "fruitless" (p. 23), Bass and Bass offer a useful, basic level definition of leadership, which like so many broad concepts is actually quite complex and multifaceted:

"Leadership is an interaction between two or more members of a group that often involves a structuring or restructuring of the situation and of the perceptions and expectations of the members. Leaders are agents of change, whose acts affect the people more than other people's acts affect them. Leadership occurs when one group member modifies the motivation or competencies of others in the group. Leadership can be conceived as directing the attention of other members to goals and the paths to achieve them. . . . [A]ny member of the group can exhibit some degree of leadership, and the members will vary in this regard." (p. 25)

With minor modifications, the preceding also provides us with a basic, top-level, definition of presidential leadership. We can replace "leadership" with "presidential leadership" and "leader" with "president." In place of the generic term "group," we can identify particular groups of importance to the president – for example, Congress, voters, leaders of other nations, cabinet secretaries, and bureaucrats, among others. It is also useful to point out from this definition that leadership is about the relationship between leaders and followers (e.g., group members) and that leadership has both behavioral and perceptual dimensions.

This definition suggests there are at least two dimensions of presidential leadership, the behavioral and perceptual. Let's define *behavioral presidential leadership* as the actions that presidents take to alter or change the behavior and/or opinions of others (e.g., members of Congress, voters, etc.) in the direction desired by the president. There are two elements to behavioral presidential leadership thus defined: (1) a president's actions and (2) the outcome of those actions, which is sometimes termed "presidential power" (e.g., Neustadt 1960, 1991) or "presidential influence" (e.g., Edwards 1997).

For instance, one presidential activity that has received considerable research attention is "going public" (Kernell 2007), or public rhetoric such as speeches, that presidents use to try to alter public opinion.[11] Behavioral presidential leadership of Congress has also received a lot of research attention, with attention to such presidential activities as going public, bargaining, doing favors, etc.[12] *Effective behavioral presidential leadership* exists when a president alters the behaviors and/or opinions of others. In a series of studies having major impact on how scholars understand the presidency, George Edwards argues that effective behavioral leadership is problematic for presidents (Edwards 1989, 2003, 2009a, 2012); that is, presidents are rarely able to alter the behavior or opinion of others. Presidential rhetoric often falls "on deaf ears" (2003) or has effects in Congress only "at the margins" (1989; also Bond and Fleisher 1990).[13]

---

11 For a review of the impact of going public on public opinion see Cohen (2010a, pp. 14–17).
12 For an extensive review of this literature see Edwards (2009a, chs. 4 & 5) and Cohen (2010a, pp. 14–17) on whether presidential going public affects success in Congress.
13 Not everyone agrees with Edwards about the limits of effective behavioral presidential leadership. Just taking the literature on the effects of going public on the issue preferences of voters, while Page and Shapiro (1984); Page, Shapiro, and Dempsey (1987); and Wood (2009) generally concur with Edwards' position, several other studies detect presidential going public effects (Cohen and Hamman 2003, 2005; Conover and Sigelman 1982; Druckman and Holmes 2004; Rosen 1973; Sigelman 1980; Sigelman and Conover 1981; Thomas and Sigelman 1984; Wood 2007). A third set of studies takes a more nuanced approach, asking under what conditions going public will move public opinion, for instance, when popularity is high, during the presidential honeymoon, or with major speeches (Cavari 2013; Mondak 1993; Mondak et al. 2004; Rottinghaus 2010; Tedin, Rottinghaus, and Rodgers 2011).

In evaluating behavioral presidential leadership, especially of Congress, we should not confuse presidential influence with success. *Presidential success*, for instance, on congressional roll calls, occurs when the president's side wins on the roll call vote. Influence occurs when a presidential action leads to a change in the (expected) roll call vote of a member of Congress. As Bond and Fleisher (1990, p. 20) state with regard to presidential influence and success in Congress: "Although presidential influence may increase success, the presidents' policy preferences may prevail for reasons that have nothing to do with influence." (Also see Beckmann 2010). For instance, presidents may be successful when their party commands majorities in Congress because presidential co-partisans hold the same policy preferences as the president. Under such conditions, presidents do not have to *act* to *win* (be on the winning side) on a roll call.[14]

Perceptual presidential leadership, the second dimension, can be defined as when the members of a group perceive the president to be a good (effective) leader or not, in other words, that the president possesses the qualities associated with good/effective leadership. Compared to behavioral presidential leadership, there is much less research on perceptions of presidential leadership. The most relevant research to date on perceptions of presidential leadership is that on public expectations of the president (Cronin 1980; Cronin and Genovese 1998; Edwards 1983; Jenkins-Smith, Silva, and Waterman 2005; Kinder et al., 1980; Simon 2009; Waterman, Jenkins-Smith, and Silva 1999; Wayne 1982). As I review and develop more fully later, these idealized expectations for presidents are one element in understanding public perceptions of the leadership of presidents in office. They provide a backdrop against which voters assess actual presidential performance.

There are several important properties or attributes of this definition of perceptions of presidential leadership. First, the voters' perception of presidential leadership is not the same as approving of the president's job in office, although the two are related. This point will become clearer after detailing voters' perceptions of presidential leadership – that is, what they mean when they say a president is a good and/or effective leader. Second, group members other than voters, for instance, legislators, leaders of foreign nations, journalists, etc., also have perceptions of a president's leadership.[15] In this study,

---

14 In fact, a president can rack up a win by jumping on the bandwagon of a bill that appears destined for passage.

15 Elite perceptions of presidential leadership is closely related to Neustadt's (1960, 1991) concept of presidential reputation. To Neustadt, a president's reputation is based on views of other political elites, those with whom the president must bargain in order to achieve his ends (1991, p. 50). Neustadt differentiates reputation from prestige. *Prestige* refers to public perceptions of the president, now commonly measured as popularity or job approval, although Neustadt had a broader conception of prestige. Gleiber, Shull, and Waligoria (1998); Grossman and Kumar (1981, pp. 244–3); and Lockerbie and Borelli (1989) are, to my knowledge, the only empirical studies that attempt to measure of presidential reputation in a systematic fashion.

however, I only look at public or voter perceptions of presidential leadership. The next section builds a theory of public perceptions of presidential leadership.

A THEORY OF PUBLIC PERCEPTIONS OF PRESIDENTIAL LEADERSHIP

A theory of public perceptions of presidential leadership must address at least three questions.

What do voters mean when they say a president is a good leader?
Where do voters' perceptions of presidential leadership come from?
What are the implications of voters' perceptions of presidential leadership
   for the president and the larger political system?

What Voters Mean by Presidential Leadership

First, voters do not have well-thought-out ideas about such complex concepts as leadership and presidential leadership. Thus, when we ask what voters mean when they say a president is a good leader, we are talking about voters' perceptions. Second, there is very little research that bears directly on the question of what voters mean when they use the term *presidential leadership*. Two literatures on public expectations of the president and on presidential approval provide some limited help in addressing this question. The public expectations studies are based on surveys that ask voters whether presidents should possess certain traits (Edwards 1983; Kinder et al. 1980; Jenkins-Smith et al. 2005; Waterman, Jenkins-Smith, and Silva 1999; and Wayne 1982), resulting in an idealized or prototypical image. Often, the lists of traits tend to be quite long and unfocused, in part because journalists designed these surveys.

Still there are several academically based surveys that aim to make sense of the mass of characteristics that voters' desire in a president. In an early such survey, Kinder and colleagues organize public expectations of the president into two sets: personality and performance. The personality sets contains such items as trustworthy, honest, and open-minded, while the performance set lists such items as strong leadership, solving economic problems, and not getting us into unnecessary wars. Waterman, Jenkins-Smith, and Silva (1999) employ a fourfold classification of expectations, or what they call leadership criteria–sound judgment, foreign affairs, ethical standard, and work with Congress. In all these conceptualizations, some aspects of personality and policy are cited as important expectation criteria. Further, and most pertinent to this study, Kinder et al. (1980) and Waterman, Jenkins-Smith, and Silva (1999) find that some expectations for an ideal president affect approval ratings and vote choice.

While the literature on public expectations is small, the literature on presidential approval is massive.[16] Perhaps the most common theme that emerges from that research is the importance of economics on job approval ratings. Numerous studies also find that foreign affairs affects presidential job approval ratings.[17] For present purposes, the important point is that the economy and foreign affairs shape presidential job approval ratings because voters hold the president responsible for these policy domains. Like the expectations literature, policy is an important element in explaining voter job approval of presidents, and policy will become an important theme in my discussion of voters' perception of presidential leadership.

Without much to draw upon on what voters mean when they say a president is a good and/or effective leader, I begin by making an assumption – voters consider a good president to be one who is both *representative* and *strong*. This perspective is useful because it allows us to develop measures of presidential representation and strength and then test hypotheses about what affects voters' perceptions about these aspects of presidential leadership, as well as the consequences of these perceptions on the presidency and American politics more generally.

Conceptually, perceptions of presidential leadership and job approval are not the same, although the two are related and thus correlated. One of the arguments of this study is that there is more to public attitudes toward presidents than job approval ratings and that we can learn much about the presidency and the political system by broadening our conceptualization of public opinion toward presidents. To make this case, I have to demonstrate empirically that factors besides job approval have systematic and substantively important effects on voters' perceptions of presidential leadership. The second related empirical task is to show that leadership perceptions affect the presidency and American politics above and beyond the effects of presidential approval. These are high empirical hurdles, given the importance of job approval in the research literature and in public discourse.

Representation and Presidential Leadership

Because *representation* and *strength* are broad and vague terms, much like *leadership*, it is important to specify in more detail what voters may mean by these terms and how they will be used in this study. This research emphasizes *policy representation* of the president toward voters, cognizant that a president can be a representative in other ways, for instance as a symbol of the nation (Greenstein 1974).[18] Here, policy representation is conceptualized in

---

16 That literature is much too massive to cite here fully. For useful reviews, see Gronke and Newman (2003, 2009).

17 For a recent review of this literature, see Newman and Forcehimes (2010).

18 In contrast, it is hard to think of the president, as an individual in a unitary office, as being descriptively representative.

distance terms, a common approach. Representation declines as policy distance widens, but improves as that distance narrows (Achen 1978; Ansolabehere and Jones 2011).[19]

More than thirty years ago, Weissberg (1978) and Hurley (1982) distinguished between dyadic and collective representation. This distinction may have relevance in studying voters' perceptions of presidential representation (Druckman and Jacobs 2009). As originally conceptualized, *dyadic representation* refers to the representational relationship between a voter as an individual and the voter's legislative representative, while *collective representation* refers to the relationship between a voter and the legislature (i.e., Congress) as whole. To measure dyadic representation, studies typically look at the consistency between the roll call votes that legislators cast and the policy preferences of their constituents. Collective representation compares the actual policies the legislature enacts with the preferences of voters. In his seminal study, Weissberg (1978) demonstrated how a voter may not be represented in a dyadic sense but is collectively represented from Congress as a lawmaking body (also Hurley 1982). Thus, the voter's representative may cast roll calls contrary to the voter's preferences – for instance, taking the liberal side of an issue when the voter holds conservative preferences, but the legislature as a body enacts the conservative policy that the voter prefers. A classic example is the case of southern blacks in the 1960s, whose representatives in Congress opposed the civil rights legislation that they preferred, yet Congress passed that legislation.

Just as Weissberg noted that there may be differences in the realization of dyadic versus collective representation in a legislative setting, there may also be tension between these two forms of representation with regard to the presidency. The basic tension arises because of the special role of the president as a representative in the American political system. As the only leader elected with a national, as opposed to a local, constituency, voters may want the president to represent the nation as a way of counterbalancing local and other special interests, interests that often appear to have extensive influence over legislative decision making.

This idea of the president as the spokesperson for the national interest to counter the hold of local and special interests in Congress is a central theme of Woodrow Wilson's critique of Congress and Wilson's prescribed role for the presidency. To Wilson, the power of localities and special interests in Congress were at their highest in the congressional committees, his observation anticipating the subgovernment theory of policy making that emerged in the mid-twentieth century. Wilson's point was that *committee government* often led Congress to enact policies that served localities and special interests at the

---

19 Sometimes, the widening or narrowing of the policy distance between voters and representatives is termed *responsiveness*. Jones and Baumgartner (2004) also distinguish policy and agenda representation. Agenda representation concerns whether the topics that policy makers deal with correspond to the concerns of voters. This study focuses on policy representation from the president.

expense of the broader, national interest. The task of the president, to Wilson, is to use his position and access to the entire nation to overcome the hold of these interests on congressional policy making.[20] In Wilson's theory, the president should collectively represent the nation, that is, the president is a "representative of no constituency but of the whole people" (Wilson 1908, pp. 67–68).

Similarly, much research on presidential representation focuses on national opinion and the consistency or responsiveness of the president to national opinion, that is, collective representation. Wlezien and Soroka (2007, p. 806) provide the rationale for this perspective: "Presidential responsiveness to public preferences is conceptually quite simple. The president represents a national constituency and is expected to follow national preferences." There is some debate in the empirical literature whether presidents are responsive to national opinion.[21] But as Druckman and Jacobs (2009, pp. 174–176) argue, in studying presidential representation, it may be useful to disaggregate national opinion, asking the question, are presidents more representative and responsive to some types of citizens than others?

For most voters, there is a trade-off between whether the president maximizes their dyadic or collective representation. Dyadic policy distance for each voter can be calculated as the distance between the voter's policy location and the president's. Collective policy distance is the difference between the president's policy location and the median voter's. Presidents maximize collective representation when their policies are located where the median voter stands, minimizing the policy distance between the president and the median voter. When the president takes the same stance as the median voter, only that voter will see no difference between collective and dyadic representation from the president. For all other voters, there will be a difference in the policy distance between collective and dyadic presidential representation.

For some voters, then, collective policy distance to the president will be greater than dyadic policy distance, while for other voters, the reverse will hold. We know very little about how voters factor in dyadic versus collective representation when evaluating presidential representation. Voters may, for instance, weight one form of representation as more important than the other, perhaps even disregarding one of these forms of presidential representation. In other words, how do voters weight the question, "How close is the president to me?" versus "How close is the president to the average American?" How much do voters value a president who is "close to me" versus a president who is "close to the average American"? Assessing the relative contribution of collective and dyadic policy distance to voter evaluations of presidential representation and leadership is, thus, an empirical question, one that is dealt

20 Compare Wilson's two major works, *Committee Government* (1885) with *Constitutional Government* (1908).
21 This debate is thoroughly reviewed in Wood (2009, pp. 19–24); see also Eshbaugh-Soha and Rottinghaus (2013).

with in detail in the analysis that follows. At this point, about all we can say is that both collective and dyadic representation may be important in voter evaluations of presidential representation and leadership.

Strength and Presidential Leadership

Where representation is conceptually rich and complex, and there is a considerable body of work to draw upon, strong leadership is less well developed, both conceptually and empirically. For instance, in their review of the massive literature on leadership, Bass and Bass (2009) never mention or refer to "strong leadership." Among political scientists, only Sinclair (1992) begins to offer a conceptual definition of strong leadership, but for the Speaker of the House, not the president. In her study, "The Emergence of Strong Leadership in the 1980s House of Representatives," Sinclair defines a strong Speaker as one who "is more active and more decisive in organizing the party and the chamber, setting the House agenda and affecting legislative outcomes" (p. 658). In the 1980s, the Speaker accumulated formal, institutional powers, which increased the Speaker's ability to affect the operations and decisions of the House. This perspective on leadership resembles my discussion of presidential leadership, as discussed earlier.[22]

Studies of public opinion on presidency that use the term "strong leadership" mainly reference polls that ask voters to assess whether an idea president should be a "strong leader" or whether the incumbent president is a "strong leader" (e.g., Kinder et al., 1980; Newman and Siegle 2010). No survey to my knowledge asks voters what they mean by strong presidential leadership. The existing literature is thus vague on what strong presidential leadership is and merely tries to assess how important strong presidential leadership is to voters, leaving the definition of strong leadership up to the individual survey respondents.

But if my theory contends that voters value strong leadership, we need to be more specific about what voters might mean when they say a president is a strong leader. Because existing research helps little in addressing this question, I will make some assumptions about how voters define strong presidential leadership. My aim is to derive testable hypotheses from these assumptions about whether voters actually think about presidential leadership in these ways.

Voters may have several ideas in mind when they say a president is strong or weak. First, they may think a president is a strong leader when that president is in front of his followers (e.g., voters, member of Congress, etc.) and the president asks them to follow him, to go along with him. For example, there may be a policy distance between the president and set of followers on an issue, and the president wants to narrow that distance by *having the followers move closer to the president's location, not by having the president move to the*

---

22 Notably, Sinclair's understanding of strong Speakers is a function of the institutional resources provided to the Speaker, not personality traits, as is more common in the presidency literature.

followers' location. Presidents may be viewed as strong when they try to narrow that distance by moving followers closer to the president. Second, voters may say a president exhibits strong leadership when they think the president is resolute, that is, determined, tenacious, and/or not willing to back down. In contrast, a weak president is one who backs down in the face of opposition. To complicate matters with regard to resolve, some voters may view resolve as stubbornness. Third, voters may think a president is a strong leader when he is tough. Presidents may demonstrate this quality when they make "tough" decisions. Tough decisions may be those that impose political costs on presidents, for instance, when strong interests or important segments of the president's party oppose the decision. Fourth, presidents may appear to be strong to voters when they appear to be in control of events, as opposed to being controlled by events (Erikson, MacKuen, and Stimson 2002, pp. 62–65).

Fifth, voters may think a president is strong when he is successful. Because presidents rarely possess command authority,[23] presidents often have to persuade others to get what they want (Neustadt 1960, 1991). A large amount of news coverage on the presidency is about presidential attempts to persuade others. The need to persuade is usually presented in news reports as challenges to the president, where the president will either succeed in his persuasion attempt or not. Journalists also tend to use game and/or contest metaphors as a news frame, but such frames require an outcome, a "win" or a "loss" for the president.[24] Wins reflect positively on presidents and losses reflect negatively. To voters, these presidential wins may mean that others are willing to accede to the president's preferences, that they are willing to follow the president. Thus, voters may view the president as strong when he prevails or wins in persuasion attempts.

All of these ideas are but conjectures at this point (and there may be other ways in which voters think that a president is strong versus weak). Although each of these is worthy of empirical study, this study focuses on the fifth way, presidential success, primarily because there are data that allow empirical analysis.[25]

---

23 Presidents have expanded their unilateral authority, such as executive orders. But executive orders can be reversed by Congress, although they rarely are, in part because presidents anticipate what Congress will allow them to accomplish through such devices (Howell 2003; Mayer 2002).

24 Presidents can realize a partial victory, receiving some of what they aimed for in their persuasion attempt – for instance, by compromising. See Peterson (1990) for use of more nuanced categories than just "win" versus "lose" in his study of presidential success in Congress.

25 There are no data on the first three voter conceptualizations of strength of which I am aware, nor do I have resources at this writing to field a survey to study these various conceptualizations. Erikson and colleagues (2002, pp. 64–7) employ computerized content analysis of media over a 20-year period to locate news items that portray the president as either in control of events or not in control. They find that "in control" stories tend to be associated with higher approval and "not in control" stories with lower approval.

There are numerous arenas in which presidents try to persuade other decision makers to comply with what the president wants. Foreign policy, for instance, occupies a considerable portion of presidential time and effort. Much foreign policy making involves the president and his administration interacting with leaders of other nations – to get foreign adversaries to back down or to negotiate treaties and accords with (prospective) allies.[26] One issue with marking when presidents are successful or not in foreign policy is that there is not necessarily a nonambiguous decision or action on the part of another nation or its leader to look at. Wars, for example, may conclude without a formal treaty or concession by one side or the other concerning who won or lost. And presidential rhetoric may be aimed at deterring the other nation from taking an action. If the other nation does not act, is it because the president deterred the other nation, or is it because the other nation was not likely to have acted anyway? Many domestic encounters are similarly ambiguous in deciding if a president was successful or not.

Due to these types of issues, I turn to presidential success on congressional roll calls. Presidents take sides on many roll calls, and it is easy to judge whether the president was on the winning or losing side. Plus, there are organizations, such as *Congressional Quarterly*, that have been tracking this type of presidential activity since the early 1950s. We can use this type of data to test hypotheses about the relationship between presidential success in Congress and voter perceptions of presidential strength.[27]

Factors Influencing Voters Perceptions of Presidential Leadership

The preceding discussion presents an argument that voters define presidential leadership as representation and strength. Although there are several ways of thinking about representation, such as symbolic and descriptive, this study focuses on policy representation, which is conceptualized and measured as policy distance. It is unclear whether voters prefer dyadic or collective representation from presidents. Voters may also hold several notions for presidential strength: being ahead of followers, resolve, and success, for instance. Due to data limitations, this study will focus on strength as success. But how do voters determine whether a president is representative and strong? What evaluative calculus do they use?

26 Wood (2012) investigates how presidential rhetorical saber rattling may affect the behavior of other nations.

27 An alternative methodology, which is not restricted to one mode of presidential success and which is superior to that used here, would be to content analyze news on the president for whether journalists reported a presidential win or loss. In fact, I am assuming that the news media report faithfully whether a president wins or losses in Congress (as well as other venues), and this type of assessment affects voter perceptions of presidential strength. Perhaps even better would be content analyses of news that portray the president as strong or weak. However, such data collection is far from trivial given the immense volume of reporting on the president and the limitations of computerized analysis of vast quantities of text (Cohen 2008).

In assessing whether a president possesses these leadership qualities, voters compare the president to expectations, or what they want in their idealized picture of presidents. This is not a study of expectations; rather expectations provide a yardstick or backdrop against which voters assess the performance and/or attributes of specific presidents while in office. In making this type of comparison between an ideal and actual president, voters can employ three decision rules: (1) They may project attributes of leadership onto the president, (2) they may think the president innately possesses certain leadership traits, and/or (3) they may evaluate actual presidential performance. These three decision rules are not necessarily exclusive.

First, voters may project leadership traits onto presidents irrespective of whether a president actually possesses or demonstrates that aspect of leadership. A voter's political predispositions may lead to projection about presidential leadership. For instance, Democratic voters may be more likely to view a Democratic president as representative and strong than Republican voters, and the reverse for a Republican president.[28] Voter political predispositions, such as partisanship, may act as a perceptual filter, affecting the type and nature of the information that the voter receives and processes (Goren 2002, 2007; Zaller 1992).

Second, perceptions of presidential leadership may derive from the personal qualities of the president.[29] There are several sources of information for voters about the possible personal characteristics and personality of presidents. For instance, a president's background may affect perceptions of the president as a representative. A president with a more modest background may be thought of as one of the people, as being able to understand and empathize with average people, perhaps as more representative of voters in general than a president whose background is more privileged. Throughout so much of U.S. history, presidents and presidential candidates have tried to convince people of their humble roots – the proverbial "log cabin" myth (Pessen 1984) – in order to create a perception of representativeness. Presidential background may also create an impression of strength and resolve – for instance, if a president overcame adversity, like Franklin Roosevelt's polio.

But presidential personality may also be revealed through his public rhetoric. As one example, psychologist David G. Winter (2002, 2005; Donley

---

28 On the importance of political predispositions on support for presidents and other leaders, see Ladd (2007, 2011); Lebo and Cassino (2007); and Lenz (2013).

29 The notion that presidential traits, such as personality and character, may affect performance in office has a long lineage in presidential studies, dating at least to Barber (1972) and most currently expressed in Greenstein (2012). There is a much smaller literature that looks at the factors that affect public perceptions of presidential traits and the implications of those traits on evaluations of presidents, such as their approval (Greene, 2001; Newman, 2003). One issue with this public opinion literature is endogeneity – that is, whether political predispositions and approval of the president affect public perceptions of presidential personality and character or visa versa.

and Winter 1970) in a series of studies has measured achievement, affiliation, and power motivation personality attributes from the public rhetoric of
presidents.[30] Just because psychologists, using sophisticated techniques, can
measure presidential personality does not imply that voters are also able to do
so, but the theoretical possibility exists that they can, at least to some degree.
Whatever type of information source voters use, they may learn about basic
traits of a president's personality.

Both the projection-predispositions and personal attributes perspectives
suggest that perceptions of presidential leadership will be relatively constant
across a president's term in office. This is because voter predispositions and
presidential personality traits are highly resistant to change across a president's term in office. Inasmuch as these factors affect voter perceptions of
presidential leadership, voters will perceive a president as either a strong and
representative president or not for the duration of the president's tenure in
office. But there is a third source of public perceptions of presidential leadership that is more dynamic within presidencies: real-world events and conditions and how presidents navigate and adjust to these changing circumstances,
what I will call *presidential performance.*

For instance, the international setting is dynamic and may shift from peace-
fulness to belligerence quite swiftly. Consider the impact of the September 11,
2001, terrorist attacks on public perceptions of George W. Bush. Prior to that
date, although still early in his presidency, Bush was viewed as a beleaguered
president, often barely registering majority support. But a few days later, the
public began to view Bush as a strong leader. For instance, on September
7–10, 2001, Gallup reports that George W. Bush had a 51 percent approval
rating. Just days later, on September 14–15, his job approval ratings hit a lofty
86 percent. On June 14–18, 2001, 54 percent of respondents to a CBS News/
New York Times poll said that Bush had "strong qualities of leadership." On
September 13–14, the figure rose to 70 percent, and a week later, on September 20–21, had marched higher to 83 percent, a 30-percentage-point rise in
three months – a remarkable, steep, and rapid alteration of strength perceptions. Similarly, in a July 10–11 Gallup/CNN/*USA Today* poll, 57 percent
thought that Bush cared "about the needs of people like you." In early October (10/4–5/2001), the percentage had risen to 69 percent. Approval of the
president, perceptions of strength, and concern with typical voters (a form of
or aspect of perceptions of representation) can change starkly in a short period
of time, in this case due to an event, the president's behavior during that event,
and how that behavior colors public perceptions of presidential leadership.

Real-world events also may have negative effects on public perceptions of
presidential leadership. The Iranian hostage crisis is a case in point. On November 4, 1979, Iranian students stormed the American embassy in Tehran, Iran,

---

30 See Song and Simonton (2007) for a review of this type of research.

taking 52 Americans hostage and holding them in captivity for 444 days, until January 20, 1981, the day Ronald Reagan was sworn in as president. In the early days of the hostage crisis, the public surged in support of Jimmy Carter, as is typical of rally events.[31]

For instance, in February 1980, three months after taking the hostages, President Carter still commanded plurality support from voters concerning his handling of the crisis. An ABC News/Harris poll of February 7–10, 1980, found that 44 percent of respondents labeled Carter's handling a success compared with 36 percent who labeled it a failure, the other 20 percent having various and noncommittal responses.[32] The same question posed to voters conducted on April 8, 1980, another two months into the crisis, saw a reversal in public perceptions of Carter's handling of the hostage taking, with only 25 percent calling it a success compared to 64 percent who called it a failure.

Carter's approval ratings also showed an initial upsurge in the wake of the hostage crisis. In the few days before the crisis (11/2–5/1979), Gallup reported a 32 percent approval and 55 percent disapproval rating for the president. A few weeks into the crisis (11/16–19/1979), Carter's approval had inched upward to 38 percent approving and 49 percent disapproving. By the end of November 1979 (11/30/1979 to 12/3/1979), Carter's approval ratings had risen steeply to 51 percent, with only 37 percent disapproving. His approval ratings stayed above 50 percent into February 1980 and then began to fall. The lengthening of the crisis accounts for much of the fall in support, which plummeted to 38 percent by mid-April 1980. Carter's approval stayed in the 32–38 percent range through the rest of his presidency.

The impact of the 9/11 terrorist attacks and the Iranian hostage crisis appeared to have a truly remarkable effect on the Bush and Carter presidencies, reinvigorating one and devastating the other. These events also dramatically altered public perceptions of these presidents. But these events also are distinctive. What about more typical and routine events, the everyday stuff of politics? Can they also affect public perceptions of presidential leadership?

Of the many types of events and conditions that may affect public perceptions of presidential leadership, this book focuses on relations with Congress for several reasons. First, interacting with Congress, such as taking a position on an issue, is a common form of presidential behavior, perhaps the most important policy–making activity for presidents. Second, those interactions and their outcome (whether the president wins or loses in Congress) are reported heavily in the news. As a consequence of the amount of news attention that presidential interactions with Congress receive, presidential

---

31 For an analysis of public opinion tides during the hostage crisis, see Callaghan and Virtanen (1993).

32 The wording of the question reads: With the (Iranian) hostages having been held for (number of) months, do you think President Carter's handling of the hostage situation has been a success, or do you think it has been a failure?

interactions with Congress and their outcomes are likely to affect public perceptions of the president and his leadership qualities.

Some Implications of Relations with Congress on Presidential Leadership

If presidents want voters to view their leadership in a positive light, presidents should behave in ways that lead voters to view them as representative and strong. Some types of events and situations may allow the president to exhibit his representation and strength simultaneously, such as during the initial stages of foreign crises. But other situations, in particular interactions with Congress, presidents may have to select being either representative or strong, that is, successful. This is because the factors that promote success in Congress undercut representation.

Party control of Congress is the most important factor conditioning presidential success with the legislature.[33] However, when the president's party controls Congress, the president's policy positions will move away from the center and toward the extremes (Cohen 2011a; Wood 2009). In as much as the median voter is located near the center,[34] then presidents will become less collectively representative when their party controls Congress. Thus, at least with regard to relations with Congress, presidents face a trade-off between strength/success and representation. This perspective suggests that presidents are somewhat constrained in their policy choices in the legislative arena (Jones 2005). Chapter Three develops this notion and provides empirical support for it.

The Implications of Public Perceptions of Leadership

Our third question asks about the implications of public perceptions of presidential leadership. Does it matter whether voters think the president is a good and/or effective leader or not? My theory argues that perceptions of presidential leadership have implications for presidents – and for American politics more generally – *above and beyond the effects of job approval.* This theory starts with the common observation that the president is important to voters, perhaps more important than any other political leader for a large number of voters. Voters generalize their attitude about presidential leadership onto

---

33 For studies that make this point see Barrett and Eshbaugh-Soha (2007); Beckmann (2010); Bond and Fleisher (1990); Cohen (2012, 2013); Cohen, Bond, and Fleisher (2013); Edwards (1989); Lebo and O'Geen (2011); Lee (2009); and Marshall and Prins (2007).

34 There is considerable evidence that even in this age of high party polarization, voters tend to be moderate on issues, and the median voter is located near the center. See Ansolabehere, Rodden, and Snyder (2006); Bafumi and Herron (2010); Fiorina, Abrams, and Pope (2005); and Levendusky, Pope, and Jackman (2008). For an alternative view, see Abramowitz (2010).

other aspects of the presidency, such as job approval and voting in presidential elections, as well as aspects of the larger political system, such as trust in government and attitudes toward Congress.

First, we see the importance of the president to voters in their attention to the president compared with other political leaders. The president is the most visible political actor in people's minds. Nearly the entire adult population can correctly identify the president, but knowledge of other political leaders quickly falls off. Only one-third can name both home state U.S. senators and slightly less than half are able to identify their representative (Delli Carpini and Keeter 1996, pp. 74–75; Greenstein 1974, pp. 121–147). As Greenstein (1974, p. 124) concludes, "[T]he President is . . . the best-known American political leader. For some people, he is the only known political leader, and for others one of the few."

For instance, only 31 percent and 36 percent of respondents could name correctly *at least one candidate* running for the House and Senate, respectively, from the 1978–2004 cumulative data file of the American National Election Studies (ANES), and only about 43 percent and 46 percent of respondents could identify correctly the majority party for the House and Senate. Compared to the modest level of information that voters know about politics and public affairs in general, the public is considerably more aware and knowledgeable about the president, nearly universally so. This comparative visibility leads voters to focus their attention on the president more than other political leaders.

Several factors account for voters' comparative knowledge of and attention to the president. First, the unitary nature of the office makes it easier for people to follow and identify with the president than a collective body like Congress. In watching the actions of the president, the public only has to focus on a single person. Interpreting politics and government from such a viewpoint is easier than trying to make sense of the many personalities of Congress, the different positions that they hold, and the complex rules that govern legislative processes. Second, school textbooks on history, government, and civics are often organized around presidents and their accomplishments (Roberts and Butler 2012; Sanchez 1996). Early in life, children come to see the president as the central figure in the political system. Similarly, the media spend more time covering the president than any other leader, presenting another president-centric portrait of American politics and government (Cohen 2009).

Additionally, voters rely on the president for psychological reassurance, especially in times of stress and uncertainty. We see this in the reactions of people to the sudden death or assassination of presidents in office. Upon learning of the assassination of John F. Kennedy, many people reported feeling distressed and suffered from psychosomatic symptoms, such as stress, unease, sleeplessness, etc. Similar reactions seem to follow each time a president has died in office (Greenstein 1974, pp. 123–124). One of the crucial functions of the president for the average citizen is to provide a sense of security in a hostile and complex political world, to indicate to people that someone is in charge and that critical matters are being taken care of (Edelman 1964, 1974).

Perhaps most important, many voters' employ a presidential frame or heuristic for understanding American politics and policy making (Kuklinski and Quirk 2000; Lau and Redlawsk 2001). Voters use heuristics to organize and make sense of political phenomena. There are two major heuristics that American voters seem to employ – a party heuristic and a presidential heuristic – and the two may overlap, especially in an age of party polarization. When employing the party heuristic, voters will see politics as a contest or differences between Democrats and Republicans. Similarly, the presidency heuristic will organize political phenomena into two competing sets: the president and his allies versus the president's competitors and adversaries.

Through the combination of the importance of the president and the use of the presidential heuristic, voters generalize their attitudes about the president, including perceptions of presidential leadership, onto political phenomena beyond the president in office. The importance that voters attach to the president means that voters heavily weight their evaluations of the president, including perceptions of the executive's leadership. Then, through the presidential heuristic, voters apply their evaluations of presidential leadership onto aspects of the political system besides the presidency, for instance, government in general (e.g., their trust in government) and Congress. Much of the second half of this book is devoted to testing this proposition – *that perceptions of presidential leadership will affect trust in government and attitudes toward Congress.*

PLAN OF THE BOOK

The rest of the chapters in this book are organized around these three questions: How do voters define presidential leadership? What factors affect their perceptions of presidential leadership? And what are the implications of voters' perceptions of presidential leadership for the president and the wider political system?

Chapter Two addresses the first question, the meaning of presidential leadership to voters, asking in particular whether there is a public demand for presidential representation and strength. To that end, I review as many public opinion surveys as I could find that asked voters questions relevant to presidential representation and strength. The existing survey evidence, however limited, indicates that voters want their president to be both representative and strong.

Chapter Three turns to the impact of Congress on presidential position taking and success. This chapter demonstrates that the factors that lead to presidential success in Congress also push the president to take comparatively extreme, as opposed to moderate, policy positions. Thus, presidents, in their dealings with Congress, face a trade-off between policy success and policy moderation. Further, the argument developed in this chapter is that voters use presidential policy positions and success with Congress in assessing whether the president is representative and strong. But for them to do so, there must be sufficient news on presidential–congressional relations. This chapter shows that there is.

Chapter Four turns to the second major question, whether relations with Congress affect voters' perceptions of presidential leadership. To test this linkage requires survey data on voters' assessments of a president's strength and representation, but the necessary survey data only exist for strength, not representation. Thus, this chapter focuses on whether success in Congress affects whether voters think a president is strong versus weak. Results of the analysis indicate such a connection: As presidential success rates rise, voters are more likely to see the president as strong.

Chapter Five turns to the question of presidential representation. Although we lack questions asking voters to rate a president's representational qualities, we can measure the policy distance between voters and the president, with the idea that a smaller policy distance indicates better representation than a wide policy distance. The analysis in this chapter then asks whether policy distance affects presidential job approval ratings. Using a variety of data, the analysis finds that presidential job approval ratings are higher when policy distance is small.

Chapter Six turns to the implications of presidential leadership on the presidency – in particular, presidential elections. The analysis finds that perceptions of presidential leadership affect whether voters like the candidates for the office as well as how they vote in presidential contests. These results hold even when controlling for presidential approval, and the effect of approval on candidate evaluations and vote choice greatly weakens when the leadership variables are used in the analysis. This underscores an important point of this research: that there is more to public evaluation of the president than job approval.

The theory offered here argues that due to the importance of the president to voters, they will generalize their attitudes about the president across the political system. Chapter Seven tests this prediction on trust in government and voter approval of Congress and their individual representative. The analysis shows that perceptions of presidential leadership affect trust and congressional and representative approval, even in the face of controls for presidential job approval ratings. When voters feel better about presidential leadership, they trust their government more and are more likely to approve of Congress as an institution and their representative in Congress.

Chapter Eight reviews the findings, highlighting some of the more important ones, as well as discusses some of the limitations of this research, unanswered questions, and directions for future research. The chapter ends with a discussion of the importance of public perceptions of presidential leadership for American democracy.

Evidence of the Public Demand for Presidential Leadership

The theory outlined in the previous chapter argues that voters define presidential leadership as representation and strength. And in evaluating whether a president is a good and/or effective leader in this sense, voters compare the actual behavior of presidents with an idealized standard. The closer a president comes to fulfilling the voter's expectation concerning representation and strength, the more positive the voter's evaluation will be of the president's leadership. This chapter reviews evidence on the theoretical assumption that voters value representation and strength from presidents, followed by a review of existing evidence relating to the public demand for representation and strength in presidents.

THE PUBLIC DEMAND FOR PRESIDENTIAL REPRESENTATION

There is neither theory nor empirical evidence to tell us whether voters prefer dyadic or collective representation from presidents or how they balance these two representational demands when they conflict. In fact, it is difficult to both design and locate poll questions or studies that have studied this issue.[1] Voters would probably say that they want both types of representation from the president. Yet, as I reviewed above, for many voters, there is a trade-off or tension between collective and dyadic representation from presidents.

In the following sections, I review what I have been able to locate that bears on the trade-off between collective and dyadic representation as it pertains to the president, and little of it is directly on point. First, Kinder et al. (1980), using 1979 survey data, asked respondents a host of questions

---

1 Another issue in studying public preferences for representation from presidents is that the voter may conflate his or her preferences for presidential representation in general with the behavior of the sitting incumbent. See Cohen (2010b) for a fuller discussion of this point.

TABLE 2.1. *Importance of Selected Traits in the President, 2007.*

Trait	Mean[a]	% Very or Strongly Important
Willingness to work with both parties	4.20	84.3
Being decisive	3.79	82.0
Understanding and sympathizing with others	3.36	69.3
Honesty and integrity	4.61	95.9
Ability to communicate well	4.41	90.5
Intelligence	4.45	90.7
Experience in Washington, DC	2.71	43.2
Strong belief in God	2.97	58.3
Having new ideas	3.56	71.4
Being likeable	3.03	39.2
Served in the military	2.31	23.0
Experience in foreign policy	4.07	74.4
Closely agrees on most issues	1.57	32.3
Ability to bring the American people together	3.98	82.1

[a] 1 = not at all important, 5 = extremely important.
Source: National Leadership Index 2007, Center for Public Leadership, John F. Kennedy, School of Government, Harvard University/*U.S News & World Report*, September 4–17, 2007.

regarding desirable traits in presidents. They do not present direct evidence that the public has a preference for representation from presidents, but several of their items relate to the concept of presidential representation. For instance, they find that 46 percent and 31 percent of respondents say it is important that presidents "communicate openly with the public" and "understand the little people," while another 32 percent and 48 percent say it is bad if presidents "become isolated from the people" and "favor special interest groups" (p. 319). Most telling is that the public desires a president who represents the entire nation and not special interests.

The National Leadership Index Poll conducted in 2007 by the Center for Public Leadership, John F. Kennedy School of Government also asked respondents questions relating to presidential representation.[2] That poll asked respondents about 14 traits, several related directly to notions of national, that is, collective representation (Table 2.1). Two items touch on collective representation: A president should be "willing to work with people in both political

2 The JFK School has been polling voters on confidence in leadership since 2005, but only in its 2007 poll did it ask respondents about desirable traits for presidents, asked in context of the upcoming presidential election.

parties," and a president should have the "ability to bring the American people together"; while a third, that the president should "closely agree with you on most political issues," relates to dyadic representation. Respondents clearly preferred the "bipartisan" and "unifying" president: 84.3 percent and 82.1 percent expressed such traits as "very" or "extremely" important. In contrast, dyadic representation was less desirable; only about one-third of respondents thought it "very" or "extremely" important that the president hold the same views on issues, while about one-fifth thought such representation was "not at all" or "slightly" important, and nearly one-half thought such policy representation was moderately important. Respondents preferred policy agreement from the president over disagreement, but national representation was more important to voters than dyadic representation. However, these questions did not ask voters to select a "bipartisan" or "unifying" president over dyadic representation from the president.

In the 2008 Cooperative Congressional Election Study, I asked a small battery of questions aimed at eliciting respondent assessments of several aspects of presidential representation (Cohen 2010b). To minimize respondents merely thinking about George W. Bush, who was in office during the survey administration, I prefaced the module of presidency questions with this statement: "For the next several questions, I would like you to think back on the past several presidents." In contrast to the Kinder et al. (1980) and the National Leadership Index Poll approaches, which asked about ideal presidential behavior, my battery asked about actual presidential performance in recent years. For each of the following questions, I asked respondents whether they strongly agreed, agreed, disagreed, or strongly disagreed; the questions were rotated randomly to avoid question order bias:

1. Presidents are too far removed from ordinary people.
2. Presidents rely too heavily on their staffers and assistants who work in the White House.
3. Presidents pay too much attention to the needs of their political parties.

Each of these questions taps into a different dimension of presidential closeness versus distance from the public, although none explicitly ask about policy representation or the trade-off between dyadic and collective presidential representation. By wide margins, the public appears discontented with the actual level of presidential representation for all items (Table 2.2). Combining the agree and strongly agree responses, more than 70 percent of respondents think that presidents are too removed from the public, slightly more than half think they are too reliant on their staffers, and about three-quarters think presidents are too concerned with the needs of their parties. Taking into account that from 7 to 14 percent of respondents answered "don't know" to these statements, these results suggest a stunning degree of representational discontent with American presidents.

TABLE 2.2. *Attitudes Concerning Presidential Representation, 2008.*

	President Is Too Removed from the Public	President Is Too Reliant on Staffers	President Pays Too Much Attention to Party Needs
Strongly agree	31%	17%	29%
Agree	42	37	45
Don't know	7	14	10
Disagree	18	29	15
Strongly disagree	2	4	1
N	811	810	812

Source: 2008 Cooperative Congressional Election Study, Fordham University Module.

Finally, some surveys asked about presidential behaviors related to the notion of national or collective representation. Table 2.3 presents results from three Pew surveys conducted in 1995, 1999 and 2003. The surveys asked respondents whether they thought it important that a president be "willing to compromise," say "what he believes, even if unpopular," have "consistent positions on issues," and be "loyal to his party." Combined, these items provide some indirect evidence on public preferences for collective versus dyadic representation.

Being willing to compromise may be the essence of policy moderation, while taking consistent policy positions may be a defining characteristic of ideologues. A president cannot simultaneously be willing to compromise but remain consistent on issue positions. Here, we see large majorities wanting a president to do both, with from 62 to 76 percent desiring a president willing to compromise but somewhat larger percentages (77–79 percent) wanting issue consistency. Large majorities, from 74 to 80 percent, also prefer that a president say what he believes, even if it is unpopular. But the public is split over presidential loyalty to his party, with roughly one-half thinking loyalty to party is important and one-half taking the opposite position. The results of these surveys provide some limited evidence that voters desire representation from presidents and may rank collective representation more highly than dyadic representation.

THE PUBLIC DEMAND FOR STRONG PRESIDENTS

Several public opinion polls present results that show the value voters place on strong leadership from presidents. In March and May 1971, then President Richard Nixon commissioned the Opinion Research Corporation (ORC) to poll voters on desirable characteristics for presidents. These polls used a

TABLE 2.3. *Public Preferences for Presidential Characteristics, 1995–2003.*

	1995		1999		2003	
	Important[a]	Unimportant[a]	Important	Unimportant	Important	Unimportant
Willingness to compromise	63	35	62	36	67	31
Saying what one believes, even if unpopular	80	18	78	20	74	22
Having consistent positions on issues	79	19	78	20	77	20
Loyalty to one's party	40	58	47	52	46	52

Question wording: "Next, I'm going to read you a list of personal characteristics or qualities. If '5' represents an absolutely essential quality in a president and '1' a quality that is not too important, where on this scale of 5 to 1 would you rate . . ."

[a] Important is defined as the percentage who answer 4 or 5; Unimportant is defined as the percentage who answer 1, 2, or 3. Important + Unimportant percentages do not add to 100% because of "don't know" responses.

Source: Princeton Research Associates, Pew Research Center (survey dates: November 11, 1995; November 11, 1999; September 9, 2003) (accessed from the Roper Poll Archive).

unique methodology for gauging public preferences. Respondents were given word pairs, like weak/strong, with the negative trait in the pair located at "1" and the positive trait at "7" and were asked to place their ideal president along the seven-category scheme. Obviously, respondents tended to place their ideal president toward the positive pole at 7. Table 2.4 lists some of the responses from the March 1971 survey; results from the May 1971 are nearly identical.

Voters want their president to be predictable over unpredictable, a unifier as opposed to a divider, sensitive rather than insensitive. By larger margins, the public associated their ideal president with presumably strong leadership characteristics, like decisiveness over indecision, strong over weak, leading rather than following, and self-confidence. Specifically, 70 percent placed their ideal president at 7 on leadership, while the percentages tagging 7 as ideal for strength, self-confidence, and decisiveness were 69 percent, 67 percent, and 57 percent respectively. In contrast, 41 percent placed the ideal president at 7 for predictability and 39 percent for sensitivity. Consistent with the argument made in Chapter One, strong leadership may entail a set of related traits and behaviors from presidents.

In a 1996 study, the Media Studies Center found similar preferences for strong leadership in an idealized vision of the president using a different study design. The Media Studies Center asked respondents to indicate how essential it is for an ideal president to possess a certain trait. Table 2.5 presents results of that survey. Combining the "essential" and "very important" categories, 93 percent want presidents to be trustworthy, 94 percent want them to have the ability to get things done, and 94 percent want them to be strong leaders. Somewhat smaller, yet still overwhelmingly large percentages of respondents want their ideal president to be consistent (85 percent), to care about people like themselves (84 percent), perhaps an aspect of representation, and to be patriotic (79 percent).

Other polls similarly find strong leadership highly desirable in a president. A Greenberg Quinlan Rosner poll conducted in August 2008 presented respondents with a list of traits and asked them to name the two most important for a president to possess (see Table 2.6). Strong leadership was the second most frequently mentioned attribute, at 31 percent, behind honesty and trustworthiness (47 percent). Other traits mentioned frequently by respondents included bringing about change (26 percent), sharing values with the voter (22 percent), caring (21 percent), and experience (20 percent).

STRONG LEADERSHIP VERSUS OTHER PRESIDENTIAL TRAITS

Surveys that ask respondents to identify a desirable character trait in a president, like those reported earlier, produce laundrylike lists. Without being forced to select one trait over another, respondents produce indiscriminant lists. An alternative, and perhaps better, method for determining what voters' desire most in a president requires then to pick one trait over another, not

TABLE 2.4. *The Idealized President, Nixon Polls, 1971.*

	Negative						Positive	No Opinion
	1	2	3	4	5	6	7	
Unpredictable/predictable	3	1	3	19	13	19	41	1
Divides/unifies	5	3	2	14	7	14	54	1
Insensitive/sensitive	2	2	3	19	13	20	39	2
Indecisive/decisive	1	2	2	10	8	18	57	2
Liberal/conservative	13	7	9	38	7	9	15	2
Weak/strong	1	0	0	5	5	19	69	1
Follower/leader	2	1	1	6	3	15	70	1
Lacks confidence/Self-confidence	2	1	1	5	7	17	67	0

"For each pair of words, please circle the number on the line which comes closest to how you would describe the ideal president." Respondents were given word pairs. The negative trait in the pair is located at 1 and the positive trait at 7. The cell entries are percentages.

Source: Opinion Research Corporation, May 12–23, 1971, and based on 1,513 personal interviews. Sample: national adult.

TABLE 2.5. *How Essential Are Certain Traits for Presidents?*

	Essential	Very Important	Somewhat Important	Not Too Important	Don't Know
Trustworthiness	52	41	5	1	1
Ability to get things done	52	43	4	1	1
Consistency	41	44	11	2	1
Strong leader	49	45	5	1	1
Patriotic	39	40	16	3	1
Really cares about people like you	42	42	12	3	1

Question: "I am going to read a list of words and phrases that might describe the ideal president. Realizing that one person is not likely to have all of these qualities, tell me how important it is that the next president have each of the following. Is this essential, very important, somewhat important, or not too important that the next president have this quality?"
Cell entries are percentages.
Source: Media Studies Center/Roper Center Unanchored Voter Poll, January 19–February 10, 1996, and based on 2,007 telephone interviews. Sample: national registered voters.

TABLE 2.6. *Preferences for Presidential Traits.*

Trait	Percentage Citing Trait Is Most Important
Honest and trustworthy	47%
Strong leader	31%
Can bring the right kind of change	26%
Shares your values	22%
Cares about people like you	21%
Experienced	20%
Patriotic	11%
Independent	9%

Question: "I am going to read you a list of attributes that some people say are important for political figures. Please tell me which two of these attributes are the most important in a candidate for president."
Source: True Patriot Survey, August 2008, by Eric Liu, Nick Hanaver; Methodology: Conducted by Greenberg Quinlan Rosner Research, August 12–14, 2008, and based on 1,000 telephone interviews.

merely to let them identify all desirable traits. This more restrictive methodology indicates that voters tend to value strong leadership over other traits.

For example, in September 1988, the NBC News/*Wall Street Journal* poll asked likely voters, "In choosing a president, do you think it is more important

that he be a tough, strong leader, or that he be a caring and compassion-
ate person?" These likely voters preferred tough, strong leadership over
care and compassion by a 62–24 margin (with 14 percent not sure). In May
2004, Ayres, McHenry & Associates asked likely voters a similar question:
"[W]hich do you think is more important in the next President of the United
States, that he is a strong leader, or that he cares about people like you?"
Results from this question were similar to the NBC News/*Wall Street Journal* poll despite question wording differences, with 42 percent preferring
the strong leader, 28 percent preferring a caring president, while 27 percent
wanted both traits, and 3 percent had no opinion.

An ABC News/*Washington Post* poll in a July 2004 survey asked a similar
question, "If you had to choose, which of these two qualities is more important
to you in a president, someone who is a strong leader, or someone who understands the problems of people like you?" Strong leadership was preferred over
understanding problems by a wide margin, 57–30, with 10 percent desiring
both traits. In one last administration of a similar question, Fox News/Opin-
ion Dynamics asked a national sample of registered voters in October 2007,
"For each of the following pairs of attributes, please tell me which one will be
more important to you in deciding your vote for president (in 2008) . . . For
the candidate to be a strong leader, or for the candidate to share your values?"
with sharing values perhaps being an aspect of representation. Again, these
registered voters preferred the strong leader over a president who shared their
values by 59–22 margin, with 16 percent wanting a combination or saying
that it depends. Results of these surveys, using different questions and asked
at different times, show a public preference for strong leadership. The most
recent of these polls, Fox News/Opinion Dynamics, may be the most telling in
that respondents valued strong leadership over representation in a president,
assuming that "shared values" triggers some notion of representation.

A number of other surveys asked respondents to choose from a larger set of
characteristics. Although a smaller percentage of respondents given these lists
of traits select strong leadership (or a variant) than for the preceding comparative questions, strong leadership still emerges as one of the most often mentioned desirable traits for a president. In one of the most recent, the Quinnipiac
University Poll of May 2008 asked a national sample of registered voters this
question (the percentage selecting the trait are in brackets): "When you decide
how to vote for president, which of the following is the single most important
quality you look for in a candidate? . . . Trustworthy [29 percent], shares your
values [16 percent], a strong leader [31 percent], competent [20 percent], inspir-
ing [3 percent]." Although strong leadership does not receive majority support,
it is the most cited first choice among these traits for voters.

Finally, a *Time*/Abt SRBI poll in November 2007 asked a national sample
of adults to name their first, second, and third most important traits for presidential candidates from this list: good judgment, strong leader, strong moral
character, cares about people like me, experienced, inspirational. Summing

across the three selections, good judgment came in first at 57.8 percent with strong leadership only slightly behind at 55.9 percent.[3] The other choices lagged behind, with 43.9 percent naming strong moral character, 34.8 percent selecting "cares about people like me," 32.8 percent for experience, and 9.9 percent for inspirational. No matter how the question is worded or the selections offered, strong leadership ranks as one of the most important traits that voters want in their ideal president. Still, as noted earlier, it is far from clear from these questions what voters mean when they say they want a strong leader.

CONCLUSION

This chapter reviewed findings from polls, which showed that voters demand representation and strength from presidents, the first piece of empirical support for the theory of public perceptions of presidential leadership developed in Chapter One. These idealized preferences for presidents provide a backdrop or standard against which voters assess or judge a president's leadership. Three factors – projection (predispositions), presidential personality, and presidential performance – may affect whether voters think a sitting president provides good and/or effective leadership. Although this study gives some attention to each of these factors, it emphasizes the effects of presidential performance on voter evaluations of presidential leadership.

Furthermore, this study singles out one type of presidential performance – relations with Congress – for several reasons. (1) We can develop unambiguous and conventionally understood measures of presidential position taking and success. Position taking has implications for presidential representation and success for presidential strength. (2) It appears voters learn about the general tenor of presidential relations with Congress because those relations receive voluminous news coverage. (3) These interactions compel presidents to choose between being representative of voters, at least in a collective sense, versus being successful, and thus appearing strong. At least with regard to relations with Congress, presidents cannot simultaneously maximize voters' demand for a representative and strong (e.g., successful) president. The next chapter turns to these questions, asking first, how strongly does Congress influence presidential position taking and success, and second, is there enough news coverage about presidential–congressional relations for voters to learn about presidential representation and success?

---

3 The fact that good judgment was placed first in the list to respondents may have had something to do with the slight edge of good judgment over strong leadership.

3

Congressional Sources of the President's Leadership Image

The theory of public perceptions of presidential leadership raises three questions: (1) What do voters mean when they say a president is a good and/or effective leader? (2) What factors influence whether voters think the president is a good leader? (3) What are the implications of these public perceptions on the president and the larger political system?

The theory assumes that voters define presidential leadership in representational and strength terms. Chapter Two presented evidence in support of this assumption. The theory also suggests that three factors – projection, presidential personality, and presidential performance – will affect whether voters think the president is both representative and strong. These pages focus on presidential performance and, in particular, relations with Congress. The contention here is that attributes of the congressional environment, especially party control and polarization, affect the kinds of positions presidents take on roll calls and presidential success on those votes.

The positions presidents take on roll calls before Congress tell us whether the president is a liberal, moderate, or conservative. From this location, we get a sense of how representative a president is, at least in a collective sense. Because voters in general and the median voter in particular tend to be moderate, the collective policy distance between presidents and voters is minimized when the president is also moderate. Policy moderation improves the quality of collective representation from presidents.

But in selecting where to locate on policy debates, presidents do not only take into account how well they represent voters. They also ask whether their side will prevail or not on congressional roll calls. Presidents care about whether their side wins or loses on roll calls. Winning allows the implementation of policies that presidents find desirable (Beckmann 2010; Cohen 2012). But winning may also affect the president's reputation for being strong in so far as victories on congressional roll calls lead voters to think of the president as strong, while loses lead them to view the president as weak. The problem for presidents is that the factors that lead to success, primarily party control, also push them to take more extreme (liberal/conservative as opposed to moderate) stances on roll calls. Interactions with Congress over policy formulation, one of the most important tasks of modern presidents, limit the ability of presidents to develop a reputation among voters as both representative and successful (e.g., strong). Presidents will come away from their legislative interactions looking either representative or successful to voters, but not both. Table 3.1 provides a schematic of this argument.

The impact of presidential–congressional relations on voters' understandings of presidential leadership hinges on voters knowledge about presidential position taking and success in Congress. At a minimum, there must be a sufficient volume of news about presidential–congressional relations for voters to learn where the president locates on the liberal–conservative spectrum and whether presidents are successful or not in their dealings with Congress. This chapter addresses these two issues: the degree to which congressional factors affect both presidential position taking and success and whether there is enough news about presidential–congressional relations for voters to learn the policy location of the president and his success with Congress.

The next section tests whether attributes of Congress affect presidential position taking. That analysis also compares this congressionally based explanation with one that emphasizes the role of party activists and the parties' selection process for presidential candidates. The following section turns to the congressional factors that affect presidential success and position taking – specifically, party control and polarization. Together, these two analyses show that factors that lead to greater presidential success in Congress also move presidential position taking away from the center and toward the liberal or conservative poles. Finally, the third major section of this chapter looks at the amount of news coverage of presidential–congressional relations. A precondition for voters using attributes of interactions with Congress in assessing presidential leadership is that there is enough news about those interactions for voters to learn about presidential positions and success.

TABLE 3.1. *Congress and Public Perceptions of Presidential Leadership.*

Dimension of Presidential Leadership Perceptions	United Control of Congress and the Presidency	Divided Control of Congress and the Presidency	
		Low Polarization	High Polarization
Representation	Unrepresentative	Moderately representative	Unrepresentative
Strength	Strong	Moderately strong	Weak

CONGRESS, PARTIES, AND PRESIDENTIAL POSITION TAKING

What influences the policy positions that policy makers take? Whether public opinion influences the policy positions that political leaders take has important implications for a democracy. Consequently, scholars have spent considerable time addressing the degree and conditions under which the public affects the policy choices of policy makers.[1] This question too has animated research on presidential policy choice, with some studies finding presidential responsiveness to public opinion (Druckman and Jacobs 2009; Erikson et al. 2002; Hicks 1984; Jacobs and Shapiro 2000; Manza and Cook 2002a, 2002b), while others do not find public opinion effects or suggest it is conditional (Canes-Wrone 2006; Canes-Wrone and Schotts 2004; Cohen 1997; Hill 1998; Lee 2012; Wood 2009; Wood and Lee 2009). Another perspective argues that personal belief or ideology determines a president's policy choices rather than public opinion pressures. Thus, presidents who have liberal beliefs will espouse liberal policies (Calder 1982; Langston 1992, 2012; McKay 1989).[2] A third perspective sees presidential policy choices as deriving from their partisan affiliation. From this perspective, Democrats will be more likely to take liberal positions than Republicans (Baer 2000; Gerring 1998; Harmel 1984; James 2006; Milkis 1994; Poole and Rosenthal 1997; Skowronek 1993; Wood 2009; but see Karol 2009).

I take a different tack. Rather than ask whether presidents adopt liberal or conservative positions, I ask: What affects whether a president's policy positions are moderate or extreme? Liberal and conservative presidents can be thought of as extreme in comparison to moderates. *Extreme*, as used here, refers to politicians who are decidedly liberal or conservative as opposed to moderate or middle of the road. This definition differs from equating extremism with radicalism of the left or right. Although the question of presidential policy moderation versus extremism has rarely been addressed (but see Cohen 2011a, 2012), two research streams suggest hypotheses about why presidents would take moderate as opposed to extreme policy positions: the party nomination process and the congressional context.

Party Activists and Presidential Policy Extremism

First, consider how the reforms of the nomination process may affect presidential policy choice. Those reforms, which were implemented primarily in

---

1 See the exhaustive reviews by Shapiro (2011) and Chong and Druckman (2013).
2 This is not merely a tautology. The policies that a president selects may differ from his preferences for a variety of reasons. Consider, for example, Nixon's imposition of wage and price controls to deal with inflation. On economic policy, Nixon preferred orthodox, conservative approaches, but reelection needs, the severity of the economic crisis, and Nixon's use of surprise actions (e.g., his trip to Red China) have been offered to explain his wage and price control policy. (See Matusow 1998.) Similarly, Ronald Reagan held strongly anticommunist attitudes, yet at times was pragmatic in diplomatic dealings with the Soviets, especially regarding arms control (Hantz 1996).

the mid-1970s, led to activists having greater influence in party politics, in particular the selection of the parties' nominees for office. As those activists tend to hold relatively extreme political opinions, some scholars implicate these reforms to the growth of polarization in the political system. Oddly, however, despite the centrality of the presidency as a political institution, rarely has research considered the effects of the nomination reforms or polarization on the presidency. As Layman, Carsey, and Horowitz (2006) state: "[T]he work on growing polarization between the parties in government has focused largely on Congress" (p. 87).[3]

Many studies contend that the increasing influence of party activists within the parties helps account for the growing polarization between the parties over the past several decades (Aldrich 1995; Aldrich and Rohde 2001; Fiorina with Abrams and Pope, 2005; Jacobson 2000; King 1997, 2003; Layman et al. 2006; Layman et. al. 2010; Saunders and Abramowitz 2004; Shafer 2003). Here we should think of party activists broadly to include those who work in candidate campaigns, financially contribute to candidates and the parties, and attend the national conventions, as well as interest groups that seek to influence the nomination and election of candidates for office.

Party activists may stimulate polarization for several reasons. First, they hold relatively extreme policy views compared to voters and rank-and-file members of parties (Carmines and Woods 2002; Jennings 1992; McClosky, Hoffman, and O'Hara 1960; Miller, Jennings, and Farah 1986). Figure 3.1 illustrates the relative policy extremism of more versus less campaign active citizens, using American National Election Study (ANES) data from 1972–2004. To measure ideological positions, I folded the seven-point ideological self-placement scale, so that 0 equals moderates, 1 equals "slightly" liberal or conservative, 2 equals liberal or conservative, and 3 equals "extremely" liberal or conservative.[4] To distinguish respondent level of campaign participation, I used the ANES campaign index scale. I recoded the scale such that 1 and 2 are categorized as low levels of campaign activity, 3 and 4 are medium campaign activity, and 5 and 6 are categorized as higher levels of campaign activity.[5]

For each presidential election year from 1972 through 2004, those higher in campaign activity are ideologically more extreme than respondents lower in campaign activity, often by a wide amount. On average, highly campaign active respondents are 0.38 units more ideologically extreme than the least active respondents, a considerable difference given that the ideology scale only ranges from 0 to 4.[6] The point here is not to provide a definitive and

---

3 There are several studies showing a growing partisan gap in approval of the president (Bond and Fleisher 2001; Jacobson 2000; Newman and Siegle 2010).

4 This is variable VCF0803 from the American National Election Study (ANES) Cumulative Data File.

5 This is variable VCF0723 from the ANES Cumulative Data File.

6 Some of the variability in the ideological placement of the most campaign active stems from the small n's involved, at times less than 20.

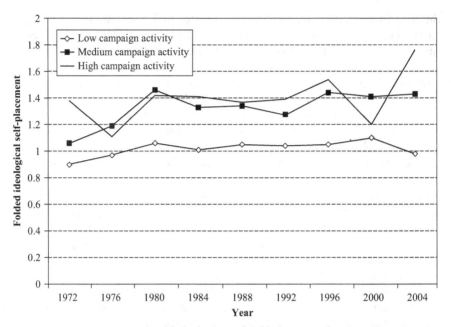

FIGURE 3.1. Comparison of Folded Ideological Self-Placement by Campaign Activity Level, 1972–2004.

Source: American National Election Study Cumulative Data File, see text for details on variable construction.

precise estimate of the ideological differences between voters and delegates to conventions – because we do not have data that easily compare convention delegates and other nomination activists with voters – but merely to illustrate that higher levels of campaign activity are associated with more extreme policy viewpoints.

Second, party activists play a critical role in selecting the parties' candidates for office, especially in the post-reform era since the early to mid-1970s. Third, the party activists provide considerable resources for candidates' primary and general election contests. Thus, in the era of party activist influence, candidates for office and office holders will either resemble the policy extremism of activists or will be responsive to their views, repaying activists for their vital electoral support and/or trying to secure their support in the upcoming election.

The reforms of the early to mid-1970s heightened the influence of activists on their respective parties. For example, one consequence of the reforms was to replace party caucuses and other devices with primaries for nominating candidates. As a result, party activists supplanted traditional party leaders in selecting the parties' nominees. Owing to their critical role in the primary and nomination process (Cohen et al. 2008), activists served as gatekeepers, ensuring that the party's nominees would reflect the activist's policy preferences. This in turn pushed the party's nominees and office holders toward the policy extremes.[7] As the influence of activists within the parties grew, the Democratic Party moved to the left and the Republican Party to the right.

The reforms of the presidential selection process in the 1970s exposed the presidency to the newfound influence of party activists. Presidents, and presidential aspirants, accommodated the growing influence of party activists within their parties through selection and/or conversion-adaptation effects. *Selection effects* means that as party activists become increasingly important in the nomination process, politically extreme candidates are more likely to gain the nomination than moderates. *Conversion-adaptation effects* means that aspirants for the nomination move to the political extremes to gain the support of the party activists. Mitt Romney's move to the right in the 2012 Republican presidential nomination contest illustrates this conversion-adaptation process.

The motivation for office, including re-nomination, link these nomination and election processes to governing, thereby affecting the policy positions that presidents take.[8] The policy positions that presidents take in office, in other words, will affect their ability to be re-nominated. If they take positions at variance with the preferences of the party activists, they may undermine their chances for the nomination. Jimmy Carter, for example, is the only incumbent president to see a strong challenge to his re-nomination in the post-reform era, perhaps because his policy positions were too centrist for the party's activists, which were located toward the left (Shaffer 1980; Stanley 2009).[9] No president seeking re-nomination has been denied it since the reforms of the mid-1970s, which may indicate that presidents cater to their party activists.[10] The lukewarm, if not cold, reception that John McCain received in 2008 among conservative Republican Party activists also illustrates the linkage between the ideological positions of presidential aspirants and nomination-election politics. Second-term presidents, too, have an incentive to cater to these party activists, even though they cannot run for the presidency again. By maintaining their "extremist" policy credentials, they insure some ability to influence who the party selects as their successor, which may be important for the president's legacy and impact on the party.

This party activist perspective leads to the hypothesis that presidents of the party reform era should be more extreme than presidents prior to those

---

7 Several studies document the influence of party activists on the policy stances of candidates since the reforms of the mid-1970s. See Masket (2007) and Miller and Schofield (2003).

8 Murray (2006), for example, finds Ronald Reagan highly responsive to the policy preferences of party activists.

9 In 1980, many Democrats felt that Jimmy Carter was too moderate, and liberal stalwart Senator Edward Kennedy challenged him for the nomination that year, an example of what may happen to an incumbent president seeking reelection who bucks the activists in the post-reform era.

10 It may also indicate the incumbency power of the presidency (Weisberg 2002).

reforms. A second hypothesis is that presidents and presidential candidates should become more extreme as the degree of polarization between the activists of the two parties has grown from the mid-1970s to the present. Layman and colleagues (2010) find that party activists – in particular, those who attended the national party convention – have become increasingly polarized on ideological and policy grounds over the past 30 years.[11] Based on this perspective, we should see presidents becoming more extreme in the positions they take on congressional roll calls in the period since the party reforms of the 1970s.

The Congressional Context and Presidential Policy Extremism

An alternative perspective looks at how the congressional context affects presidential policy choice. Because Congress is so important to the enactment and implementation of presidential policies, this perspective argues that presidents will take Congress into account when establishing their policy positions (Cohen 2012). There already exists some evidence that presidents alter their policy positions depending upon party control in Congress. For instance, Wood (2009, pp. 113–17) finds that presidents are less liberal when government is divided (when the opposition party controls one or both houses), compared to his criterion situation of Democratic control of Congress and the presidency.[12]

Let us begin with the assumption that all a president cares about is winning in Congress. Given this assumption, what policy position should a president take on bills before Congress? Simply, the president should adopt the position that a majority of members of Congress will accept. Let's compare what presidents have to do to win when their party controls Congress as opposed to when the opposition party is in control.

Let us further assume that the median of the party that controls Congress is the key member that a president needs to bring on board if his policy is to win. By definition, the presidential party median is closer to the president than the opposition party median. The president has a much smaller distance to move from his preferred policy position when his party is in control than when the opposition controls Congress. Consequently, there will be a larger proportion of roll calls in which the president's side wins with majority control than with opposition party control. This, however, is a trivial result. More consequential for the argument here is that because the president has to move farther when

---

11 They compare the policy preferences of delegates to the national nominating conventions from 1972 through 2004 on three policy dimensions: social welfare, racial issues, and cultural issues. On a 0 to 1 scale, with 0 indicating no difference and 1 indicating maximum difference, the difference between the party's delegates was about 0.1 on cultural issues and about 0.4 for both racial and social welfare issues. In 2004, delegate differences were between 0.5 and 0.6 for all three issues (p. 331).

12 Wood (2009, pp. 115–16) has too few cases of Republican control of both houses and the presidency for reliable estimates for that configuration.

the opposition party is in control than his own party, presidents will be more moderate during divided than united government.

Impressionistic evidence suggests some support for the divided government-moderation prediction. Eisenhower, a minority president for most of his term, had a good working relationship with Senate Democratic Majority Leader Lyndon Johnson, as well as a reputation for policy moderation (Collier 1994). Richard Nixon did not have such cordial relations with the Democratic majority but managed on several occasions to forge compromises on legislation and, in retrospect, does not appear an especially doctrinaire conservative (Evans and Novak 1972). In contrast, George W. Bush, who developed a reputation of staunch conservatism, did not seem to moderate much during the last two years in office when the Democrats held Congress (Aberbach and Peele 2011). Importantly, Eisenhower and Nixon served when the parties were not highly polarized, which was the political context that George W. Bush faced.[13]

How does polarization – one of the signature characteristics of modern American politics – affect presidential interaction with Congress? First, party polarization should have little implication for the president when his party controls Congress. The policy distance between the president and his party is likely to be slight under almost all circumstances and should not vary systematically when polarization is high or low. Polarization should have little consequence, then, for either presidential victory rates or presidential moderation during united government. No matter the level of polarization, during majority government, presidents will take comparatively extreme policy positions, reflecting the ideological tendency of his party.

But polarization will make it harder for the president to work with Congress when controlled by the opposition party. For instance, polarization increases the cost of presidential movement toward the key opposition party member, the member that the president needs to win (e.g., the opposition party median). Polarization should also increase the costs for that key member to work with a president of the opposition party. The president's party, in and out of Congress, may oppose, reject, or challenge a president who moves toward the opposition and/or tries to work with the opposition party. Thus, during divided government, presidents will not moderate their position taking when polarization is high but will be more likely to do so when polarization is low. Furthermore, because minority party presidents during polarization maintain their relatively extreme policy positions, they should win less often than when polarization is at lower levels.

This discussions leads to several hypotheses:

H1: Presidents will be more moderate during divided than united government.
H2: Presidents will moderate less during divided government as the level of polarization between the parties increases.

13 For an extended treatment of the effects of divided government on the president, see Conley (2002).

H3: Presidential success will be higher during united than divided government no matter the degree of polarization, but as polarization increases, presidential success will decline during divided government.

This model differs from Wood (2009), who focused on divided government but not the conditional effects of polarization on presidential moderation. Wood found that Democratic presidents become less liberal when they lose majority control of Congress, which is similar to saying that they become more moderate when they lose party control of Congress.

This model also has implications for the president's public image. Due to the high victory rate of majority party presidents, the public will tend to view them as strong leaders, in part equating success in Congress with strong leadership. But majority party presidents will also be viewed as relatively extreme, where the public prefers moderation in its presidents. Majority party presidents cannot fulfill the public's ideal image that a president be both strong and representative – that is, moderate. In contrast, minority party presidents cannot develop an image of leadership strength (success) through their interactions with Congress because of the comparatively high rate of defeat they suffer compared with majority party presidents. Minority party presidents can mitigate this problem somewhat by moderating their policy stances. Such moderation will increase their success rates with Congress somewhat – as compared to if they did not moderate their policy positions – and such moderation may improve the president's representational image. Polarization may have dire public image consequences for minority party presidents – they will lose even more frequently than presidents who moderate during divided government, undermining how strong the public perceives them to be; plus, voters will view them as extremists, undercutting their representational image with voters.

Variables

To test these ideas, we need measures of presidential policy extremism, presidential success, polarization in Congress, and party reform. In earlier analyses on Congress as a source of presidential policy extremism (Cohen 2011a, 2012), I found that adjusted Americans for Democratic Action (ADA) measures were more sensitive to the congressional environment than DW-Nominate scores, mainly because the ADA scores can vary across years, while the DW-Nominate scores are repeated for the two years that make up a Congress.[14] For this

14 There are issues with using ADA roll calls for creating a comparable time series, primarily agenda composition effects; that is, the votes/issue across years are not comparable. Groseclose, Levitt, and Snyder (1999) have developed a method to adjust the ADA scores across time to provide greater temporal comparability. The analysis here uses these ADA scores, adjusted as Groseclose and colleagues (1999) recommend, averaging the ADA presidential scores for the House and Senate. Also see Anderson and Habel (2009).

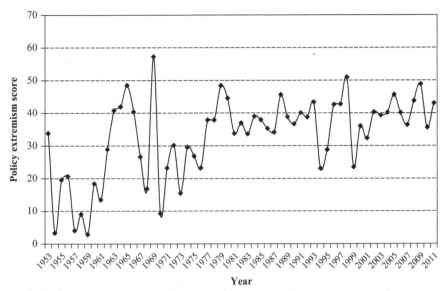

FIGURE 3.2. Presidential Policy Extremism, 1953–2010.
Source: Based on Adjusted Americans for Democratic Action (ADA) scores, see text for details.

reason, I again use adjusted ADA scores, which now run from 1953 to 2010.[15] Because the ADA scores are scaled from 0 to 100, with 0 indicating no support for the liberal side and 100 indicating complete support, I fold the ADA scores at the series mean to create the presidential extremism score.[16] High values indicate presidential extremism and low values presidential moderation. Figure 3.2 plots the presidential extremism scores from 1953 to 2010.

The party activist hypotheses is tested with a pre-/post-reform dummy, coded 0 for 1951–76 and 1 for 1977–2010. The dummy tests whether post-reform presidents are more extreme than pre-reform presidents. Based on the party activist theory, we should expect a positive and statistically significant coefficient for the reform period dummy. There is some initial support for this hypothesis, as presidents are more extreme in the reform era (1977–2010) than the pre-reform era (1952–76), 38.8 compared to 24.0.

The congressional context hypotheses require a variable for divided government and congressional party polarization, plus their interaction. Divided government is measured with a dummy variable, coded 1 if the opposition

15 In my earlier analyses (Cohen 2011a, 2012), the ADA scores only ran from 1953–2002. I thank B. Dan Wood for providing me with the updated adjusted presidential ADA scores. The ADA has been collecting information on the liberalism of members of Congress and the president since 1947, but I begin the analysis with 1953, the first year that we have data on congressional polarization variable used in the analysis.

16 The formula is Absolute value × (Annual adjusted ADA score – 38.52).

party controls at least one house and 0 for united government. To measure congressional polarization, I average the annual percentage of party votes in the House and Senate. A party vote is defined as when 50 percent plus one of Democrats vote in opposition to 50 plus one of percent Republicans.[17] The interaction of divided government and polarization multiplies these two variables. Under united government, the interaction equals 0 but takes the party polarization value with divided government. The congressional context theory suggests a negative sign for divided government; that is, presidents will moderate under divided government. Higher polarization will be associated with greater presidential extremism, as will the interaction term.

RESULTS

Table 3.2 presents results of several estimations of the impact of the congressional context and party reform on presidential extremism.[18] Diagnostics did not detect any nonstationarity problems with the presidential extremism variable, but other tests indicated heteroskedasticity and autocorrelation issues.[19] Four estimations are presented in the table: ordinary least squares (OLS), OLS with robust standard errors, Newey-West regression, and OLS with robust standard errors correcting for second-order autocorrelation.[20] All of the

17 This differs from my earlier analyses, which used the absolute value of the difference in DW-Nominate scores for the median member of the two parties in each chamber, averaging distance for the two chambers. I changed to the party votes instead of the DW-Nominate measure because, as noted earlier, the DW-Nominate measure does not vary across years within a Congress, but the unit of analysis here is the year, not the Congress. The party vote measure and the DW-Nominate measures are still highly correlated, over 0.90.

18 In my earlier analyses (Cohen 2011a, 2012), I also included a variable for public opinion, the Stimson public mood variable. Those analyses found a positive and significant effect of the public mood on presidential extremism: When the public was more liberal, presidents became more extreme, a finding that is hard to interpret. The finding makes a bit more sense when we realize that across the entire series, the public is always net liberal. I repeated the earlier analysis by including the mood variable, which again attained significance with a positive sign, but its inclusion did not affect the other variables in the estimation. I also ran equations with two other public opinion variables, symbolic liberalism from Ellis and Stimson (2012) and the annual percentage of independents, taken from the Gallup polls. Symbolic liberalism is the net percentage of voters who identify as liberal versus conservative. Neither of these two additional opinion variables was statistically significant. Because the finding with the mood variable is hard to interpret substantively and because it does not affect the other variables, the table does not report findings with the mood variable.

19 The Dickey-Fuller test statistic for presidential extremism was -4.59 compared to a critical value of -3.57, and the augmented Dickey-Fuller test statistic with trend included but no lags was -6.25 compared to a critical value of -4.13. Tests found lag functions were not statistically significant. Because the presidential extremism series is stationary, we can perform the analysis on the variable in levels. This differs from the earlier analysis in Cohen (2011a, 2012), which found that presidential extremism was not stationary, and thus used error correction techniques.

20 After estimating the OLS, the Breusch-Pagan/Cook-Weisberg test found significant heteroskedasticity, $X^2(1) = 7.06$, $p = 0.008$. Newey-West regression helps correct for heteroskedasticity.

TABLE 3.2. *Impact of Party Reform and Congressional Context on Presidential Policy Extremism, 1953–2010.*

	OLS	OLS (with robust standard errors)	Newey-West Regression (4 lags)	Arima Regression (robust standard errors, AR(2))
Reform dummy	15.57***	15.57***	15.57**	15.08***
	(3.25)	(3.31)	(5.28)	(4.18)
Divided government	−37.87**	−37.87*	−37.87**	−44.13***
	(15.19)	(15.77)	(15.77)	(13.88)
Congressional polarization	−0.56*	−0.56*	−0.56**	−0.69*
	(0.25)	(0.29)	(0.21)	(0.31)
Interaction (divided × polarization)	0.71*	0.71*	0.71**	0.86***
	(0.31)	(0.33)	(0.29)	(0.26)
Constant	53.02	53.02	53.02	58.42
	(11.91)	(14.99)	(10.85)	(16.58)
AR(2)	—	—	—	0.38**
				(0.14)
/sigma	—	—	—	9.00***
				(0.85)
N	58	58	58	58
R^2/Adj. R^2	0.40/0.36	0.40	Na	Na

*p < 0.05
**p < 0.01
***p < 0.001
Source: See text for details.

estimations point to the same substantive conclusion, providing support for both the party reform and congressional context hypotheses.

First, presidents are some fifteen points more extreme in their policy choices during the party reform era than prior to those reforms. This finding is somewhat stronger than my earlier analysis, which found reform presidents about ten points more extreme than pre-reform presidents (Cohen 2012, p. 204). There are several notable differences between the two analyses that might account for the difference in the effect of the reform dummy. First, the analysis here has ten additional data points, and presidents have grown increasingly extreme in their policy stances during the last ten years of the series. For instance, from 1977 to 2000, the reform years in the early analyses, presidential extremism averaged 37.7, compared to 41.3 for the last ten years (2001–10). The reform dummy variable merely picks up whether the average level of extremism differs across the two periods. Adding so many highly extreme data points could lead the reform dummy to being significant in this analysis when it was not so in the earlier one. One major weakness of the reform dummy is that it does not isolate the actual effect of the reforms of the 1970s, but lumps into the variable all differences between the pre-reform and reform eras.

The second difference between this and the earlier analyses has to do with the stationarity of the presidential extremism variable. For the shorter time span, presidential extremism was found to be nonstationary, thus requiring error correction (ECM) regression. ECM regression differences the dependent variable, and the earlier analysis also first differenced the independent variables. Although not necessary with the data used here (because the extremism series is stationary), I performed an ECM regression by differencing all the variables used in Table 3.2 and including a lagged dependent variable. In that estimation, all the variables performed as expected, except that the reform dummy was no longer statistically significant. Nor might we have expected it to be significant, as differencing that variable is asking if there is any difference in the level of presidential extremism from 1976 to 1977. A differenced dummy variable is constant for all values except the first where the switch from 0 to 1 occurs. The analytical decisions required in the earlier analysis severely hindered the ability to test for pre-/post-reform effects.

The results in Table 3.2 also provide support for the congressional context hypotheses. First, as expected, presidential extremism declines by approximately thirty-eight points when facing an opposition Congress. This is less than found in the earlier analyses (fifty-five), but still substantively meaningful and statistically significant. Second, polarization leads to lower levels of extremism, about 0.56 points less for each 1 percent increase in polarization. The sign for the direct effects of polarization is contrary to expectations, but sign reversals are common in interaction models, and so we should not make much out of this apparently wrong sign.[21] More important is the positive and significant sign for the interaction term: during divided government, as polarization increases by 1 percent, presidential extremism increases a corresponding 0.7 percent.

Figure 3.3 graphically illustrates the impact of increasing polarization for presidents serving during united and divided government. The figure plots the actual level of presidential extremism for united and divided government presidents at different polarization levels. The graph shows a slight decline in presidential extremism during united government as polarization rises, but the effect is not statistically significant. As hypothesized, presidential policy choice during united government is not responsive to the level of congressional polarization. Presidents during united government always select policies near

---

21 For a discussion about why sign reversals may happen in interaction models see Brambor, Clark, and Golder (2006); Berry, Golder, and Milton (2012); and Friedrich (1982).

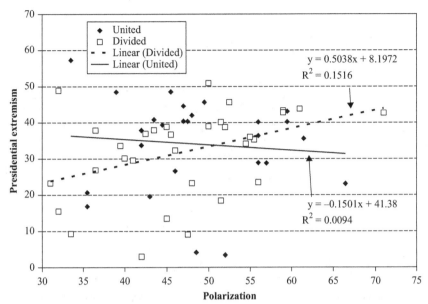

FIGURE 3.3. Impact of Divided Government and Polarization on Presidential Extremism, 1953–2010.
Source: See text for details.

their party medians, which tend to be relatively extreme. In contrast, presidential policy choice during divided government is highly responsive to the level of polarization in Congress. The slope of the regression line for divided government presidents is relatively steep. When polarization is low, presidents are about twenty points less extreme in their policy choice than when polarization is high.[22]

The analysis of this section demonstrates that presidential policy choice is responsive to the congressional context. Majority presidents are routinely extreme in their policy choice because they can win by selecting policy options close to their party medians in Congress. In contrast, minority presidents must moderate their policy stances if they are to have any chance of winning on the floors of the legislature's chambers. However, their ability to moderate declines as polarization between the congressional parties widens. The next section tests whether the key independent variable, party control, also affects presidential success. If it does, then we have empirical support for the trade-off that presidents face between representation and strength/success.

22 The effects of polarization do not appear quite as strong as found in the earlier analyses. For instance, when using the Newey-West regression results in Table 3.2, divided government presidents will be about 6 points more extreme during the highest level of polarization (71) than when at the lowest level (31). The greater impact of the reform dummy variable in part accounts for the weakened, albeit significant, effect for polarization.

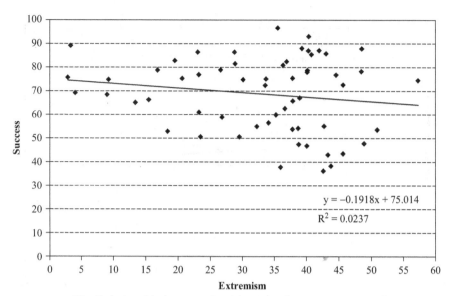

FIGURE 3.4. The Relationship between Presidential Policy Extremism and Success, 1953–2010.

Source: For presidential policy extremism and presidential ADA positions, see the text for details. For success, see *Congressional Quarterly*'s annual vote studies on presidential support in Congress.

CONGRESSIONAL CONTEXT AND PRESIDENTIAL SUCCESS

This section looks at the sources of presidential success, but unlike the rest of the huge literature on the sources of presidential success, I focus on the relationship between presidential extremism/moderation and success. I do this to establish that there is a systematic trade-off between moderation and success. Figure 3.4 presents a scatter plot between presidential extremism and congressional concurrence with the president from 1953 to 2010. Concurrence is defined as the average annual percentage of roll call positions that the president's side won, weighted by the number of roll calls in each chamber.[23] As the scatter plot reveals, there is no simple relationship between presidential extremism and success ($r = -0.15$, $p = 0.25$). But as demonstrated later, the relationship between presidential policy extremism and success is more complex and depends on the congressional context.

Party control is clearly the most important factor determining presidential success in Congress, a finding repeated in study after study.[24] Presidents

---

23 The data source is Ragsdale (2009, pp. 500–2), which I have updated through 2010 from *Congressional Quarterly*'s annual vote studies on presidential support.

24 The literature on this point is too massive to cite fully here. For several recent studies see Barrett and Eshbaugh-Soha (2007) and Beckmann (2010); Cohen (2012); and Cohen, Bond, and Fleisher (2013).

are more likely to receive support for their policy positions from members of their own party than the opposition for several reasons: (1) Members of the president's party are likely to share his policy preferences. (2) Presidential co-partisans in Congress will run for reelection on the president's record as well as their own, which creates another incentive to support the president. Lebo and O'Geen (2011), for instance, find that presidential success has a positive effect on presidential party performance in the subsequent congressional election. (3) The majority party controls important levers of power in Congress, including committees, access to the floor, and rules governing debate and roll call voting, which gives the president some advantages when his party controls Congress.

When the president's party controls Congress, all the president needs is the support of his co-partisans to win on floor votes. Extreme policy positions can win as long as the president's party is in the majority; thus, presidents have no incentive to moderate their policy stances. The situation differs when the opposition party controls Congress. By definition, the president will need some members of the opposition to support his side if he is to win. To gain the roll call support of opposition members, presidents will have to compromise, that is, move toward the opposition.[25] Minority presidents need to moderate their policy stances if they are to win on congressional roll calls. The previous section demonstrated that minority presidents do moderate, conditional on the level of polarization. When polarization is high, minority presidents are less prone to moderate than when polarization is low. This has implications for the legislative success of minority presidents. Policy moderation by minority presidents should be associated with success. But is this the case?

The dependent variable for this analysis is total annual House and Senate concurrence (percentage agreement) with the president from 1953 to 2010. Concurrence is the number of roll calls supporting the president's side divided by the total number of roll calls on which the president took a position, averaged across the two chambers and weighted by the number of roll calls per chamber. I use the concurrence scores of the two chambers combined because the idea put forth here is that presidents will moderate when the opposition party holds at least one chamber.

The strategic moderation-success hypothesis argues that moderation only leads to success during divided government. Moderation implies that presidents move closer to the policy preferences of the opposition party and away from their own party. By moving closer to the opposition party's policy preferences during divided government, the president should increase the likelihood of forging a legislative compromise with the opposition, thereby increasing presidential success. Presidents need some opposition support to win during divided government. If, on the other hand, during divided government

---

25 Some opposition party members also must be either willing to compromise their positions and/or to work with the president on legislation.

presidents do not moderate, but take positions close to their own party, the likelihood of success should fall. Presidential extremism in the face of divided government reduces the ability of picking up support from opposition legislators, which is necessary for success on roll calls. In contrast, presidents do not have to moderate when their party controls both legislative chambers but, instead, should locate near their party's center. As long as their party stays cohesive, presidents do not need opposition support to prevail on roll calls during united government.[26] To test this interaction model, I use the following equation:

$$
\begin{aligned}
\textit{Presidential success} = &\ \textit{Constant} + b_1(\textit{Divided government}) \\
&+ b_2(\textit{Presidential policy extremism}) \times b_3(\textit{Divided government} \\
&\times \textit{Presidential extremism}) + e
\end{aligned}
$$

As discussed earlier, divided government is a dummy variable, coded 1 if the opposition party controls at least one legislative chamber and 0 otherwise. Presidential policy extremism is the annual, corrected, folded ADA presidential score as defined earlier. High scores indicate presidential extremism, while low scores indicate presidential moderation. The strategic moderation hypothesis predicts a statistically significant and negative sign for the interaction term, which is the multiplication of divided government and presidential extremism.[27]

Table 3.3 presents the results. Diagnostics revealed that the concurrence (success) series is stationary, but autocorrelation and heteroskedasticity may be present. Thus, the table presents several estimations: simple OLS, OLS with robust standard errors, Newey-West regression, and an ARIMA model that corrects for first-order autocorrelation.[28] All estimations report the same substantive results.

As predicted, presidential extremism has no effect on concurrence (success) when the president's party is in the majority. Nor does extremism have a direct impact on concurrence. But the interaction term between extremism and divided government is significant, indicating that as minority presidents become more extreme in their policy stances, their success with Congress ebbs. The effect is substantively meaningful as well. Each one-point increase

---

26 This assumes that the president's party is large and united enough to overcome filibusters in the Senate or that the opposition is unlikely to threaten the president with a filibuster.

27 In my earlier analysis I included several other control variables, including dummies for the 3rd and 4th year of a president's term, dummy variables for presidents Nixon and Reagan, and presidential approval (Cohen 2012, p. 251). Because my aim here is to describe the relationship between moderation and success, conditional on party control, not to provide a full causal model of presidential success in Congress, there is no need to add control variables.

28 The Dickey-Fuller test statistic for success is -4.44 against critical values of -3.57 at the 0.01 critical level. Trends and lags were not found to be significant. The Breusch-Pagan/Cook-Weisberg test for heteroskedasticity for the uncorrected OLS model on Table 3.2, with a X^2 (1) = 5.77, p = 0.02.

TABLE 3.3. *Impact of Party Control and Presidential Policy Extremism on Success in Congress, 1953–2010.*

	OLS	OLS (with robust standard errors)	Newey-West Regression (4 lags)	Arima Regression (robust standard errors, AR(1))
Divided government	−4.92 (6.68)	−4.92 (5.54)	−4.92 (4.36)	−4.86 (5.33)
Presidential extremism	0.03 (0.14)	0.03 (0.12)	0.03 (0.12)	−0.02 (0.11)
Interaction (divided × extremism)	−0.59** (0.19)	−0.59** (0.16)	−0.59** (0.14)	−0.61*** (0.17)
Constant	80.92 (4.94)	80.92 (4.58)	80.92 (4.01)	82.78 (4.49)
AR (1)	—	—	—	0.33** (0.13)
/sigma	—	—	—	8.17*** (1.03)
N	58	58	58	58
R²/Adj. R²	0.69/0.67	0.69	NA	NA

* p < 0.05
** p < 0.01
*** p < 0.001
Source: See text for details.

in presidential extremism leads to a 0.59 percentage decline in success with Congress. During divided government, presidential extremism varies from a low of 2.9 to a high of 50.9, with an average of 31.9. Based on these values, when minority presidents are least extreme, they can expect a success (concurrence) score of 74.4, but a score of 58.2 when they are at the average extremism levels and 47.5 when they are most extreme. The difference in concurrence for the least and most extreme minority presidents is 26.9 percentage points.

Figure 3.5 graphs the relationship between success and extremism separately for majority and minority presidents. Superimposed on the scatter plot is the regression line. That line for majority presidents is essentially flat. As majority presidents get increasingly extreme in their policy stances, their success level with Congress remains unchanged. Matters are much different for minority presidents. The regression line falls as minority presidents become increasingly extreme. For example, they win on approximately three-quarters of roll calls when they are moderate but win less than half the time when they are highly extreme. In fact, there is not much difference in the success

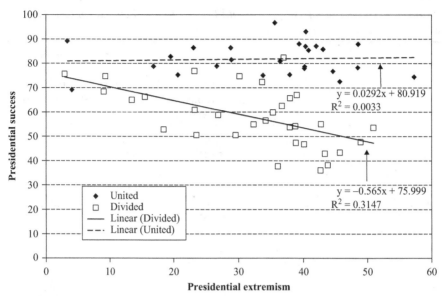

FIGURE 3.5. Impact of Divided Government and Presidential Extremism on Presidential Success in Congress, 1953–2010.
Source: *See text for details.*

levels of success of minority and majority presidents when both are moderate. Moderate minority presidents appear to be able to attract enough opposition support to win most of the time. Thus, extremism matters for the success level of minority presidents, but not for majority presidents.

Summary: Congress and Presidential Position Taking and Success

The results of the two analyses have implications for the theory developed here. First, the congressional context has systematic implications for presidential position taking and success. Second, there is a trade-off between presidential extremism in policy choice and success. Generally, presidents cannot be both moderate and successful at the same time. Majority control of Congress promotes presidential success, but it also tends to pull presidents to take more extreme positions. Policy moderation is only associated with success in Congress for minority presidents, but minority presidents appear able to moderate only when polarization levels between the parties are not high.

In terms of shoring up their leadership image with voters, presidents, through their interactions with Congress, can develop an image as either representative or strong, but not both. Minority presidents in office during periods of high polarization are in the most precarious position when it comes to their leadership image among voters. Their extremism, forced on them due to high polarization, will undermine the representational side of their image, and that same degree of policy extremism in the face of an opposition-controlled Congress will depress their success level, which will undermine the strength aspect of their leadership image. Minority presidents who take extreme policy stances will be regarded as unrepresentative and weak – the worst of all possible worlds. The troubles for extreme minority presidents mount insofar as members of Congress are responsive to the presidential leadership image in deciding whether or not to support the president.[29]

The overall argument that links presidential–congressional interactions to the president's leadership image among voters has yet to be substantiated empirically. For those interactions to affect how voters assess the leadership of presidents requires that voters develop a leadership image of the president based on the president's interaction with Congress. We do not expect that voters should have much detailed information about presidential relations with Congress, but the news media, through its coverage of presidential interactions with Congress, is critical in linking what goes on between the president and Congress and voter perceptions of the president. At a minimum, there needs to be enough news about the president for voters to learn about the general tenor of presidential position taking and success for voters to evaluate the president's leadership qualities. In reporting on presidential–congressional interactions, the news media must also help voters interpret those interactions in light of the two aspects of presidential leadership emphasized here, representation and strength. The next section takes a stab at providing empirical evidence that the news media provide this type of information and interpretation for voters in enough quantity and clarity for them to evaluate the president's leadership, although we will see that we do not have the necessary data to test all of these causal paths from presidential–congressional interactions, to news coverage of those interactions, to voter use of that news in shaping their leadership image of the president.

THE LEGISLATIVE PRESIDENCY IN THE NEWS

Thus far, this chapter demonstrated that the congressional context – in particular, party control and polarization – has systematic effects on presidential policy moderation and success. The theory developed here contends that voters use information about presidential interactions with Congress in assessing the president's leadership qualities. When presidents take moderate positions on issues before Congress, voters will more likely view the president as being collectively representative than when a president takes more extreme policy positions. This is because the policy distance between presidents and voters

---

29 This suggests that public attitudes toward the president and success in Congress are endogenous, unlike most existing research, which suggests that public attitudes, like approval, are exogenous to success. I return to this point in the next chapter.

collectively narrows as presidents locate themselves in the center, that is, near the median voter. Similarly, when presidents are successful, they will be looked upon as strong but will be viewed as weak when they lose frequently on congressional roll calls. This is because voters associate winning with being strong.

But for voters to use these interbranch relations to assess a president's leadership qualities, they must be aware of the tenor of presidential–congressional interactions and be able to understand the implications of those interactions. The news media are vital in this regard. It is through the news media that voters learn about political events, and many voters also rely on new media reporting to help them interpret the implications of those events (Cohen 2010a, ch. 8). Several studies imply that news coverage on presidential–congressional relations may affect public assessments of the president. For instance, Nicholson, Segura, and Woods (2002; also Newman and Lammert, 2012) argue that presidents enjoy higher approval ratings during divided than united government. They argue that divided government confuses voters over whom to blame, the president or Congress, a version of the clarity of responsibility idea (Powell and Whitten 1993). During united government, in contrast, with the president's party in control of the two branches of government, voters are more likely to blame the president and his congressional co-partisans for policy failures. Although Nicholson and colleagues do not identify news reporting as a mechanism for establishing this linkage, it is easy to suggest that during divided government, news stories mention the fact of divided government, parceling blame in some proportion to both the president and the opposition-controlled Congress.

Groseclose and McCarty's (2001) congressional blame game also implies that news coverage of presidential–legislative interactions will affect presidential approval. In the congressional blame game, the opposition-controlled Congress passes legislation in the run-up to a presidential election, with the expectation that the president will veto that legislation. Vetoes impose "audience costs" on presidents, signaling to voters that there is conflict between the branches. Vetoes, in the blame game model, signal to voters that presidents are extreme: "When a veto occurs in equilibrium, the president's type must be in the region that voters dislike" (p. 110); in other words, the president holds extreme policy preferences. Again, although Groseclose and McCarty do not address directly the role of news coverage in their model, it is not hard to argue that news coverage of veto episodes affects public approval of the president by highlighting to the public that there is conflict between the branches and perhaps implying the limits of presidential leadership during these episodes.

To date, while there are some studies that try to track the amount of news on the president, as well as select characteristics of that news, like its tonality, we have little idea of the amount of coverage on the legislative side of the presidency. This chapter represents an initial effort to gauge the amount of news on the legislative presidency. The next section reviews the literature on presidential and congressional news. Then I introduce the data used to estimate the amount of news on the legislative presidency, the content analysis of *The New York Times* from the Policy Agendas project (http://www.policyagendas.org/). That section provides some descriptive information on the volume of news on the legislative presidency, suggesting a sufficient volume for voters to learn about aspects presidential interactions with Congress.

Existing Research on Presidential and Congressional News

Let us define the *legislative presidency* as the interactions between the president and Congress in policy making. News coverage of the legislative presidency, thus, reports on those interactions. While past research on both news coverage of the president and Congress is relevant to our understanding of legislative presidency news, there is little research that directly bears on news of the legislative presidency. Consequently, we know little about how frequently the legislative presidency is covered in the news, conditions that affect the volume of news coverage on the legislative presidency, the topics covered, or the stage of the policy making process.

Despite a relatively large volume of research on news coverage of Congress, even that literature helps little for our current purposes. For the most part, studies on news coverage of Congress look at which types of members of Congress are likely to receive more news coverage than other types of members, for instance, leaders versus rank and file members, majority party versus minority party legislators, men versus women, whites versus minority members (Cook 1986, 1989; Kuklinski and Sigelman 1992; Miller 1977, 1978; Niven and Zilber 1998; Robinson and Appel 1979; Schaffner and Seller, 2003; Sellers 2010; Squire 1988; Tidmarch and Pitney 1985; Vermeer 1987; Vinson 2003; Zilber and Niven 2000). Another stream of research looks at coverage of congressional elections (Goldenberg and Traugott 1984; Levy and Squire 2000) and scandals (Rozell 1996). To my knowledge, Susan Miller's (1977, 1978) now dated work is the lone examination of news coverage of Congress as an institution across stages of the policy making process. Her study found that such news focused on the end stages of the congressional policy-making process, primarily floor roll call votes, and, to a lesser degree, final committee reports to the floor.

Similarly, there is now a growing body of work on news coverage of the presidency (see the review in Cohen 2009). Much effort in recent research has aimed at measuring historical trends (Balutis 1977; Cohen 2008; Cornwell 1959; Kernell and Jacobson 1987) and the tone of presidential news (Brody 1991; Cohen 2008, 2010a; Erikson et al. 2002; Farnsworth and Lichter 2006; Groeling 2010; Grossman and Kumar 1981); the former is useful for understanding the development of the public presidency, and the latter set is most important for understanding the impact of news coverage on presidential approval. None of that research, however, looks at the legislative presidency.

Three studies, to my knowledge, directly compare the presidential and congressional news. Larson (1988) argues that the president receives more news coverage than Congress. Insofar as news coverage enhances the power of an institution, as news coverage tilts to the president over Congress, there should be an increase in presidential power at the expense of Congress, according to Larson. Her article, however, only reviews existing studies of presidential and congressional news; she provides no additional data on their relative news coverage.

Shields and Goidel (1996) content analyze the Vanderbilt Television News Archive from 1990 to 1993, focusing on the relative amount of news coverage of the president and the House and Senate on the national debt issue. Again, they find more news coverage of the president than the legislature. Importantly, they find that about one-quarter of news stories mention both the president and Congress, while two-thirds of the total time (in broadcast seconds) mentions both branches. That their study looked at only one issue raises questions of generalizability.

Cohen (2009) overcomes this limitation in his long time series of *New York Times* front-page news coverage, which presents the percentage of congressional news stories that also mention the president. He finds that, over time, the president appears more frequently in congressional news. By the 1970s, more than half of all congressional news mentions the president. Cohen's data, however, do not indicate the topic covered or the stage of the policy-making process. Based on the scanty existing research, we know little about news coverage of the legislative presidency.

The Legislative Presidency in the News, 1946–2005

The preceding discussion points out the limitations and barriers to studying the legislative presidency in the news. Here, I use the content analysis of *The New York Times* (1946–2006) from the Policy Agendas Project (PAP). Before turning to a description of these data, it is necessary to justify the use of *The New York Times* as a general indicator of news coverage. Studies of the news media often use *The New York Times*. The idea here is that *The New York Times* sets the news media's agenda, especially with regard to national and international news – the intermedia agenda setting hypothesis. In other words, due to the respect accorded to the *Times*, as well as limitations on the ability of most news organizations to collect in-depth news on national and international events, many organizations turn to other news organizations that they can trust and rely upon. *The New York Times* plays that role; thus, much of the national and international news that news consumers receive may be thought of as filtered *New York Times* news reporting.[30]

30 Other major news organizations, such as the *Washington Post* and the major television networks, also play that role. At least when it comes to national news, these major news organizations seem to report similarly, known as the consonance hypothesis. Comstock and Scharrer (2005, pp. 178–82) review the literature on both intermedia agenda setting and news media consonance. There is strong support for both of these hypotheses; also see Cohen (2010a, pp. 123–5).

The PAP sampled the first entry on odd-numbered pages in *The New York Times* Index, which results in 46,459 cases (index entries) for analysis from 1946–2006, about 762 per year. Within years, this provides us with a random sample of indexed stories. But because the Index changes font and page size over this sample period, the PAP also provided several estimates to use for weighting across years. In the following analysis, I use the estimated total number of articles per year for weighting purposes.

There are two attributes of this data collection that recommend it for our purposes: (1) It covers an extended period of time, unlike most other content analyses of media. This data set is temporally comprehensive. (2) It samples all news, not just news on presidents, Congress, or specific policies (e.g., Shields and Goidel 1996). Unlike Cohen (2008, 2009) who looked at front-page coverage only, the PAP collected news across the entire newspaper, allowing us to compare legislative presidency coverage on the front and back pages of *The New York Times*, thus deepening our understanding of such news coverage.

However, there are several limitations in using these data for our purposes. The designed was aimed at measuring the policy agenda. Thus, we are using these data for a purpose not originally intended. The PAP coded whether the Index mentions the president and Congress in two separate dummy variables, which will be our primary variables of interest.[31] *The New York Times* Index, due to its brevity, may understate the amount of presidential or congressional news because the president and Congress are only mentioned in the Index if the indexer thought the president or Congress was a major participant in the story. Presidents may be secondary actors in many stories. But this restriction of the president and Congress as major participants in a story may be to our advantage. Public impressions of the president and presidential–congressional relations are most likely when the president plays a prominent, as opposed to secondary, role in a news story. Another limitation of these data is that the coding does not record the stage of the policy-making process, such as presidential initiation of legislation, committee hearings, floor debates, and/or roll call voting. Thus, we will not be able to pinpoint the policy-making stage of news coverage of the legislative presidency. Still, these data provide us with a comprehensive account of presidential and congressional news over

---

31 The codebook describes the president variable (variable 12) this way: "mentions the current President or his staff (including 'White House,' 'Clinton Administration,' 'Presidential spokesman'). Also includes historical references to past presidents concerning actions while in office. Also includes the Vice President. Also includes presidential advisory bodies, commissions, etc." For the Congress variable (variable 13), the codebook uses this language, "mentions the Congress, the House or Senate, Members of Congress, staff members, or the legislative process. Also includes congressional advisory bodies, Library of Congress, other legislative branch activities of the federal government. Also includes discussion of legislative debates where they clearly took place in Congress, even if Congress is not specifically mentioned. Does not include discussion of previously passed legislation unless Congress is specifically mentioned."

TABLE 3.4. *Frequency of News on the Legislative Presidency, Presidential News that Does Not Mention Congress, and Congressional News that Does Not Mention the President in* The New York Times, *1946–2006.*

	Nonpolicy News (%)	Policy News (%)	All News (%)
All other news	99.49	67.82	86.79
Congress without president	0.15	13.57	5.54
President without Congress	0.33	13.64	5.67
Legislative presidency	0.02	4.96	2.01
N	27801	18625	42426

These data are weighted to take into account changes in the number of stories per page in *The New York Times* Index.
Source: Policy Agendas Project, http://www.policyagendas.org/.

a relatively long period of time and allow us to say something about the incidence of news coverage on the legislative presidency.

For this analysis, *legislative presidency news* is defined as when both the president and Congress are mentioned in the coded index story. Table 3.4 presents a breakdown of the frequency of legislative presidency news, other presidential news, and other congressional news, for policy-related, non-policy-related, and all news stories, weighted by the number of estimated articles per year.

First, nonpolicy news swamps policy news in overall frequency. This makes sense given the expansiveness of the PAP sampling scheme and the variety of content in *The New York Times* (and other general news media). Policy news, that is, news that mentions a public policy, accounts for 43.8 percent of all news, still a healthy fraction. Second, the table indicates that when the president and/or Congress are mentioned in the index, it is in a policy story. There are very few nonpolicy stories that mention the president and/or Congress. Based on these figures, I calculate only 10 nonpolicy stories annually on the legislative presidency, less than one per month.[32] Nonpolicy stories on the president, however, are more common, about 159 per year, about one every other day. Congress nonpolicy stories, too, are rare, 72 per year, or about one every five days. These totals pale when compared policy stories on the legislative presidency, 1,255 (3.4 per day); presidency stories that do not mention Congress, 3,451 (9.5 per day), and Congress stories that do not mention the president, 3,444 (9.4 per day). Policy stories in which the president and/or Congress appear are frequent: On any given, day a reader of *The New York Times* can expect multiple stories on the two branches and their interactions. News coverage of these policy-making institutions is frequent. Moreover, that the president and/or Congress overwhelmingly appear in policy stories, and

32 This is based on a weighted average of 73,412 total stories per year.

rarely in nonpolicy ones, underscores the policy-making role and responsibilities of these two institutions over their celebrity.

This point also raises speculation that even when the president and/or members of Congress are involved in symbolic and ceremonial occasions, either they or the news media link those occasions to policy matters. This finding contrasts with Waterman, St. Clair, and Wright's (1999) argument that symbolism and image management are more important than policy for the public presidency. Presidential image management and policy making may be linked, at least in news coverage of the president. And insofar as news coverage affects public orientations to the president and/or Congress, then the symbolic and policy image of these policy makers may be intertwined.

This is not to say that presidents do not use symbols and image to bolster their policy leadership. Symbol manipulation – such as strong leadership, competence, morality, and patriotism – may be used to foster policy leadership. But, possibly, policy leadership can also burnish the president's symbolic leadership image. Speaking about certain policies in particular settings in particular ways may help the president convey an image of competence and confidence to voters. Recall that after uttering the famous line, "the only thing we have to fear is fear itself" from the opening paragraph of his first Inaugural Address (March 4, 1933), Franklin D. Roosevelt then proceeded to discuss the policy options and directions that his new administration would take. This is but one example of symbolic manipulation – here, the demonstration of presidential confidence used in the service of policy leadership. There might not be as bright a line separating symbol from policy as the Waterman, St. Clair, and Wright (1999) thesis suggests.[33]

Table 3.4 also indicates that the president and Congress appear frequently in policy news. Together, the two institutions account for approximately one-third of all policy news, shared about equally between the two branches. Further, legislative presidency news accounts for a significant proportion of policy news on the president and/or Congress, about 15 percent. Still, these figures suggest that the bulk of news about the president or Congress focuses on one branch at a time, not the two working together, a finding a variance with Cohen's (2008, 2009) estimates. The major difference between these figures and Cohen's is that Cohen collected data on the front page only, whereas these PAP data cover the entire newspaper.

Table 3.5 presents the PAP data for the front page only. In comparison with the entire newspaper, policy-related news appears in much greater frequency on the front page, about 46 percent of all front-page stories. However, the front page, compared with the entire newspaper, accounts for only 6.6 percent of all newspapers stories. Based on this estimate, there will be about 1.5 legislative presidency news stories per week and slightly more than four per week for the president and Congress alone on the front page. One reason

33 See Cohen (1997) for more on the connections between symbolism and policy.

TABLE 3.5. *Frequency of Front Page News on the Legislative Presidency, Presidential News that Does Not Mention Congress, and Congressional News that Does Not Mention the President in* The New York Times, *1946–2006.*

	Nonpolicy News (%)	Policy News (%)	All News (%)
All other news	98.86	53.86	69.22
Congressional without president	0.00	14.11	9.30
President without Congress	1.04	22.11	14.92
Legislative presidency	0.11	9.91	6.57
N	979	1889	2868

These data are weighted to take into account changes in the number of stories per page in *The New York Times* Index.
Source: Policy Agendas Project, http://www.policyagendas.org/.

that legislative presidency stories may not appear more frequently on the front page is if such news tends to be about the passage of legislation or roll call voting on important legislation that the president has taken a side on, as Miller (1977, 1978) found. These final outcomes of the legislative process are not frequent events themselves – Congress does not enact major legislation every day of the week.

If the front page is reserved for what editors consider the most important news, then we have an indication here of newspaper editors privileging policy over nonpolicy news. The comparatively frequent placement of legislative presidency news on the front page, compared with placement of such news on the back pages, may signal to readers the importance of this aspect of the presidency. If newspaper readers adopt the editors' definition of importance, such as front-page location, then we may surmise that readers also view the legislative presidency as important and perhaps use their understanding of presidential interactions with Congress in judging the president's leadership and job performance.

Where legislative presidency news accounted for about 15 percent of all news on the Congress and the presidency, on the front page it accounts for more than 21 percent of all such news. On average, news of the legislative presidency is thought to be more important by editors than news on either the presidency or Congress. Still, this 21 percent figure falls well shy of Cohen's figures, but again, differences in data collection probably account for this gap. Recall, the PAP uses *The New York Times* Index, and the brief accounts in the Index only record whether an actor is prominent in the news story. Cohen used the entire text of the news story, coding whether the president and a leader of Congress was mentioned. He did not assess the relative importance of the president or the congressional leader. Thus, his data collection method is less discriminating. More importantly, both point to the importance of the legislative presidency in the news.

The simple cross-tabulations presented thus far hide the temporal variation in government and policy news. Cohen (2008), for instance, reports an increase in the proportion of news on the president across the twentieth century, peaking in the 1970s and falling thereafter. He attributes much of this cycle of news attention to changes in the structure of the news media, especially the diffusion of cable television and other forms of new media.

Figure 3.6 plots by sets of ten years, beginning with 1946–55 through 1995–2006, the proportion of legislative presidency news for news overall, policy news, and front-page news. All three of these trend lines show peaks in the 1966–75 period. The more restrictive measures, especially those for front-page news, show a modest uptick in legislative presidency news in the last decade (1996–2006) from a post-peak bottom in the 1976–85 decade. Still, the news totals for that final decade are much lower than the peak decade of 1966–75. In contrast, the broadest indicator of news share – that is, for all news – shows that after the peak of 1966–75, the amount of legislative presidency news stays flat, at slightly under 2 percent (compared with nearly 4 percent during 1966–75). These trends show the displacement of hard news (i.e., policy news) by nonpolicy and softer news, a trend that has been noted elsewhere (Baum 2003; Baum and Kernell 1999, 2007; Cohen 2008; Kernell and Rice 2011; Patterson 2000). But still, legislative presidency news makes it on to the front page with some frequency, even in the era of soft news.

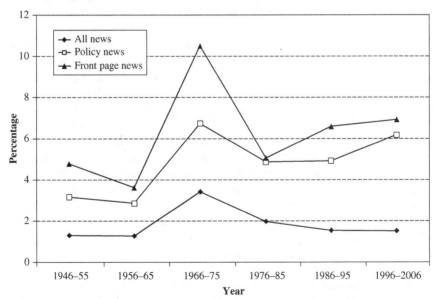

FIGURE 3.6. The Legislative Presidency in the News by Decade, 1946–2006.
Source: Policy Agendas Project, http://www.policyagendas.org/. See text for details.

CONCLUSION

The analysis in this chapter demonstrated that conditions in Congress – in particular, party control and polarization – affect the positions presidents take,
as well as presidential success, on congressional roll calls. Although the effects
of party control and polarization have been well documented before (Cohen,
Bond, and Fleisher 2013; Fleisher, Bond, and Wood 2008), there has been
much less attention to whether these congressional factors also influence the
president's policy positions (Cohen 2011a, 2012). Presidents' positions move
to the extremes when their party controls Congress, while divided government leads presidents to moderate their positions, conditional on the degree
of polarization between the parties. This set of findings is important for this
study for two reasons: (1) It establishes the effect of Congress on presidential
positions and success, attributes that voters use in assessing the president's
representation and strength. (2) Due to the impact of Congress on presidential
positions and success, presidents face a trade-off between being representative
(by taking moderate positions) and strong (by winning on roll calls).

The last section of this chapter tested whether there was enough news
about presidential–congressional relations for voters to use when assessing a president's leadership qualities, that is, presidential representation and
strength. Analyzing more than 50 years of the content analysis of *The New
York Times* Index from the Policy Agendas Project found a sufficient amount
of presidential–congressional news for voters. Presidential interactions with
Congress, labeled legislative presidency news, appeared frequently in the
pages of the *Times* and, with some frequency and regularity, appeared on the
front page of that newspaper, too.

Still, this chapter left some important questions unanswered. The analyses here did not demonstrate that voters use news reporting on presidential–
congressional interactions in evaluating presidential leadership qualities. This
assumption seems reasonable because other research shows that those who pay
more attention to the news are more knowledgeable about politics and public
affairs (Delli Carpini and Keeter 1996; Jerit, Barabas, and Bolsen 2006). I
will demonstrate later in this text that voters are quite accurate in where they
locate presidents along a liberal–conservative space; that is, the positions that
presidents take on roll calls predict where voters locate the president. Still, it
would be useful to have direct evidence that voters learn about presidential
positions and success with Congress from news reports.[34] Second, the theory
of public perceptions of presidential leadership argues that success with Congress affects whether voters perceive the president as strong or weak. This
assumption is tested in the next chapter.

---

34 Not every voter needs to attend to news coverage to learn about presidential positions and
   success. Voters who read newspapers and watch news broadcasts could inform the less atten-
   tive through conversations, for instance. For more on this type of information flow, see
   Cohen (2010, ch. 8).

4

Success in Congress and Perceptions
of Presidential Strength

"Winning isn't everything, it's the only thing"
Vince Lombardi, Fordham University Football Star and Coach

"America loves a winner. America will not tolerate a loser."
General George S. Patton, Final Pep Talk Speech to U.S. Troops before
D-Day Invasion, May 17, 1944

This chapter turns to the second major question of the theory of public perceptions of presidential leadership – the factors that affect those perceptions. The
theory identified at least three possible sources of those perceptions – voter
projection of leadership qualities onto the president, the individual traits of
presidents, and presidential behavior and performance in office. Although this
chapter will address each of these factors, the greatest emphasis will be given to
presidential performance – in particular, presidential relations with Congress.
As detailed in Chapter One, due to the importance accorded to and the volume
of news on presidential relations with Congress, such relations should have
strong and significant effects on voter perceptions of presidential leadership.

The theory of public perceptions suggests two hypotheses that link relations with Congress to perceptions of presidential leadership: (1) Presidential
positions on roll calls should affect whether voters think the president is a
good representative or not. (2) Presidential success on those roll calls should
affect whether voters think the president is strong versus weak. Unfortunately,
I am unable to test the positions-representation hypothesis directly because,
to my knowledge, no poll asks voters whether they think a president is a good
representative or not.[1] Later in this study, I test this hypothesis indirectly by
looking at whether policy distance, a measure of presidential representation,

1 I scanned the Roper Poll archive in vain for questions of this sort but was unable to locate any
relevant questions.

affects approval of the president. Thus, this chapter only tests the linkage between success and perceptions of strength.

The success-strength perceptions hypothesis reverses that casual arrow in most studies of presidential relations with Congress, which argues that public opinion, usually approval ratings, affect success.[2] Here, I am arguing in addition that relations with Congress can affect public opinion about the president. Although this perspective is uncommon, close Washington observers seem to think that presidential relations with Congress may affect the president's image with voters, and there are hints in the political science literature on this linkage as well.

I used two types of data to test this hypothesis, at the aggregate and individual levels. For the aggregate test, I collected all polls that asked voters to assess presidential strength, referring to specific presidents, not ideal presidents. From 1976–2011, there were 424 relevant polls questions. I used the cumulative data file of the American National Election studies (ANES) for the individual level test. From 1980–2004, the ANES has routinely asked respondents to rate presidents on various qualities, including strength. Both tests find support for the success-strength hypothesis. Before turning to the empirical analysis, let us review the literature on the effects of success in Congress on public attitudes toward the president.

FROM PRESIDENTIAL SUCCESS TO PUBLIC OPINION

Barely a year into his presidency, Jimmy Carter saw a deep erosion in his public standing, as his approval ratings slid from approximately 70 percent upon taking office in January 1977 to the mid-40s in April 1978. While a worsening economy accounted for some of the decline in public support, Washington observers also blamed Carter's rocky relations with Congress. Despite Democrats controlling both houses of Congress by comfortable margins, Carter got off on the wrong foot by threatening to veto popular water projects (Scheele 1978). In hopes of restoring his public standing and repair damage with congressional Democrats, Carter felt he needed a high-profile legislative victory. The administration identified Senate ratification of the Panama Canal treaties for that task.[3] Washington insiders concurred with the president about the

---

2 The literature on the effects of presidential approval on success in Congress is huge, and need not be cited fully here. Important studies that find an approval-support association include Barrett and Eshbaugh-Soha (2007); Brace and Hinckley (1992); Canes-Wrone and Demarchi (2002); Edwards (1976, 1980, 1989, 1997); Lebo and O'Geen (2011); Ostrom and Simon (1985); and Rivers and Rose (1985). However, Bond and Fleisher (1980, 1984, 1990); Bond, Fleisher, and Northrup (1988); Borrelli and Simmons (1993); Cohen et al. (2000); Collier and Sullivan (1995); and Lockerbie, Borrelli, and Hedger (1998) fail to detect such an association. A good review of the literature is found in Edwards (2009b).

3 The first, the Permanent Neutrality Treaty, was ratified on March 16. It declared the Canal neutral and open to vessels of all nations. The second, the Panama Canal Treaty, was ratified on April 18. It provided for joint Panama–U.S. control of the Canal through December 31, 1999; thereafter, control would shift to Panama.

potential public implications of a major legislative accomplishment. Hedrick Smith, *New York Times* reporter, contended that ratification of the Panama Canal treaties would "produce the kind of turnaround in Mr. Carter's public image that he has long been seeking" (Smith 1978). After a concerted effort by the administration, in March and April 1978, the Senate ratified the two treaties by 68–32 margins.[4]

Forty years later, congressional Republicans, stung by losing the presidency to Barack Obama in 2008, designed a legislative strategy they hoped would recapture the White House and Congress. That strategy entailed refusing to cooperate with the Obama administration on policy making (Grunwald 2012). Although policy distance between the Republicans and the administration in part underlies this noncooperation strategy, congressional Republicans also took into consideration the potential implications of legislative accomplishments for public perceptions of Obama's presidential leadership. Republicans assumed that denying the president legislative accomplishments would weaken his image among voters and would harm Democratic prospects in the 2010 elections and Obama's reelection in 2012. Like the Carter example, Washington insiders again assumed that presidential success in Congress would affect public perceptions of presidential leadership, job approval ratings, and election outcomes.

A modest political science literature also finds that presidential relations with Congress can affect his standing with the public. There are two sets of relevant studies. The first set looks directly at the impact of success on approval, while the second set provides indirect evidence that presidential relations with Congress may affect presidential approval.

The first set consists of only two dated and one more recent study. Using monthly data from 1953–80, Ostrom and Simon (1985) detect an endogenous relationship between approval and success; however, their estimation approach raises several issues. Among these issues, they measure success as the monthly cumulative percentage of presidential victories on roll calls. This measure is problematic because no, or only a small number of, roll calls may be held during a particular month. They note this issue (p. 340, ft. 4) and use the cumulative measure to smooth out month-to-month volatility caused by the sparse number of monthly roll calls, but this cumulative measure may lead to a temporal mismatch between approval and success. Finally, their roll call measure only uses domestic policy votes. A case can be made that foreign policy success will also affect voters' assessment of the president. Brace and Hinckley (1992) also test for endogeneity between approval and success using annual data from 1953–88 and find that approval and success affect each other. Still there are several issues in Brace and Hinckley's data. Most importantly, it is unclear that they have properly identified instruments to

---

4 The votes were held on March 16 and April 18, with 52 Democrats and 16 Republicans voting in favor, and 10 Democrats and 22 Republicans voting against.

implement their simultaneous equation (two-stage least squares) estimation.[5]
More recently, Cohen (2011b) uses simultaneous equation models on aggregate data spanning nearly 60 years (1953–2011). He finds that approval affects
success but, more relevant for present purposes, success also affects approval.[6]

A second set of studies do not bear directly on the relationship between
approval and success in Congress but suggest that aspects of presidential–
congressional relations may affect job approval ratings. First, Nicholson and
colleagues (2002) hypothesize and find that presidential approval will be
higher under divided than united government, arguing that divided government confuses voters as to which branch should be blamed: the president
(and his party) or the opposition Congress. Thus, during divided government,
some blame is deflected from the president onto Congress, resulting in higher
approval during divided than united government. Second, Groseclose and
McCarty (2001) develop a congressional blame game in which an opposition-
controlled Congress passes legislation in presidential reelection years, expecting the president to veto it. They argue vetoes harm the president's reputation
with the public, making him look politically extreme. Their analysis shows
dips in approval subsequent to presidential vetoes.[7]

Third, Groeling (2010) finds that costly criticism/support by members of
Congress affects presidential approval. *Costly criticism* is when presidential
co-partisans criticize the president, and *costly support* is when opposition
party members laud him. According to Groeling, the news media are more
likely to report costly communications than cheap talk (e.g., opposition criticism, co-partisan support). His analysis demonstrates that costly criticism/
support affects approval but cheap talk does not. Finally, Kriner and Schlicker
(2014), using monthly data from 1953–2006, find that congressional investigations of the executive branch negatively affect presidential approval.[8] All
of these studies suggest that presidential relations with Congress may affect
the president's approval ratings. Extrapolating from these studies, presidential

---

5 Brace and Hinckley have three endogenous variables: annual approval, success, and the number of presidential positions on roll calls. But their analysis of the success model does not
identify a unique exogenous variable, which is necessary for estimation of the two-stage least
squares (2SLS) technique. It is possible to perform 2SLS in a two-step fashion, first estimating the instrumented endogenous variables and then estimating the endogenous effects of the
instrumented variables in separate equations. This technique may affect the standard errors
in the second step, unless corrected. Brace and Hinckley do not provide enough detail to
determine if they used corrected standard errors.

6 Still, Cohen admits to issues in estimating the simultaneous equations because of limited
variables to use as instruments.

7 Another possibility is that vetoes indicate to the public that the president cannot get Congress
to accept his policies, that he is a weak leader, which will also harm his public reputation.

8 Kriner and Schlicker also argue that there may be an endogeneity between congressional
investigations and approval because Congress may be less willing to investigate the president
and executive branch when the president is popular and more willing to do so when he is
unpopular.

relations with Congress may affect other voter assessments of the president, such as perceptions of strength and representation.

AN AGGREGATE MEASURE OF PRESIDENTIAL STRENGTH, 1976–2011

To create the aggregate, time-series indicator of presidential strength of leadership, I searched the Roper Poll archive for all questions that asked respondents to assess this presidential attribute. The specific search queried the data archive for the president's last name (e.g., Carter, Reagan, Obama) and the word "leader" or "leadership." This search located 508 questions from 1976–2011 that asked respondents to rate a president's leadership. From this set of questions, 424 asked specifically about the president's strength of leadership. The analysis in this chapter is based on the strength of leadership questions. See the Appendix to this chapter for details on questions and sources.[9]

To test the effect of success on perceptions of presidential strength requires questions that ask voters to rate a specific president's strength of leadership, not questions on leadership in general nor expectations of an ideal president. Questions about a president's leadership in general are not specific enough to test the success-strength hypothesis. Voters may have several things in mind other than or instead of strength when answering a general question about a president's leadership. In addition, questions that ask about traits in an ideal president are not asking respondents to evaluate the strength of a specific president. Only questions asking voters to assess whether the president is strong or not are useful for testing the congressional success-strength hypothesis.

But as noted earlier, factors other than mere success in Congress may affect voter assessments of presidential strength. Presidents may rack up wins and losses in other arenas, for example, in foreign affairs. Although it would be useful to have measures of presidential success that encompasses noncongressional forms, doing so is difficult due to ambiguity in what constitutes a presidential success versus a defeat, and the data collection at this time is prohibitive. In contrast, there are conventional and unambiguous ways of determining success in Congress through roll calls. Also, voters think that one of the most important job duties of modern presidents is legislative policy leadership. Thus, despite these limitations, there is much to recommend success in Congress to test the success-strength linkage.

---

9 I chose to limit the analysis on the questions that ask about strength of leadership, and not merely leadership, because it is unclear what voters may be thinking when only asked about presidential leadership. They may be thinking about strength, but could also be thinking about representation, moral character, issue positions, or something else. The strength of leadership questions, in contrast, are unambiguous, at least in the sense of tapping attitudes on the aspect of leadership of concern in this chapter. The excluded questions are numbered 3, 8, 10, 13, and 32 in Appendix Tables 4.2 and 4.3.

Besides success, there are other factors that may affect voter perceptions of presidential strength. For instance, voters may project strength assessments onto presidents, perhaps due to their political predispositions, such as their partisanship. Thus, co-partisans may be more likely to view the president as being strong than opposition party identifiers or independents. From this perspective, perceptions of presidential strength are mere rationalizations of preexisting attitudes (Erikson 2004; Kramer 1983). Moreover, voters may learn about the individual traits, such as background and personality, and think that presidents are strong or not because of these traits. Both the projection and traits perspectives hypothesize stability in strength within presidencies. In contrast, the congressional success hypothesis predicts that presidential strength perceptions can vary within presidencies in as much as presidential success varies within presidencies.[10]

The search procedure identified 424 questions on presidential strength from nineteen polling organizations, using thirty-two different questions, from 1976 through June 2011.[11] No usable questions were asked prior to 1976, restricting the temporal range of the series, and the number of questions per year varied tremendously. Appendix Table 4.1 presents the breakdowns of the number of questions by year. No strength questions were asked in 1985, and a strength question was asked of voters fewer than ten times for nineteen of the thirty-six years in the series. The largest number of times that strength of leadership questions was posed to respondents was in 2004, with fifty. Overall, strength question are asked an average of 11.8 times per year with a standard deviation of 11.0. Presidential strength questions have become more common in recent years, especially since 2000, but still there is only one administration of such a question in 2008, and a strength question was asked only six times in 2007. Obviously, presidential leadership strength has not been a routine part of the polling arsenal of questions on presidents, like the presidential job performance question, or more recently, favorability/likability questions.

Pollsters who query respondents about presidential strength have not settled on a standard question. Even some polling firms have used several different questions. The irregularity of the series, in both temporal and question format senses, complicates the construction of an aggregate presidential leadership opinion series. My original intention in collecting these data was to use James Stimson's WCALC algorithm to create a presidential strength time series.[12] Stimson's algorithm requires overlap within time units of different question series. From this overlap, the marginals across questions can be compared

---

10 Any event that the public views as a success, whether congressionally based or not, should affect voters' perceptions of strength.

11 Even when two different polling houses used the same question, I count this as two questions due to possible house effects in the administration of surveys to respondents.

12 Stimson's WCALC program can be accessed at http://www.unc.edu/~jstimson/Software. html. The process was first introduced in Stimson (1999), with construction of the famous public mood indicator. Since then, it has been employed in numerous studies to construct time series from a variety of survey questions.

and adjusted, and a latent underlying dimension can be extracted. For this procedure, there cannot be any gaps in the series. Despite the large number of polls that I collected, these conditions are not met. Not only are there no polls for 1985, but only 201 of the 426 months (from January 1976 through June 2011) had any leadership poll, 47 percent of these months. Even collapsing the data by quarter fails to help, as there are no polls for 41 of the 142 quarters (29 percent). Thus, the analysis will use each of the 424 polls as separate data points. While this poses some complications for the analysis, it also allows estimation of simultaneous equation models. Before turning to that analysis, the next two sections address two key questions: How stable are these perceptions of presidential strength within administrations? And, how similar are these strength perceptions to presidential job approval?

Intra-Administration Stability of Leadership Perceptions

The projections and individual presidential characteristics perspectives predict intra-administration stability of public perceptions of presidential strength. In contrast, the presidential performance perspective predicts considerable intra-administration variability in how the public rates a president's strength of leadership – as a president wins more frequently, voters should be more inclined to view the president as strong, but as the president begins to lose with frequency, voters should begin to see him as less strong, as weak. Summed over individual voters, there should be an association between the percentage of times a president wins during a time period and the percentage of voters who view the executive as strong versus weak.

To test these competing hypotheses, using the survey marginals of the 424 strength of leadership questions, I first calculated a net positive score by taking the percentage of positive responses and dividing them by the addition of the percentage of positive and percentage of negative responses.[13] This calculation corrects for differences in "no opinion" responses across the different survey questions.[14] Then, I regressed these net positive scores on dummy variables for the question used and the number of response categories. The regression also clusters on the month of the survey to correct possible non-independence of observation when multiple surveys were conducted in the same month. As expected, differences in the question posed and the number of response categories affects the net positive response and accounts for 24 percent of the variance.[15]

---

13 Net positive leadership score = (Percentage of positive responses)/(Percentage of positive responses + Percentage of negative responses).

14 This calculation procedure was first recommended by Beyle, Niemi, and Sigelman (2002) in their study of the popularity of governors, senators, and presidents at the state level, using multiple question formats across a variety of surveys and polls.

15 Clustering does not appear to affect the performance of the estimation, as the R^2 remains 21 percent.

TABLE 4.1. *Impact of Presidential Dummy Variables on Aggregate Perceptions of Presidential Strength, 1976–2011.*[a]

Variable	b	SE	t	p
Carter	−5.43	3.56	−1.53	0.13
Reagan	17.11	3.13	5.45	0.000
Bush 1	18.04	2.62	6.89	0.000
Clinton	6.96	2.34	2.98	0.003
Bush 2	11.56	2.51	5.61	0.000
Obama	18.18	2.84	6.40	0.000
Number of categories	−2.18	3.19	−0.68	0.50
Constant	52.79	6.95	7.60	0.000
R^2	0.40			
N	424			

[a] Clustered on year-month of survey
Source: See text for details.

Next, I added dummy variables for each president, with Ford as the criterion case, into this estimation. If the projections and/or presidential characteristics perspectives were valid, we should find the presidential dummies to be strong predictors of these leadership scores. In contrast, the presidential performance model hypothesizes that there will still be a considerable amount of variation in these aggregate public perceptions left unaccounted. Table 4.1 presents the results of the presidential dummy estimation. The table does not report the specific coefficients associated with question wording.

There is some support for the projections/presidential trait perspectives. The addition of the presidential dummy variables increases the R^2 to 40 percent, a 16 percent increase over the estimation that did not include the presidential dummies. Still, this leaves a substantial amount of the variance unaccounted for. All of the presidential dummies are significant, except for Carter. The constant captures the effect of the criterion case – here, Ford – which indicates that Ford on average received a strength rating of 52.8. The dummies for the other presidents indicate how much higher or lower their strength of leadership ratings are compared with Ford. All except Carter have positive signs, indicating that respondents on average rated all of the other presidents as stronger than Ford, sometimes by large amounts. For example, Obama and George H. W. Bush are eighteen points higher and Reagan is seventeen points higher in strength than Ford. The insignificant Carter coefficient suggests that his leadership ratings, on average, are no different from Ford's.

Figure 4.1 provides a visual perspective on these presidential strength ratings. Because there are differences in the ratings presidents receive across questions due to question wordings and response categories, we cannot simply

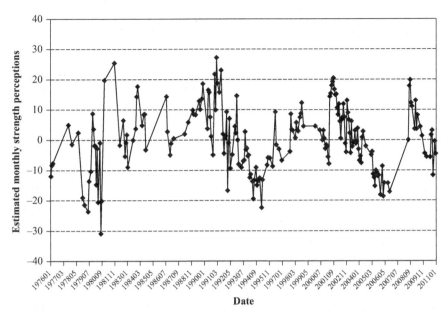

FIGURE 4.1. Trends in Presidential Strength Ratings, Estimated Monthly Ratings, 1976–2011.
Source: See text for details.

take the average of surveys conducted the same month (or quarter). To produce a valid and useful visual portrait of trends in presidential leadership ratings, I saved the residuals from the regression that used the question dummies and number of response categories as predictors; the presidential dummies are not used in this estimation. The resulting scores are now the strength ratings purged of the question and number of response categories, making the strength perception scores across questions comparable. Then, I averaged these residuals by the month of the surveys to create the monthly presidential strength scores, which are plotted on Figure 4.1.[16] On the figure, positive values indicate higher strength perception scores and negative ones indicate weaker strength perceptions. Thus, the highest value (27.2) can be interpreted as 58.1 percent stronger than the lowest residual value (–30.9). For now, the most important information conveyed on the figure is the variability in the scores, which suggests considerable variation within presidencies. But from

16 Residuals are the variance left unaccounted for by the predictor variables, in this case, the question dummies and response category variable. The size of the residual is the distance from the prediction to the actual value. Residuals may be either positive or negative, which tell us whether the predictive model over- or underestimates the actual value. Large residuals, either positive or negative, imply that the predictive model does a poor job in accounting for variance. Thus, the plot in Figure 4.1 has positive and negative values, with 0 indicating perfect prediction by the regression model.

TABLE 4.2. *Descriptive Statistics of Monthly Averaged Estimated Presidential Leadership Strength Ratings.*

President	n	Mean	Standard Deviation	Minimum	Maximum
All	201	0.3	10.6	−30.9	27.2
Ford	3	−9.3	2.3	−12.0	−7.7
Carter	19	−7.6	13.1	−30.9	19.7
Reagan	22	4.1	8.2	−9.0	25.4
Bush 1	30	7.5	10.1	−16.7	27.2
Clinton	47	−3.4	8.4	−22.4	14.6
Bush 2	62	0.2	10.0	−18.6	20.5
Obama	18	3.8	8.6	−11.6	19.9

The values are residuals after regressing the strength perceptions on dummy variables for question wording. Then the residuals are averaged by month.
Source: See text for details.

the visual inspection alone, we cannot determine if that within-presidency variance is random or not.

Table 4.2 presents descriptive statistics for the plot on Figure 4.1 by president. The standard deviation indicates considerable intra-administration variance. Generally, there is a good deal of variance within administrations, ranging from eight to ten for most presidents, except for Ford, who has a low standard deviation, which is a function of the few data points, and Carter, who has the largest standard deviation, at more than thirteen. Yet, from inspection of Figure 4.1 and Table 4.2, it is not clear what drives intra-presidency variance in leadership ratings, whether that variance is random or systematically determined.

The preceding discussion provides, at best, a weak test of the projections/presidential characteristics models of public perceptions of presidential leadership strength. All that the regression with the presidential dummies can test for is differences in the average level of leadership ratings across presidents. These regressions do not provide a direct test of the impact of projections or particular traits on perceptions of presidential strength.

Furthermore, my discussion of the predispositions and traits perspectives may unfairly caricaturize them. Predispositions, such as partisanship, are likely to be highly stable within administrations, but not necessarily static, as my discussion assumes.[17] Plus, as presidents gain experience on the job, and learn better how to be president, they may make improved use of the traits

17 Numerous studies have investigated the dynamic properties of party identification at the individual level. For a recent study with a good review of the past literature, see Bartels et al. (2011).

that enhance their performance and less use of traits that harm their performance. Light (1982, 1999), for example, argues that there is a cycle of increasing effectiveness for presidents – the longer they are in office, the more effective they are as president.[18] Finally, partisanship does not exhaust the political predispositions relevant for strength of presidential leadership. Presidential job approval may also be thought to be an important political predisposition. Job approval ratings are not stable within administrations. Insofar as voters use these assessments to rate presidents on strength of leadership, then we would expect some intra-administration volatility in strength ratings too. From this perspective, political predispositions will determine voter ratings of presidential strength, the predisposition being job approval. In other words, perceptions of presidential leadership strength may be nothing more than another way of measuring job approval. This raises the question of whether these leadership ratings are anything but presidential approval ratings, the topic of the next section.

Are Perceptions of Strength and Job Approval Merely the Same Thing?

Whether public ratings of presidential leadership strength and job approval are the same is in actuality a question of the nature of public opinion regarding the presidency. Are voters naïve and simplistic in the attitudes and assessments of presidents? Or are voters more discriminating and complex in how they assess presidents?

Voters' lack of interest and information about politics and public affairs (Delli Carpini and Keeter 1996) and their high and unrealistic expectations for presidents (Simon 2009), suggest they are naïve and simplistic in their assessments of presidents. Still, the visibility and the volume of news coverage on the chief executive suggest the potential for voters to be more discriminating in their evaluation of presidents. The public receives a considerable amount of information about presidents, much of it easy to understand. For instance, a voter might learn that the sitting president wins roll call after roll call in Congress, as well as the ideological orientation of the policies that the president has advocated and promoted. This president's high legislative victory rate might lead the voter to think the president is a strong leader. But what if the voter disagrees with the policy direction that the president took on his legislative agenda? This latter consideration might lead the voter to disapprove of the president's job performance. In other words, a president may be viewed as a strong leader because he is a winner but as doing a poor job because of voter disagreement with his policy decisions. It is an empirical question whether voters are naïve and think highly

18 For some evidence in support of the cycle of increasing effectiveness, see Krause and O'Connell (2011).

of any president who they happen to like on whatever basis or whether they are more discriminating.

There is some empirical work that suggests voters are somewhat discriminating in their evaluations of presidents. First, the public apparently distinguishes between presidential character traits and job performance, although the two are related (Greene 2001; Newman 2002, 2003, 2004). If such assessments were identical, their relationship would be so strong that nothing else would emerge as a statistically significant predictor. But Greene and Newman show that factors besides character affect job approval, such as the state of the economy.[19] A second distinction has been made between job approval ratings and emotional affect toward the president, usually labeled *favorability* or *likability*.[20] Several studies find differences between job approval and favorability ratings – in particular, that Bill Clinton's job performance ratings did not suffer much during the Lewinsky scandal–impeachment period, although his favorability ratings declined more severely (Cohen 1999a, 1999b, 2000; McAvoy 2008). Kiousis (2003) argues that news coverage has different effects on presidential job approval and favorability. A third perspective suggests that voters evaluate presidential job performance differently across policy areas. For example, Nickelsburg and Norpoth (2000) demonstrate that foreign policy approval and economic policy approval differentially affect overall job approval, implying that voters discriminate between these two policy realms when assessing the overall performance of the president in office (also Cohen 2002a, 2002b; McAvoy 2006; Newman and Lammert 2011). Thus, a case can be made, both conceptually and empirically, that the public discriminates in evaluating presidents across different dimensions. Is this the case for strength of leadership and job approval?

To begin answering this question, Figure 4.2 overlays the monthly job approval ratings onto the monthly estimated presidential leadership strength ratings (as presented on Figure 4.1). In general, there is some consistency between the two series, but there are many instances of (large) gaps between the approval and strength ratings. The two series, however, are correlated strongly with a Pearson's r of 0.71 (p = 0.000). But note also that a correlation of 0.71 equates with an R^2 of 0.50.[21] Only one-half of the variance in the two series is shared.

Figure 4.3 presents the scatter plot between the approval and strength series, with a regression line overlaid. The regression line's slope tells us that

19 Neither Greene nor Newman considers that perceptions of character traits and job approval may be endogenous. Their analyses treat character traits as exogenous, as affecting job approval, but that approval does not affect perceptions of presidential character traits. If perceptions of traits and job approval are endogenous, this type of model misspecification may affect their results.

20 Ragsdale (1991) is the first to my knowledge to study the sources of emotional reactions to presidents and to distinguish them from job approval.

21 In other words, the two series only share half of their variance with each other, leaving a considerable amount of variance that is independent or different across them.

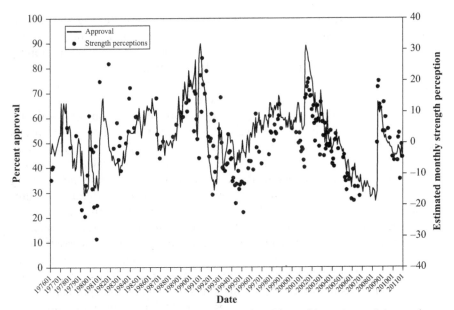

FIGURE 4.2. Monthly Presidential Job Approval and Monthly Estimated Strength Perceptions Compared, 1976–2011.

Source: See text for details.

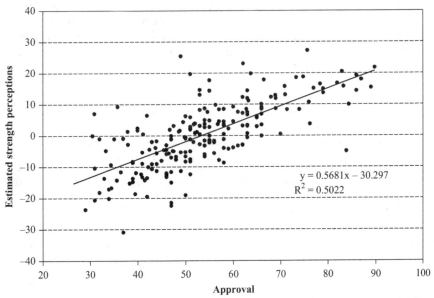

FIGURE 4.3. Scatter Plot between Monthly Estimated Strength Perceptions and Job Approval Ratings, 1977–2011.

Source: See text for details.

as job approval ratings go up, so do the strength ratings. But the scatter plot also indicates variability around the regression line – many data points are not on or near the line. There are several possible sources of the differences between leadership and approval ratings. In particular, the leadership ratings may contain considerable measurement error or noise, which may be due to combining many different types of questions.

The ANES allows us to test the relationship between job approval and strength ratings at the individual level because those surveys have asked voters about both types of assessments in almost all of its surveys from 1980–2004. Table 4.3 presents a cross-tabulation of the presidential approval and leadership ratings. There is a positive relationship between approval and respondent rating of presidential leadership, as in the aggregate analysis, but a significant number of respondents, approximately 60 percent, fall into the off-diagonal cells. Moreover, as for the aggregate data, there is only a modest correlation between the two types of presidential ratings (see the various correlation coefficients displayed on Table 4.3). Although approval and leadership ratings are related, voters seem to discriminate between the two standards. Perhaps voters employ different standards in evaluating presidential strength and job approval.

The next sections details the sources of public assessments of presidential strength of leadership and tests the primary hypothesis of this research: that victory rates in Congress will have a statistically significant impact on whether voters view the president as a strong or weak leader. When victory rates are high, everything else being equal, voters will be likely to view the president as strong, but as victory rates fall, voters will increasingly see the president as a weak leader. This analysis proceeds in two stages, presenting first the analysis on the aggregate leader data and then utilizing the individual level data from the ANES.

TABLE 4.3. *Relationship between Presidential Strength and Approval Ratings at the Individual Level, 1980–2004.*

Presidential Approval	Presidential Leadership			
	Not Well at All	Not Too Well	Quite Well	Extremely Well
Strongly disapprove	60.7	32.4	8.9	3.4
Disapprove	23.9	33.5	22.2	11.2
Approve	6.7	14.1	21.6	14.2
Strongly approve	8.8	20.0	47.3	71.2
N	3,074	6,305	4,038	1,573

Cells are column percentages.
Question: Does "he provides strong leadership" describe "president's name"?
Gamma = 0.61, p = 0.007, Kendall's tau_b = 0.45, p = 0.006, Pearson's r = 0.45, p = 0.000
Source: American National Election Studies, 1980–2004.

DOES SUCCESS IN CONGRESS AFFECT
PERCEPTIONS OF STRENGTH?

Aggregate Tests

The key hypothesis under consideration is the effect of success in Congress on public perceptions of presidential leadership strength. The specific hypothesis tested here looks at the president's success rate in Congress, not the size of his victory (defeat) margins. Although the size of the victory/defeat margin may be important, to apply that standard in evaluating presidential strength requires a level of knowledge that voters may not have. Thus, the analysis uses the less restrictive assumption about voter knowledge: that voters will have a vague idea about the overall success level of the president in Congress rather than specific details.[22]

To measure presidential victory rates in Congress, I use the average of the House and Senate vote concurrence rates from Ragsdale (2009, Table 9.7, pp. 500–2). Vote concurrence is the percentage of roll calls in which the president's side won (p. 477), what is often called *success* in the literature.[23] I supplement Ragsdale's collection, which ends with 2007, by turning to the *Congressional Quarterly* (CQ) Presidential Support Scores results for 2008–11 from their annual stories on the topic. CQ is the primary source that Ragsdale relies on for the concurrence measures. For the final measure of success (*concurrence*, using Ragsdale's term), I average the House and Senate concurrence scores, assuming that voters do not distinguish House from Senate success.[24]

There are several statistical issues to deal with in testing the success-strength perceptions hypothesis. First, variables besides success in Congress may affect public perceptions of presidential strength. Earlier we found, for instance, a correlation between job approval and perceptions of presidential

---

22 We lack information on voter knowledge about presidential–congressional relations and can only test for the direct effects of presidential success on voter strength perceptions, not those effects mediated through the news nor mediated through voters' knowledge and understanding. In this sense, the tests offered here are conservative and will be the hardest to find support for.

23 Ragsdale calls *success* "concurrence" and calls *member support* "member concurrence" (2009, p. 477). Member concurrence is the percentage of times a member voted on the same side as the president.

24 There are issues with the decision to average all roll calls on which a president takes a stand. Most importantly, such a measure lumps together important and less important votes, and the news media are not very likely to report on the less important items. But in the aggregate, measures of presidential success on important (e.g., CQ key votes) and less important roll call votes tend to be highly correlated. Moreover, the blunter measure used here, which not only uses all presidential positions but averages them across the two congressional chambers, probably does a good job of indexing to voters whether a president generally is victorious or not. See Bond and Fleisher (1980), Edwards (1985), King (1986), and Shull and Vanderleeuw (1987) for discussions of the properties and relationships across various measures of presidential success in Congress.

strength. The analysis needs to control for these other factors – in particular, approval – to ensure that any statistical association between success and strength perceptions is not spurious. Second, success, approval, and strength perceptions may be endogenous; that is, each may affect the others. If these variables are endogenous, it may be difficult to sort out the causal relationships among them, especially using standard statistical techniques, like regression, which assume the independent variables are exogenous to the dependent variable. A major order of business for the analysis is determining the causal structure among these variables, whether they are endogenous or exogenous.

Because each statistical approach forces some analytical compromises and because this is the first time that perceptions of presidential strength have been given any serious empirical inspection, I do several different types of analyses on several different ways of measuring perceptions of presidential strength. The first set of analyses uses the aggregate presidential leadership scores; the second set uses the individual level data from the ANES. The aggregate analysis begins with the strength scores from the 424 individual surveys from 1976–2011. Congressional success is measured annually, which means the same success value will be used for each of the strength polls taken during a year. I also use the Gallup approval reading for months with presidential leadership surveys. For months where there are multiple presidential leadership polls, this means that the Gallup approval reading of such a month also will be used repeatedly. Using the success and approval readings repeatedly creates a statistical issue by violating the independence of observation assumption for regression. The advantage in using the 424 strength readings is that they allow me to use the thirty-two question dummies as exogenous variables for the simultaneous equation estimation (two-stage least squares) to determine if strength perceptions and success in Congress are endogenous. Still, all the analyses using the 424 strength perceptions data show that success in Congress is positively associated with those perceptions, as the hypothesis predicts.

A second set of aggregate analyses use the 201 monthly estimated strength scores because of the preceding statistical issues, primarily the violation of the independence of observation assumption.[25] Assuming that success is exogenous to strength perceptions, I can turn to techniques that control for the fact that success is an annual measure. These analyses also show support for the success-strength hypothesis.

As a final set of analyses, I use the individual-level data from the ANES, which include measures of public perceptions of presidential strength as well as job approval. Similar to the aggregate analyses, disentangling the endogeneity between strength perceptions and approval is daunting. But these data are structured such that we can make stronger claims that success is exogenous

---

25 Recall these 201 monthly scores are based on combining the strength scores from the 424 polls when there are one or more such polls per month, as described previously.

to the strength perceptions (and approval) because the ANES surveys are conducted at the end of the year, after all roll calls that are used to construct the success variables have been taken. This temporal ordering – where success comes before measuring strength perceptions and job approval – allows us to argue that success is exogenous to the strength perceptions and job approval ratings. Again, the analyses show a positive and statistically significant effect of success in Congress on voters' perceptions of presidential strength. For an extended discussion of the endogeneity issue and the selection of instruments for use in the analysis, see the Appendix to this chapter.

Results

Table 4.4 presents the results of the two-stage least squares (2SLS) estimation. (Results of the first-stage estimation are presented in Appendix Table 4.3.) First, the three equations fit the endogenous (dependent) variables well, with R^2s of 0.63 for strength perceptions, 0.69 for presidential approval, and 0.82 for

TABLE 4.4. *Two-Stage Least Squares Estimation of Strength Perceptions, Success, and Approval, 1975–2011.*

	Endogenous (Dependent) Variable					
	Strength Perceptions[a]		Success		Approval	
Variable	b	SE	b	SE	b	SE
Strength perception	—		−0.05	0.09	0.51***	0.06
Success	0.65***	0.07	—		0.27**	0.08
Approval	0.56***	0.06	−0.02	0.08	—	
Divided	21.99***	2.41	63.58***	8.96	10.99***	3.17
Misery Index (lagged)[b]	—		—		−3.57***	0.35
Events	—		—		2.47***	0.62
Second term	—		−3.04***	0.99	−5.90***	1.11
Polarization	—		30.25***	6.21	—	
Divided × Polarization	—		−127.21***	12.03	—	
Constant	−21.44	6.38	73.56	4.24	22.72	6.32
N	424		424		424	
R^2	0.63		0.82		0.70	

[a] Also controls for seven question dummy variables used as instruments.
[b] Lagged one month
* p < 0.05, ** p < 0.01, *** p < 0.001
Source: See text for details.

success in Congress. The most important findings are those for the effects of the endogenous variables on each other. Taking strength perceptions first, as anticipated by earlier findings, approval strongly affects perceptions of presidential strength. The coefficient indicates that each 1 percent shift in approval corresponds to a 0.56 percent shift in strength perceptions. A one-standard-deviation shift in approval corresponds to a 7 percent shift in strength perceptions.[26] Of greatest interest is the impact of success on strength perceptions. The coefficient for success is positive and significant, with each 1 percent change in success corresponding to a 0.65 percent shift in strength perceptions. A one-standard-deviation change in success (16.4) leads to a 10.5 percent change in strength perceptions. Not only is this effect statistically significant (t = 8.66, p = 0.000), but it is substantively meaningful as well.

Strength perceptions and success also affect presidential approval. Each 1 percent change in strength perceptions produces a 0.51 shift in approval. A one-standard-deviation change in these perceptions (12.2) will lead to slightly more than a 6 percent shift in approval. Success in Congress also positively affects approval, but not as strongly as success affects strength perceptions. With a regression coefficient of 0.27 and a standard deviation of 16.4, a one-standard-deviation increase in success leads to a 4.4 percent increase in approval.

Turning to the success equation, neither approval nor strength perceptions appear to affect success; coefficients for both fall short of statistical significance. The insignificance of approval on success is especially troubling. Although there is a debate in the literature on the effects of approval on success, most aggregate studies find that approval affects success.[27] Recall, success is measured annually, while approval is measured monthly, and there are multiple strength perception readings per month for some months. The mismatch in temporal units might account for the lack of effect of strength perceptions and approval on success. But this mismatch should have weakened the impact of success on the two presidential attitudes because the roll call votes used to create the annual success measure may occur after the opinion measure. A roll call vote during the second half of a year cannot affect opinion during the first half of the year, for example, unless presidential success on roll calls is relatively constant across the year.[28] One way to deal with this

---

26 The standard deviation of approval is 12.5.

27 There are numerous issues in the literature on estimating the effects of approval on success. For good conceptual discussions see Edwards (1997, 2009b) and Cohen (2011b). The literature on the question is massive; again, see Edwards and Cohen for reviews of that literature.

28 This is a plausible if we assume that the actual success rate reflects the probability of a presidential victory at any point in time across the year. This is all the more likely because factors that affect success tend not to vary across the year, like party control and polarization levels. But that scenario also assumes that all presidential roll calls are likely to occur with an equal likelihood at any time across the year. Krehbiel (1998), in contrast, argues that bills more likely to pass will occur earlier in a Congress, giving rise to the honeymoon effect.

mismatch is to construct a success variable, for instance, a running tally of success for roll calls that come prior to the opinion measures.[29] Another is to use multilevel modeling approaches that help control for the nesting of the opinion measures within the time units of the success measures, a technique employed in the next section.

Finally, a brief discussion of the control variables is in order. First, presidents are considered stronger during divided as opposed to united government. The effect appears massive, too, with divided government presidents receiving 22 percent higher strength perceptions than united government presidents. It is not clear why this effect is so large. One possibility is that the equation to estimate strength is too sparse, that it lacks several important control variables. But such underspecification would only matter if the absent controls were correlated with success. Another possibility is that divided government actually has large effects on public perceptions of presidential strength. For example, although divided government lowers a president's success rate in Congress, divided government probably also increases the number of times that the president must confront Congress over policy differences. Perhaps presidents look better to voters in these policy disputes, and thus, when presidents stand up to recalcitrant opposition congresses, their reputation among voters soars. All of this is speculation, which deserves further elaboration.

Several control variables also significantly affect approval. Again, divided government presidents are more popular than united government ones, here by about 11 percent, a very strong result, much higher than found by Nicholson and colleagues (2002). The positive–negative event variables also affect approval. Positive events boost approval about 2.5 percent, with negative events depressing approval also by that amount. Presidents will be 5 percent more popular during a month of positive events compared with a month of negative events. The results also indicate that second-term presidents are less popular, by nearly 6 percent. Finally, economic misery lowers presidential approval 3.5 percent for each 1 percent uptick in misery. A one-standard-deviation shift in the Misery Index will swing presidential approval approximately 5.6 percent, while a president serving during the worst of times will be about 24.5 percent less popular than a president serving during the best of economic times.[30]

Finally, consider the impact of controls on the success equation. The results are somewhat complicated because of the interaction between divided government and polarization. For both of the constituent variables of the interaction, the signs are opposite to what is normally expected because they are positive. But we should not interpret these signs and coefficients in an interaction model as we would without interactions; the coefficients are conditional and

---

29 This is the approach that Ostrom and Simon (1985) take.
30 The Misery Index in these data ranges from about 3.8 to 10.6, and with a standard deviation of 1.6.

depend on all the relevant variables in the equation. For instance, consider the effects of united government for three polarization conditions: least (0.51), average (0.75), and highest (0.91). For all three conditions, presidential success will be about 63.6 percent.[31] Now consider the effects of divided government during the same three periods of polarization. Under divided government, presidents can expect to win about 78 percent of the time during the lowest level of polarization, 55 percent when polarization is at average levels, and 39 percent when polarization is at its highest. These results repeat the effect of polarization on minority presidents – as polarization increases, success falls.

A MULTILEVEL MODEL OF PRESIDENTIAL STRENGTH PERCEPTIONS

The preceding analyses suggest that neither approval nor strength appears to affect success in Congress; that is, success is exogenous to approval and strength perceptions. But, the 2SLS estimation could not take into account the mismatch in the temporal units used to measure the three variables – most importantly, the annual measurement of success compared with strength perceptions, which often are measured multiple times per month. Multilevel modeling, in which some variables are nested within other variables, is one approach to help resolve this measurement mismatch. Here, we can think of both strength perceptions and approval being nested within year, the time unit for success.

In this section, I use an estimation technique that combines instrumental variable estimation and multilevel modeling.[32] This technique, however, is limited—it can only perform a two-equation 2SLS and only allows for one nesting level. The data here are measured with several levels (i.e., time units) – within months for strength perceptions, months for approval, and years for success. Thus, a mixed-level, simultaneous equation estimation cannot handle all of the complexity of the data structure. But because it corrects for at least one of the issues of the preceding analysis, it can help check to see if the results are stable across different estimation techniques. For this analysis, we must assume that success in Congress is truly exogenous to approval and strength perceptions; this may be a problematic assumption as the earlier discussion points out.

---

31 This is because the value of united government = 0, and thus, all the terms other than the constant drop out. That the president's success level remains the same under united government – no matter the degree of polarization – has been found in other research, for instance, in Chapter Three in this book.

32 For instance, the xtivreg command in STATA 11.0, which I use later. The xtivreg procedure uses the Balestra and Varadharajan-Krishnakumar G2SLS random effects estimator. Technical details of the estimator can be found in Balestra and Varadharajan-Krishnakumar (1987). I used the random effects (re) xtivreg model, which assumes that the congressional success variable is a random sample of all possible values of success. Using the re model allows us to see the statistical effect of success on strength perceptions, our primary hypothesis.

TABLE 4.5. *Multilevel, Simultaneous Equation Estimation of Approval, Success, and Strength Perceptions, 1975–2011.*

Variable	Approval				Strength			
	b	SE	z	p	b	SE	z	p
Approval	—				0.50	0.11	4.43	0.00
Question 4	0.95	2.48	0.38	0.70	−0.19	2.02	−0.09	0.93
Question 19	0.11	1.45	0.07	0.94	1.33	1.17	1.13	0.26
Question 26	−2.19	2.72	−0.80	0.42	−12.69	2.20	−5.76	0.00
Question 27	2.83	4.15	0.68	0.50	11.89	3.40	3.50	0.00
Question 28	−0.02	2.67	−0.01	0.99	14.86	2.16	6.88	0.00
Question 34	2.48	1.31	1.89	0.06	4.32	1.09	3.96	0.00
Question 36	−0.03	4.82	−0.01	1.00	−18.99	3.89	−4.89	0.00
Success	0.40	0.15	2.71	0.01	0.50	0.11	4.53	0.00
Divided government	15.92	4.86	3.27	0.00	18.82	3.85	4.89	0.00
Misery Index (lag)	−3.28	0.60	−5.42	0.00	—			
Events	2.44	0.63	3.86	0.00	—			
Second term	−6.42	3.26	−1.97	0.05	—			
Constant	40.39	12.07	3.35	0.00	−8.42	9.73	−0.87	0.39

N = 424, R^2 (overall) = 0.62, sigma_u = 5.55, sigma_e = 5.36, rho = 0.52
Source: See text and Table 4.4 for details.

Table 4.5 presents results of the multilevel, simultaneous equation estimation, using the same variables as in Table 4.4. Substantively, the results closely resemble those in Table 4.4, although some of the coefficients, such as divided government, are muted slightly. Most important are the effects of success and approval on strength perceptions. Recall that approval is instrumented in this estimation, while success is not, and the multilevel model assumes that success is measured in annual time units. Both approval and success retain their strong effects on strength perceptions, but the coefficients are smaller than found in Table 4.4. This suggests that modeling choices may have some impact on the size of the effect, but differences in statistical modeling choices do not upend the impact of approval or success on strength perceptions. In the multilevel model, the coefficient for approval is 0.50 (compared with 0.56 earlier), is nearly the same, and is significant at p < 0.000. The success coefficient drops from 0.65 (given previously) to 0.50 in the multilevel model, with a p = 0.000. For both approval and success, a one-percentage-point shift produces a 0.5 percent shift in strength perceptions. A one-standard-deviation shift in approval (about 12 percent), leads to a 6 percent change in strength perceptions, while a one-standard-deviation change in success (about 16 percent) corresponds to an 8 percent alteration in strength perceptions. Importantly, for the main hypothesis under investigation here, success has pronounced effects on voter perceptions of presidential strength of leadership.

AN AGGREGATE TEST USING MONTHLY ESTIMATED
STRENGTH PERCEPTIONS

This section turns our attention to the 201 monthly estimated presidential strength perceptions, which are plotted on Figure 4.1. Recall that these monthly estimations first purge the effects of question wording and number of response categories on the 424 individual strength perception questions and then average these purged results for questions asked in the same month. This produces 201 monthly measures of strength perceptions. It is useful to turn to a monthly measure because, sometimes, there are multiple strength perception questions per month, but approval is measured monthly, leading to a mismatch in the time units of these two key variables. The annual measure of success in Congress compounds the time unit mismatch. The previous section used a multilevel model to account for the annual measurement of success, but the mismatch between strength perceptions and approval remained.

But there are also complications using the monthly strength perceptions indicator. First, the number of cases (n) falls to 201 as a result of combining the multiple polls per month. Second, and perhaps more important, we can no longer use the question wording dummies to instrument strength perceptions. Those dummies unambiguously met the exclusion restriction and strength of instrument requirements for instrumental variable estimation (see the Appendix of this chapter for details). Our lack of knowledge of the predictors of presidential strength perceptions erects a hurdle to finding other instruments, especially ones that would not affect approval. Thus, the analysis presented here should be viewed as exploratory, much like that of the previous sections of this chapter.

Table 4.6 presents the simultaneous (2SLS), multilevel model estimation of approval (instrumented) and success on the monthly estimated strength perceptions. The control variables are the same as those in Table 4.5, except that we can no longer use the question wording dummies as instruments for strength perceptions. Thus, strength perceptions are not instrumented; only approval is.

The substantive results repeat those of the earlier analyses. Both approval and success are significant and positive, as hypothesized, although their coefficients are smaller than found in the earlier analyses. The coefficient for approval is now 0.36, compared with 0.50 in Table 4.5, the multilevel estimation that used the 424 actual strength perception readings. This coefficient indicates that a one-percentage-point shift in approval leads to a 0.36 percent change in strength perceptions. A one-standard-deviation change in approval, about 13.1 in these data, will produce a 4.7 percent shift in strength perceptions. The coefficient for success is 0.37, compared with 0.50 in Table 4.5.

TABLE 4.6. *Multilevel, Simultaneous Equation Estimation of Approval, Success, and Monthly Estimated Strength Perceptions, 1975–2011.*

Variable	Approval				Strength Perceptions			
	b	SE	z	p	b	SE	z	p
Approval	—				0.36	0.11	3.18	0.00
Success	0.43	0.13	3.26	0.00	0.37	0.09	4.07	0.00
Divided government	17.36	4.38	3.96	0.00	14.10	3.19	4.42	0.00
Misery Index (lag)	−4.20	0.75	−5.64	0.00	—			
Events	3.04	0.99	3.06	0.00	—			
Second term	−8.11	2.95	−2.74	0.01	—			
Constant	45.05	10.45	4.31	0.00	−51.67	8.46	−6.11	0.00

N = 201, R^2 (overall) = 0.56, sigma_u = 4.02, sigma_e = 6.10, rho = 0.30
Source: See text for details.

A one-percentage-point shift in the annual success rate in Congress corresponds to a 0.37 change in monthly strength perceptions, while a one-standard-deviation change (17.1) will alter strength perceptions about 6.3 percent. The impact of both of these variables is substantively important, as well as statistically significant. Finally, the control variables behave similarly in this analysis, as in Table 4.5. Notably, the impact of divided government, while still large in both instances, falls compared with the earlier analyses. Most importantly, these results again find that success affects strength perceptions, our primary hypothesis. The Appendix presents additional analyses, including some robustness tests ("Robustness Tests for the Multilevel Analysis") and a technique for analysis of time series when there are gaps in the dependent variable ("Monthly Strength Perceptions as a Time Series with Gaps"). These additional aggregate tests continue to demonstrate the effects of congressional success on strength perceptions.

SUCCESS IN CONGRESS AND STRENGTH PERCEPTIONS: AN INDIVIDUAL LEVEL TEST

This section tests our primary hypothesis, but with individual-level data instead of aggregate data, as used in the preceding sections. There are several important limitations to the aggregate-level tests, the most important being whether success in Congress is endogenous or exogenous to strength perceptions. We can argue that members of Congress respond to public regard for the president; thus, when the public thinks more highly of the president, either in approval or strength terms, the president should win more frequently in Congress. But that is not what was found earlier. Instead, success only affected approval and strength perceptions; approval and strength perceptions did not seem to affect success. The lack of approval effects on success contradicts an enormous body of work that finds such approval effects, especially with aggregate level data (for reviews of and citations to that large literature, see Cohen 2011b; Edwards, 1997, 2009b). The mismatch between the measurement of the success and the presidential opinion variables may partially account for this contrary finding.

There is a second issue: The underlying theory is about individual–level behavior and attitudes. This section turns to the American National Election Studies (ANES), which have asked respondents about their approval of the president, as well as perceptions of presidential strength, for almost every survey taken from 1980 through 2004. These data provide us with approximately 15,000 individual-level observations across seven presidential election years to test the success-strength perceptions hypothesis. Moreover, the timing of the ANES surveys allows us to make strong statements about causality between success in Congress and strength perceptions. The ANES surveys are always conducted late in the year, from September through early November, after almost all the presidential roll calls have been held.

Still, like the aggregate analysis, there are several complications that we must confront. First, the strength perceptions and approval questions offer respondents four response categories, from strongly agree to strongly disagree for approval and from extremely well to not well at all for whether the president can be described as a strong leader.[33] With four ordered categories, we should employ ordered probit or logit techniques in analyzing these variables. But as approval and leadership perceptions are endogenous, we need an appropriate simultaneous estimation technique, such as 2SLS. Two-stage least squares, however, requires scaled, not ordered categorical variables. Thus, the first analytical compromise is that the analysis uses regression techniques on nonscaled variables.[34] Second, to implement the two-stage least squares estimation requires unique exogenous variables to instrument approval and leadership. Although theory is far from clear as to variables that we can use to instrument strength perceptions, the ANES include a very large battery of questions that may help in that regard. Third, unlike the aggregate analysis discussed previously, we do not have to instrument success. Finally, like the earlier discussion, I use multilevel, simultaneous techniques to deal with the annualized measure of success.

---

33 The wording for the approval question is, "Do you approve or disapprove of the way {President's Name} is handling his job as President?" followed up with another question, "Do you (dis)approve strongly or not strongly?" The strength perceptions question is worded, "In your opinion, does the phrase, 'he provides strong leadership' describe {President's Name}?"

34 I attempted to implement a two-stage ordered probit (and logit) instrumental estimation using the cmp command in STATA 11.0, but they would not converge.

Instruments for Approval and Strength Perceptions at the Individual Level

The discussion in the Appendix on instruments for approval and strength perceptions ("Endogeneity and Instrumental Variable Techniques") provides guidance in selecting appropriate instruments for this individual-level analysis. Earlier, we used the question number dummies to instrument strength perceptions, but obviously we cannot do that here. Moreover, there is little theory to guide us on instruments for strength that do not have either a direct effect on approval or whose effects are felt through other variables that affect approval. Fortunately, for this analysis, instrumenting presidential strength perceptions is not necessary, because our primary interest is in the effects of success on those perceptions. To estimate the 2SLS, we only need to instrument approval.

Previously, I argued that the economy serves as a good instrument for approval. Whether the economy is in good shape or not should not affect public perceptions of presidential strength. Recalling the example used earlier, Reagan was thought a strong leader despite the weak economy during the early years of his tenure. Rather than use the Misery Index, as I did earlier, I use the economic retrospections questions posed to respondents in the survey. The economic retrospection question asks respondents whether they think the economy has gotten better, worse, or stayed the same. I recoded this variable on a scale from 1 to 3, with 3 the "gotten better" option. Inasmuch as economic retrospections mediate the effect of the real economy on attitudes to the president, the retrospections are closer casually to those attitudes. Still, economic retrospections and approval of the president may be endogenous to each other at the individual level (Erikson 2004; Kramer 1983). To control for possible endogeneity, I use the average economic retrospection of all respondents for each survey. This gives us an aggregate measure of economic retrospections at the time of the survey.

Second, policy distance between the respondent and the president can also be used to instrument approval. The closer the policy positions of the president to the respondent, the more likely the respondent will approve of the president; that is, liberal (conservative) respondents will have a tendency to approve of liberal (conservative) presidents and disapprove of presidents on the opposite side of the policy spectrum. But ideological distance should not affect perceptions that a president is a strong or weak leader. Respondents who are ideologically close to a president may think that president is weak, while those distant ideologically can also think a president is strong. For example, liberals could easily regard Jimmy Carter as weak, while those same liberals might regard Reagan as strong. In 1980, self-identified strong liberals and liberals rated Carter, on average, a 1.4 and 1.2 on the strength scale that runs from 0 to 3, only ever so slightly toward the strong pole. Strong liberals and liberals in 1980 rated Reagan 2.3 and 2.0, clearly strong, and much stronger than their ratings for Carter. Ideological distance between the respondent and the president should not affect perceptions of presidential strength. Thus, we can use ideological distance, which should be related to approval, as an instrument for strength perceptions. To measure ideological distance, I take the absolute value of respondent self-placement and mean placement of the incumbent president on the seven-point ideological scale (Wlezien and Carman, 2001).[35]

Control Variables

This analysis also controls for several variables as a check against spuriousness. First, I control, in both the approval and strength perceptions equations, for political predispositions – in particular, party and ideological identification. Both questions use a seven-point scale, from strong Democrat (or liberal) to strong Republican (or conservative). I have rescaled these variables so that they point in the same direction as the sitting president, that is, a respondent is scored 7 when she or he is a strong identifier of the president's party and 1 when a strong identifier of the opposition. The same is used for ideological identification, with 7 signifying a respondent who is a strong "liberal" when the president is reputed to be a liberal and the same for conservatives when the president is a conservative. I label these two variables *co-partisanship* and *co-ideology*. They are both expected to be positively associated with leadership perceptions and approval. Still, the high correlation between partisanship and ideology may lead to multicollinearity, rendering neither variable significant when the other is included in the estimation. As detailed later, this does not prove to be the case.

Second, I include a series of demographic variables that previous research has found related to approval. They are age, gender (female = 1), and education.[36] Following Nicholson and colleagues (2002), I also add a variable for whether the respondent knows which party controls the House, hypothesizing that knowledge will depress assessments of strength. Unknowledgeable respondents are more likely to hold naïve understandings of American politics, which overstate the role of the president in the political process. Using the same logic, I also control for political interest, using the three-point scale from little interest to much interest in politics.[37] Third, I also employ several contextual or aggregate variables that have been found to be related to approval,

35 Using the mean placement of the "per year" helps correct for bias and noise in some individuals' placement of the president. That is, some respondents will overstate the distance or closeness of the president to them, perhaps because they like the president or they have no idea of the president's ideological stance.

36 A substantial literature exists on factors that affect approval at the individual level. See Cohen (2010a); Gilens (1988); Goidel, Shields, and Peffley (1997); Greene (2001); Gronke and Newman (2003); Krosnick and Brannon (1993a, 1993b); Krosnick and Kinder (1990); Miller and Krosnick (2000); Mutz (1992, 1994); Newman (2003); Nicholson, Segura, and Woods (2002); Tedin (1986); Valentino (1999); Waterman, Jenkins-Smith, and Silva (1999); and West (1991).

37 VCF0310, interest in the election.

TABLE 4.7. *Multilevel, Simultaneous Equation Estimation of Approval, Success, and Strength Perceptions, ANES, 1980–2004.*

Variable	Approval (First-Stage Results)				Strength Perceptions (Second-Stage Results)			
	b	SE	z	P	b	SE	z	p
Approval	—				0.23	0.03	7.09	0.00
Co-partisanship	0.28	0.00	61.90	0.00	0.10	0.01	9.99	0.00
Co-ideology	0.10	0.01	11.39	0.00	0.06	0.01	9.49	0.00
Midterm	0.04	0.02	2.11	0.04	−0.06	0.02	−3.42	0.00
Divided government	0.43	0.03	12.85	0.00	0.47	0.03	14.94	0.00
Success	0.01	0.00	8.41	0.00	0.01	0.00	8.98	0.00
Female	−0.05	0.02	−2.78	0.01	−0.06	0.01	−4.23	0.00
Interest in elections	−0.04	0.01	−2.99	0.00	0.06	0.01	6.24	0.00
Age	0.00	0.00	−0.85	0.39	0.00	0.00	−3.18	0.00
Education	−0.01	0.01	−2.63	0.01	−0.03	0.00	−6.08	0.00
Know party that controls the House	−0.08	0.02	−4.07	0.00	−0.13	0.02	−8.72	0.00
Policy distance	−0.08	0.01	−6.59	0.00	—			
Economic retrospections	1.76	0.08	22.77	0.00	—			
Wald chi-square, p	8276	0.000			5366.3	0.000		
Constant	−3.20	0.19	−16.49	0.00	−0.28	0.08	−3.50	0.00

N = 11,261; overall R² (for the second stage) = 0.42, sigma_u = 2.53e-10, sigma_e = 0.66, rho = 1.46e-19

Source: American National Election Studies, Cumulative Data File, 1980–2004. See text for details.

although it is unclear what their relationship will be to strength perceptions: (1) whether government was divided (coded 1) and (2) whether it is a midterm (1) or presidential election year (0).[38]

Table 4.7 presents the results of the multilevel, two-stage least squares estimation.

38 I also used an event variable, like that in the earlier analyses, coded 1 = positive event for that year, 0 = no event or positive and negative events cancel, −1 = negative event. But that variable never reached statistical significance, probably a function of the limited number of years in this analysis and, thus, the restricted variance on the variable. For the 13 years for which there are data, 1980–2004, only 2 years are scored −1 and two scored +1, the other 9 are scored 0. Thus, the event variable is dropped from the analysis and presentation.

First, the overall model fit for the strength perceptions equation at $R^2 = 0.42$ is impressive given these are individual-level survey data. The prime hypothesis concerns the impact of success on strength perceptions, which is found to be statistically significant and positive.[39] The coefficient for success is 0.008, which may appear tiny, but recall the dependent variable is a 0 to 3 scale. A 10 percent increase in success translates into a 0.08-step increase in strength perceptions. The success variable ranges from 43 to 88 percent, a 45 percent difference. This 45 percent difference corresponds to about 0.36 step on the 0 to 3 scale. Thus, there are substantively important effects of success on strength perceptions when we compare the extremes of the success variable. In addition, such large swings in success are not uncommon, given the impact of divided government on success, especially in an age of polarized congressional parties. I also ran a 2SLS estimation using the variables in Table 4.7, but this time without the multilevel component. These results (not shown) are substantively identical to the multilevel results in Table 4.7, and success is again significant and positive with a coefficient of 0.008.

Other variables also affect strength perceptions. As expected, approval is positively related to those perceptions. The coefficient indicates that a one-step increase in approval (on the 0 to 3 scale) corresponds to a 0.23-step increase in strength perceptions. That this effect is not larger confirms that approval and strength perceptions are related but not identical. Voters discriminate between approving of the president's performance in office and assessing the president's strength of leadership.

Individuals of the same party and ideological leaning of the president think the president is stronger. Also, knowledgeable respondents are less likely to think a president is strong, but contrary to expectations, interest is positively associated with strength. This reversed sign is not a function of the correlation between interest and knowledge. Interest retains its positive and significant sign if knowledge is dropped from the estimation. Women, older respondents, and those with more education are also less likely to rate a president as strong. During midterm election years, respondents think presidents are weaker, but the effect is small, with a coefficient of only 0.05. Finally, strength perceptions improve when government is divided, repeating results found earlier. During divided government, presidential strength perceptions are nearly one-half-step higher than during united government.

CONCLUSION

The theory of public perceptions of presidential leadership argues that voters define presidential leadership in representational and strength terms. This chapter addressed the question, What factors affect public perceptions of presidential leadership? Theory suggests three possible sources of those leadership

---

39 With such a large n, it is relatively easy for variables to reach conventional levels of statistical significance; thus, more weight should be placed on substantive significance.

perceptions: projection, presidential traits, and performance in office. To test for the effect of projection, presidential traits, and performance requires data on public assessment of the quality of presidential representation and strength. Unfortunately, no survey questions ask respondents whether they think the president is doing a good job of representing them and the nation or not. Thus, we are unable to test whether projection, presidential traits, and performance affect perceptions of presidential representation. But on numerous occasions, polls asked respondents whether they think the president is strong or weak.

Two sets of analysis were conducted, one using an aggregate measure of presidential strength and the other performing an individual-level analysis using ANES data. Some support was found for each of these three sources of voters' perceptions of presidential strength. For example, the aggregate analysis found that strength perceptions varied with the president; voters gave some presidents, like Reagan, consistently higher strength ratings than others, like Carter. Plus, the individual-level analysis suggested projection effects because voters sharing the president's party and/or ideological orientation were more likely to view a president as strong than opposition party and opposition ideological identifiers, who tended to view the same president as weaker.

Most of the emphasis in the chapter, however, looked at the effect of performance – in particular, success in Congress – on strength perceptions. Both the aggregate- and individual-level analyses, using a variety of statistical modeling techniques, found a positive association between success in Congress and perceptions of presidential strength: As presidential success rates rose, so did perceptions of presidential strength. Still, there are several limitations of this analysis. It used only one form of presidential success – success in Congress. Voters may use other types of presidential accomplishments and victories in assessing whether a president is providing strong leadership or not – for instance, international diplomacy and conflict. Further, the analysis here combined all roll calls on which presidents took positions. Future analysis might disaggregate presidential roll call positions – for instance, by the importance of the vote (e.g., CQ's key votes) and/or policy area – to see if voters weigh some types of roll calls more heavily than others in assessing presidential leadership strength.

One last important point emerged from this analysis regarding the relationship between strength perceptions and approval. Although the two were found to be correlated, they are not identical. This is consistent with other studies that find similarities, but also differences, between presidential job approval and favorability questions (Cohen 1999a, 1999b, 2000; McAvoy 2008); that assessments of presidential traits, like character, affect approval (Greene 2001; Newman 2002, 2003, 2004); and that voters differentially assess presidential performance across policy areas, such economic versus foreign policy (Cohen 2002a, 2002b; Nickelsburg and Norpoth 2000). We need more research on the similarities and differences across questions that tap public opinion toward the president. Those opinions appear to be more complex and richer than merely approval or disapproval of the president.

Appendix for Chapter 4

Questions Used to Construct the Presidential Leadership Series

Question 1: Please tell me whether the following statement applies to xxxx, or not? He is a strong leader.
Yes. No. No opinion

Question 2: From what you have seen thus far, do you think President xxxx has shown he is a strong leader, or not?
Strong leader. Not a strong leader. Mixed response. Don't Know. Refused.

Question 3: The following are phrases some people use to describe political leaders. For each phrase, please tell me if it describes xxxx very well, somewhat well, slightly well, or not at all well: He is a strong leader.
Very well. Somewhat well. Slightly well. Not at all well. Don't know.

Question 4: In your opinion, does the phrase "is a strong leader" describe xxxx extremely well, quite well, not too well, or not well at all?
Extremely well. Quite well. Not too well. Not well at all. Don't know/ Refused.

Question 5: I'd like to know if you think any of these statements describe the candidates running for President this year (xxxx). If you don't think any of them apply, just say so.) Do you think that xxxx is a strong leader?
Yes. No.
(Note: This question was only used for incumbent presidents running for reelection.)

Question 6: Do you think that xxxx is a strong leader?
Yes. No. No opinion

Question 7: Thinking about the following characteristics and qualities, please say whether you think it applies or doesn't apply to xxxx: Is a strong and decisive leader.
Applies. Does not apply. No opinion.

Question 8: From what you know of the following presidential candidates, do these descriptions apply? Do you think "strong leader" applies to xxxx?
Yes. No. Don't know/Refused.
(Note: This question was only used for incumbent presidents running for reelection.)

Question 9: Now, I am going to read you a list of words and phrases that people use to describe political figures. For each word or phrase, please tell me whether it describes xxxx very well, well, not too well, or not well at all: Strong leader.
Very well. Well. Not too well. Not well at all. Don't know/Refused.

Question 10: Do you think President xxxx is a strong leader or not? Is. is not. Not sure.

Question 11: I will read you a list of personal qualities. Please tell me for each one whether you rate President xxxx excellent, good, fair, or poor: A strong leader.
Excellent. Good. Fair. Poor. Not sure.

Question 12: Do you think xxxx has strong qualities of leadership, or not?
Yes. No. Not sure.

Question 13: Would you say xxxx is a strong leader, or not?
Yes. No. Don't know.

Question 14: How would you rate xxxx as a leader? Would you say he is a very strong leader, a strong leader, a weak leader, or a very weak leader?
Very strong leader. Strong leader. Weak leader. Very weak leader. Not sure.

Question 15: How would you rate xxxx on the following qualities, using a five-point scale on which a 5 means a very good rating, a 1 means a very poor rating, and a 3 means a mixed rating? Having the strong leadership qualities needed to be president.
5–Very good. 4. 3–Mixed. 2. 1–Very poor. Cannot rate (volunteered).

Question 16: I'd like to read you a few of the qualities that a President might have, and you tell me how closely you think each one describes xxxx using a scale of 1 to 5, based on a five-point scale, on which a rating of 5 means the quality describes him very well and a rating of 1 means it does not describe him well at all: A strong leader.
1–Does not describe him well. 2. 3. 4. 5–Describes him very well. Cannot rate.

Question 17: As I read some pairs of opposite phrases, tell me which one best reflects your impression of xxxx so far. Does xxxx impress you as a strong leader or not a strong leader?
A strong leader. Not a strong leader. Neither particularly (volunteered). Don't know/Refused.

Question 18: Please tell me whether or not you think each of the following phrases describes xxxx: Has strong leadership qualities? Does this describe xxxx, or not?
Yes, describes. No, does not. Don't know.

Question 19: Would you say that xxxx has strong leadership qualities or not?
Yes. No. Don't know/No answer.

Question 20: Now I would like to read you a series of words and phrases. For each one, please tell me, in your opinion, whether each one of these words or phrases is a very good, good, or not so good description of xxxx: Strong leader. Very good. Good. Not so good. Unsure.

Question 21: Do you think xxxx is doing a good job or a poor job providing strong leadership for the country?
Good job. Poor job. Not sure.

Question 22: I'm going to read to you a list of words or phrases and for each one I'd like to know if you feel it describes xxxx or if it does not describe him: A strong leader.
Describes. Does not describe. Not sure (volunteered).

Question 23: Do you have high expectations, some expectations, or no real expectations that the xxxx administration will make progress in each of the following? Providing strong leadership in government.
High. Some. No real. Not sure.

Question 24: If elected President in xxxx, would you expect xxxx to be a very strong leader, a fairly strong leader, or not a strong leader?
Very strong. Fairly strong. Not strong. Not sure.

Question 25: If elected, would you expect xxxx to be a very strong leader, a fairly strong leader, or not a strong leader?
Very strong. Fairly strong. Not strong. Not sure.
(**Note**: This question was only used for incumbent presidents running for reelection.)

Question 26: If elected President in xxxx, would you expect xxxx to be a very strong leader, a fairly strong leader, or not a strong leader?
Very strong. Fairly strong. Not strong. Not sure.
(**Note**: This question was only used for incumbent presidents running for reelection.)

Question 27: Now I'd like you to rate xxxx on the following items using a scale from 1 to 6, where 6 is the top rating and means excellent and 1 is the lowest rating and means poor: Is a strong leader.
6–Excellent. 5. 4. 3. 2. 1–Poor. Not sure.

Question 28: I am going to read you some statements. As I read each one, please tell me whether or not the statement applies to xxxx: He is a strong leader?
Yes. No. Not sure.

Question 29: What would you describe the leadership that President xxxx is providing for the country?
Very strong, Strong, Moderate, Weak, or Very weak

Question 30: Now I would like to read you a series of words and phrases. For each one please tell me, in your opinion, whether each is a very good, good, or not so good description of President xxxx: Strong leader.
Very good. Good. Unsure.

Question 31: Now, I'm going to read you some characteristics that are often used to describe political leaders. As I read each one, please tell me if you

think it is an excellent, good, only fair, or poor description of President xxxx: Has the strong leadership qualities this country needs.
Excellent. Good. Fair. Poor. Don't know.

Question 32: Think about xxxx. In your opinion, does the phrase "he provides strong leadership" describe xxxx extremely well, quite well, not too well, or not well at all?
Extremely well. Quite well. Not too well. Not well at all.

APPENDIX TABLE 4.1. *Number of Presidential Leadership Questions by Year.*

Year	N	Percentage
1976	3	0.71
1977	1	0.24
1978	2	0.47
1979	9	2.12
1980	18	4.25
1981	2	0.47
1982	4	0.94
1983	7	1.65
1984	12	2.83
1985	0	0.00
1986	2	0.47
1987	3	0.71
1988	2	0.47
1989	5	1.18
1990	10	2.36
1991	12	2.83
1992	17	4.01
1993	21	4.95
1994	20	4.71
1995	12	2.83
1996	8	1.89
1997	2	0.47
1998	22	5.19
1999	3	0.71
2000	2	0.47
2001	29	6.84
2002	24	5.66
2003	30	7.08
2004	50	11.79
2005	25	5.90
2006	13	3.07
2007	6	1.42
2008	1	0.24
2009	21	4.95
2010	16	3.78
2011	10	2.36

Source: Questions that ask respondents to rate presidents on strength of leadership, Roper Poll Archive. See text for details.

APPENDIX TABLE 4.2. *Frequency of Presidential Leadership Questions by Polling Firm.*

Question Number	N	Percent	Polling Firm
1	48	9.45	ABC News/*Washington Post*
2	1	0.20	AP
3	9	1.77	AP/GFK
4	1	0.20	Brigham Young University
5	82	16.14	CBS News/*New York Times* Poll
6	12	2.36	CBS News/*New York Times* Poll
7	1	0.20	CNN
8	26	5.12	Gallup
9	21	4.13	Greenberg
10	7	1.38	Harris
11	3	0.59	Harris
12	4	0.79	*Los Angeles Times*
13	3	0.59	*Los Angeles Times*
14	9	1.77	NBC
15	25	4.92	NBC/*Wall Street Journal*
16	7	1.38	NBC/*Wall Street Journal*
17	11	2.17	Pew
18	14	2.76	PSRA/*Newsweek*
19	5	0.98	Quinnipiac
20	1	0.20	Tarrance
21	49	9.65	*Time*/CNN
22	8	1.57	*Time*/CNN
23	3	0.59	*Time*/CNN/Yankelovich
24	9	1.77	*Time*/Yankelovich
25	4	0.79	*Time*/Yankelovich
26	2	0.39	*Time*/Yankelovich
27	2	0.39	*Time*/Yankelovich
28	3	0.59	Tipp
29	39	7.68	Tipp
30	1	0.20	*US News*
31	2	0.39	Wirthlin
32	12	2.36	American National Election Studies (ANES)

Source: Collected from a search of the Roper Poll Archive. See text for details.

Endogeneity and Instrumental Variable Techniques

One of the critical issues for testing the success-strength perceptions hypothesis is that the two variables may be endogenous; in other words, they each may "cause" the other. Complicating the analysis is that job approval, which has been found to be strongly correlated with strength perceptions, may also be endogenous with those perceptions. To estimate the impact of each of the three variables (success, strength perceptions, and job approval) on the others requires dealing with this possible endogeneity. Simultaneous equation models, such as two-stage least squares (2SLS), can be used to account and correct for endogeneity among variables. To estimate a two-stage least squares model requires that we have at least one instrumental variable for each of the three endogenous variables. There are at least two standards that an instrumental variable must meet – the exclusion restriction and the strength standard (Sovey and Green 2011).

For expository purposes, consider the effects of success (the instrumented variable) on strength (the outcome variable), while other variables (covariates) will also affect the outcome variable. The exclusion restriction requires that the instrument only affect the outcome variable through its impact on the instrumented variable, not directly or indirectly through any covariate. But "the plausibility of the exclusion restriction hinges on argumentation; it cannot be established empirically" (Sovey and Green 2011, p. 190). The strength standard requires that the instrument be correlated strongly with the instrumented variable. We can test the strength assumption with an F-test comparing estimations for the instrumented variable with and without the instrumental variable. An F of 10 or greater indicates a strong instrument (Stock and Watson 2007). Weak instruments do a poor job of removing the endogeneity bias between the two dependent variables (Sovey and Green 2011).

Because we are concerned with the impact of each of our three variables on the others, we need instruments for each. First, collectively, the thirty-two question dummies may be ideal instruments for strength perceptions. They meet the exclusion restriction because we cannot make an argument that question wording for the strength items will affect monthly approval or annual success in Congress.

Second, research finds that party control, polarization, and the interaction of party control and polarization strongly affect presidential success in Congress (Bond, Fleisher, and Wood 2003; Cohen, Bond, and Fleisher 2013; Fleisher, Bond, and Wood 2008). The polarization variables should affect neither strength perceptions nor approval at the aggregate level. I measure polarization in Congress as the percentage of party conflict votes, averaged across the two chambers. Party conflict votes are defined as those in which 50 percent + 1 of one party vote against 50 percent + 1 of the other party. Divided government may affect approval levels, as argued in Nicholson and colleagues (2002), who find that presidential approval is higher during divided than united government. Divided government is defined as opposition party control of at least one chamber of Congress.

As to polarization, although there are indications that increases in elite polarization may have led to greater levels of mass party identification after a period of high levels of independence (Hetherington 2001), debate exists over whether voters have polarized in the same way as the political class (Fiorina with Abrams and Pope 2005). Further, it is unclear that there are any aggregate implications of growing polarization on presidential approval. Several studies have noticed a widening partisan gap in presidential approval (Bond and Fleisher 2001; Newman and Siegle 2010), but this pattern may not matter much when looking at presidential approval trends for the public as a whole. The mean level of presidential approval has remained roughly the same in the era of higher polarization compared with the period of lower polarization.[40] Furthermore, at the aggregate level, independents and weak partisans account for most of the temporal movement in approval because the partisans' conflicting evaluations of the president cancel each other out. Thus, congressional party voting plausibly meets the exclusion restriction.

Our greatest difficulty is finding an instrument for approval that meets the exclusion restriction. A vast literature has shown that economic factors, such as the Misery Index, affect approval, but should not have a direct effect on success in Congress (Cohen 2013). In the following discussion, I use the monthly Misery Index, the addition of the unemployment and inflation rate, as the instrument for approval. The only effect that economic factors should have on success should be mediated through approval. There are two possible paths through which economic factors may affect success in Congress directly, neither convincing.

First, the economy may affect members' calculations to support/oppose the president. On the one hand, members of Congress may decide to distance themselves from a president when the economy is weak so as not to be associated with a president reputed to be doing a poor job of managing the economy. But this argument raises the importance of a president's reputation, a form of public opinion. Thus, this argument is no different from the one that argues that the effects of the economy on success are felt through the president's approval. It makes little sense that a member will oppose the president when the economy is weak if the president happens to also be

---

40 From 1953–80, presidential approval averages 56.0 percent compared with 53.3 percent for the 1981–2011 period, a difference that is not statistically significant (t = 0.88, p = 0.38).

popular – as is sometimes the case for newly elected presidents who happened to win the election because the incumbent administration was blamed for the economy.

The other pathway is that the economy may affect the positions that a president takes. If the economy weakens the president's bargaining situation in Congress, then we may expect presidents to take fewer positions when the economy is weak. But a weak economy also creates incentives for the president and Congress to propose and implement policies to deal with the economic plight. Public pressure to deal with the economic problem may not only create incentives to act, but also the conditions for legislative success. Thus, it is unclear whether, in the aggregate, presidents will take more or fewer positions when the economy is weak. Either is possible.

Insofar as approval and strength perceptions are highly related, we might expect economic factors to affect those strength perceptions. However, the effect of the economy should be felt on strength perceptions only through approval. Conceptually, job approval and strength perceptions are asking voters to rate different aspects of presidents. Job approval is primarily a performance measure; in approving or disapproving of the president, voters are essentially blaming (or rewarding) them for all manner of performance, even things that the president cannot control. Whether the economy is weak or strong, however, should not affect perceptions of presidential strength. (1) If strength is strongly a function of success, as argued earlier, there are no clear implications of the economy on success except through approval. (2) Presidents can be thought of as strong even when the economy is weak. During some of the weakest periods of the U.S. economy, such as during the Great Depression and the early 1980s, both Franklin Roosevelt and Ronald Reagan were considered to be strong presidents. The self-confidence and optimism of both presidents inspired and assured voters when times were economically bleak. Thus, a case can be made that economic factors will only affect strength perceptions through approval.

Tests for the strength of the instruments meet the 10.00 standard in all cases, as long as insignificant question number dummies are excluded.[41] The following question dummies were employed (the numbers refer to the corresponding question on Appendix Table 4.2) – 3, 15, 22, 23, 24, 29, 31. The F-test for strength is 19.92, 16.50 for approval, and 201.89 for success. Thus, the instruments appear to meet the exclusion restriction and strength standard.

---

41 Inclusion of insignificant variables, while also causing overidentification problems, may cause insignificant F-tests because degrees of freedom and cases determine the F-distribution. Excluding the insignificant question number dummies does not affect the performance of the other variables.

APPENDIX TABLE 4.3. *First Stage Results for Two-Stage Least Squares Estimates for Table 4.4.*

Variable	Strength Perceptions				Approval				Success			
	b	SE	t	p	b	SE	t	p	b	SE	t	p
Question 4	5.85	3.48	1.68	0.09	7.46	3.69	2.02	0.04	6.43	2.19	2.94	0.00
Question 19	3.39	2.10	1.61	0.11	1.50	2.22	0.68	0.50	0.83	1.32	0.63	0.53
Question 26	−18.22	3.58	−5.09	0.00	−8.35	3.80	−2.20	0.03	5.62	2.25	2.50	0.01
Question 27	12.05	5.68	2.12	0.03	3.85	6.02	0.64	0.52	3.21	3.57	0.90	0.37
Question 28	10.82	3.68	2.94	0.00	−2.00	3.90	−0.51	0.61	−4.52	2.31	−1.96	0.05
Question 34	11.83	1.75	6.75	0.00	7.45	1.86	4.01	0.00	0.45	1.10	0.41	0.68
Question 36	−24.54	6.92	−3.54	0.00	−4.55	7.34	−0.62	0.54	5.61	4.35	1.29	0.20
Divided	106.69	10.87	9.81	0.00	67.92	11.53	5.89	0.00	39.54	6.83	5.78	0.00
Misery Index (lag)	−1.51	0.39	−3.84	0.00	−3.83	0.42	−9.20	0.00	1.33	0.25	5.38	0.00
Events	2.76	0.75	3.69	0.00	4.73	0.79	5.95	0.00	2.94	0.47	6.24	0.00
Second term	−7.84	1.47	−5.34	0.00	−9.52	1.56	−6.12	0.00	0.51	0.92	0.55	0.58
Polarization	61.84	8.08	7.65	0.00	34.64	8.57	4.04	0.00	14.96	5.08	2.94	0.00
Divided × Polarization	−135.37	14.64	−9.25	0.00	−83.64	15.52	−5.39	0.00	−95.38	9.20	−10.37	0.00
Constant	22.88	6.22	3.68	0.00	50.43	6.59	7.65	0.00	61.18	3.91	15.65	0.00
F (13,410)	19.92				201.89				16.50			
R²/Adj. R²	0.39	0.37			0.86	0.86			0.34	0.32		

N = 424
Source: See text and Table 4.4 for details.

The final step is identification of other covariates that affect the three endogenous variables to guard against spuriousness. For the strength perceptions equation, I added a dummy for divided government. The rationale for the divided government dummy follows from Nicholson and colleagues (2002) and predicts a positive sign. For the approval equation, I added the following variables: divided government, an event variable, and a dummy for second terms. Nicholson and colleagues (2002) justify the divided government variable. Many studies of presidential approval find that events may either lift or depress approval (Brace and Hinckley 1992).[42] The event dummy is coded +1 for months with one or more positive events and no negative events, −1 for months with one or more negative events, and 0 for months without either a positive or negative events or when both positive and negative events occur, leading them to cancel out each other's effect. The list of events comes from Newman and Forcehimes (2010), updated through 2011 using their procedures. Finally, presidents tend to have lower approval during their second than first terms. The success equation includes control variables for second term because second-term presidents tend to have lower success levels.

---

42 See Newman and Forcehimes (2010) for a good discussion of the variety of ways that events are used in presidential approval studies.

Robustness Tests for the Multilevel Analysis

There are several important criticisms and limitations of the analysis associated with Table 4.6. First, it is not clear that success in Congress is exogenous to strength perceptions and approval. As the literature on success in Congress has often found that approval affects presidential success, it is surprising that this analysis did not detect such an effect. The use of monthly approval data may, in part, account for this nonresult. Second, we have assumed that the economy, the Misery Index, has no direct impact on strength perceptions, that its effect on perceptions is only felt through approval, making it an appropriate instrument for approval. Finally, the analyses employ only a few control variables for the strength equations. The effects of success and/or approval may thus be spurious. Because the impacts of success and approval have their weakest effects on strength perceptions using the monthly estimated data, this section attempts to deal with at least the second and third criticisms.

First, I added other control variables to the strength perceptions equation. These controls included the events variable, polarization, the interaction between polarization and divided government, the second-term dummy, and dummies for individual presidents. Of these variables, only some of the presidential dummies were found to be statistically significant, and only the George H. W. Bush dummy was consistently significant.[43] The addition of the Bush I dummy did not have an appreciable effect on the success or approval variables, slightly raising the coefficient for success to 0.40.

To test the exclusion restriction for the Misery Index, I added it as a control, with the Events variable now serving to instrument approval because it never significantly affected strength perceptions. In estimations with and without the other control variables used in Table 4.6 and mentioned earlier, the Misery Index never got close to significance, with its z-test always less than 1.00, and usually less than 0.50, and the corresponding p-values ranging from 0.5 to 0.9.

---

43 The Bush I dummy was also significant in the face of controls for the Gulf War, which did not attain significance. To preserve space, I have not presented the results of these tests, which can be obtained upon request from the author.

Monthly Strength Perceptions as a Time Series with Gaps

The aggregate analyses of presidential strength employ cross-sectional statistical techniques. Because the presidential strength data are measured over time, they are probably best considered as a time series. The numerous gaps over time in the measurement of the presidential strength variable raise important issues in treating those data as a time series. For instance, of the 424 months from 1975–2011 for which we have strength perceptions data, there are data for only 201, or less than one-half of the months. For this reason, the aggregate analyses used cross-sectional statistical techniques. But if there are time dependencies in the strength perceptions data, then the findings may be spurious, especially if success and strength perceptions share a common trend. Only time-series techniques can detect and statistically correct for such issues, but it is hard to diagnose times series for properties such as stationarity or autocorrelation when there are gaps in the data series.

There are two common approaches to "filling in" the gaps in a time series: interpolation and Kalman filtering. When there are many missing data points, interpolation produces a noisy and unreliable series, even for the more sophisticated techniques that utilize the relationship between the series and covariates of the series that do not have missing data (King et. al. 2001). An alternative approach is to use the Kalman filter to identify the time-series properties of data with many missing data gaps.[44] Kalman filtering takes known values of a data series and, using recursive techniques and probabilities, estimates the values of the missing data, weighted by data points with the higher certainties.

Time-series analysis also provides an alternative technique for dealing with the endogeneity between approval and strength perceptions that makes use of temporal ordering, in effect arguing that past events affect current (or future) events, but not the reverse. Thus, a past value of approval can affect the current value of strength perception; at the same time, we cannot argue that the current value of the perception will affect the past value of approval. In other words, a past value on variable X (i.e., approval) has to be exogenous to the current value on variable Y (strength perceptions). This can be simply modeled by regressing strength on the lag of approval. The time-series analysis will still

---

44 For examples of the Kalman filtering technique when there are numerous gaps in time-series data, see Bankert and Norpoth (2013); Baum and Kernell (2001); Green, Gerber, and de Boef (1999); Pickup and Wlezien (2009); and Sidman and Norpoth (2012).

leave us with the problem that success is measured annually, while perceptions and approval are measured monthly.

Appendix Table 4.4 displays the results of the time-series regression of strength perceptions regressed on the one-month lag of approval, plus divided government and success in Congress. Diagnostics revealed statistically significant coefficients for AR(1) and AR(3) processes. The substantive results are comparable with those reported in the other aggregate analyses. Divided government is positively associated with strength perceptions. When government is divided, presidential strength scores will be about 16 percent higher than during united government. Lagged approval also strongly affects strength perceptions. Each one-percentage-point difference in lagged approval is associated with a 0.44 shift in strength perceptions. In these data, approval has a standard deviation of 13.4. A one-standard-deviation in lagged approval will correspond to nearly a 6 percent point shift in strength perceptions.

Most important for current purposes, success in Congress still retains its statistically significant impact on strength perceptions. The coefficient indicates that a one-percentage-point change in success will lead to a 0.45 shift in strength perceptions, a magnitude of effect in line with the findings from the other aggregate estimations. With a standard deviation of 17 percent, a one-standard-deviation shift in congressional success will result in a 7.7 percent change in strength perceptions. From a different perspective, the most legislatively successful president (96.7) will have a 27 percent higher strength rating than the least legislatively successful president (36.2) – a massive amount.

Finally, into the estimation on Appendix Table 4.4, I entered, individually and in groups, several other variables to see if any other variables

APPENDIX TABLE 4.4. *Times-Series Analysis (with gaps) of Estimated Monthly Strength Perceptions, 1975–2011.*

Variable	b	SE	z	p
Success	0.45	0.06	7.96	0.00
Divided government	16.83	1.97	8.55	0.00
Approval (one-month lag)	0.44	0.06	7.93	0.00
Constant	−62.16	5.58	−11.14	0.00
AR(1)	0.24	0.07	3.74	0.00
AR(3)	0.39	0.07	5.65	0.00
/sigma	6.15	0.30	20.31	0.00

$N = 201$, $R^2 = 0.62$, Ljung-Box $Q = 0.01$, probability of $Q = 0.91$
Source: See text for details.

affect these strength scores and to see how well the results hold up under controls. These additional variables included the Misery Index lagged on month, the event variable discussed earlier, and congressional polarization. None of these variables ever reached statistical significance. (Results are not shown but can be obtained from the author.) Thus, no matter how we statistically model the effects of success in Congress on strength perceptions, higher victory rates in Congress are associated with higher strength perceptions.

5

Presidential Representation and Public Opinion

"I would remind you that extremism in the defense of liberty is no vice. And let me remind you also that moderation in the pursuit of justice is no virtue."[1] Barry Goldwater's famous line from his 1964 presidential nomination acceptance speech may have warmed the hearts of true believers and ideologues, but voters appeared to have given his sentiment a cold shoulder, handing him one of the most devastating electoral defeats in presidential history. In contrast, Ronald Reagan, who voters also perceived as being politically extreme, handily defeated incumbent president Jimmy Carter in 1980.[2]

Barack Obama took a different tack, trying to stake out the political center or at least the appearance that he was a moderate. In his policy struggles with Congress, Obama would routinely excoriate the Republicans for their unwillingness to strike policy compromises. In summer 2011, during the midst of the debt ceiling negotiations, Obama criticized the congressional Republicans,

"[t]he fact of the matter is that's what the American people are looking for, is some compromise, some willingness to put partisanship aside . . . [t]o their credit, Nancy Pelosi, Harry Reid, the Democratic leadership . . . they were at least willing to engage in a conversation because they understood how important it is for us to actually solve this problem. And so far I have not seen the capacity of the House Republicans in particular to make those tough decisions."[3]

1 Barry Goldwater, acceptance speech, 1964 Republican nominating convention, to be its candidate for president. July 16, 1943, San Francisco, CA. Accessed June 6, 2012, http://www.presidency.ucsb.edu/nomination.php.
2 For instance, using the 1980 American National Election study, on a seven-point scale (1 = liberal, 4 = moderate or middle of the road, and 7 = conservative), voters located Carter at 3.74, nearly dead center compared with Reagan at 5.2. Charges of political extremism hounded Reagan for much of his career.
3 President Barack Obama, Remarks on the Federal Budget and an Exchange with Reporters, July 22, 2011, accessed from the American Presidency Project, on June 6, 2013, http://www.presidency.ucsb.edu/ws/index.php?pid=90653&st=compromise&st1=#.

Throughout his re-election campaign, Obama criticized Republicans for their rigid, uncompromising stance. Typical of his campaign speech, Obama said this at a rally in Denver, Colorado: "They [the Republicans] engineered a strategy of gridlock in Congress, refusing to compromise even on ideas that, in the past, both Democrats and Republicans agreed on."[4] Obama, too, extolled the virtues of moderation, implying that opponents of moderate policies were unreasonable. In a major speech in support of gun control legislation in the wake of the Sandy Hook elementary school shootings, Obama railed against the National Rifle Association and its congressional supporters, "[w]hile this compromise didn't contain everything I wanted or everything that these families wanted, it did represent progress. It represented moderation and common sense. That's why 90 percent of the American people supported it."[5]

Some columnists agreed with President Obama that there was strong popular sentiment in support of political and policy moderation, crediting this middle of the road approach for his reelection victory. Based on their reading of the election results, reporters Douglas E. Schoen and Jessica Tarlov (2012) of the *New York Daily News*, argued that voters "are crying out for a middle course . . . these numbers are representative of an electorate that wants both sides to slay their share of sacred cows in service of the greater good. . . ." Plus Schoen and Tarlov saw "a rejection of extremism across races at all levels" and that "Romney himself suffered for extreme positions that he took in the primaries."

These vignettes show that presidents and presidential candidates variously are associated as being moderate or politically extreme. But, sometimes, extremists are successful and win the election, as we might argue is the case for Ronald Reagan, but sometimes extremists lose to moderates, for instance, Barry Goldwater. This chapter asks: What are the political implications of a president taking extreme versus moderate policy positions? Do voters prefer policy moderation in their presidents and presidential candidates?

POLICY LOCATION AND PRESIDENTIAL REPRESENTATION

Whether presidents are moderate or extreme – that is, decidedly liberal or conservative – relates to presidential representation. Representation is one standard that voters may use in judging a president's leadership. Defining representation in policy distance terms, we can think of presidents as representing the nation overall (*collective* representation) or as representing individual

4 Barack Obama, Remarks at a Campaign Rally in Denver, Colorado, November 4, 2012, accessed from the American Presidency Project, on June 6, 2013, http://www.presidency.ucsb .edu/ws/index.php?pid=102625&st=compromise&st1=.
5 Barack Obama, Remarks on Senate Action on Gun Control Legislation, April 17, 2013, accessed from the American Presidency Project on June 6, 2013, http://www.presidency.ucsb .edu/ws/index.php?pid=103499&st=moderation&st1=.

voters (*dyadic* representation). It may be optimal, in terms of generating support, for presidents to also locate near the center, to take moderate stances on policies and issues. First, because voters in general, and the median voter in particular, locate near the center, collective representation reaches its peak when the president also positions near the center. Plus, assuming that there are more voters who are moderate as opposed to liberal or conservative, dyadic policy distance will be minimized for the largest segment of voters when presidents also position near the center.[6]

But as already discussed, there are trade-offs for presidents when deciding to take moderate versus extreme policy stances. For instance, when the president's party controls Congress, there are strong incentives for the president to represent his congressional party – control of Congress provides perhaps the best opportunity for the enactment of policy congenial to the party. Consequently, presidents will take liberal (or conservative) policy positions rather than moderate ones when their party controls Congress. Doing so may cost the president support among voters if they prefer a president who represents them – that is, one who takes policy positions that minimize the distance between his policy positions and theirs.

Depending upon the voter's and the president's policy locations, there may be a difference between the collective and dyadic policy distance from a voter to the president. But how do voters regard presidents when collective policy distance is small but dyadic policy distance is large (which occurs when the president is moderate but the voter is not)? Under these conditions, do voters reward presidents for minimizing collective policy distance? How do voters weigh collective and dyadic policy distance in assessing presidents?

There is very little research on the effects of policy distance on evaluations of presidents and no research that compares the effects of collective and dyadic policy distance. Gronke (1999) and Newman (2003) show that at the individual level, dyadic policy distance appears to affect approval of the president. Zaller (1998) suggests that moderate presidents do better in election contests than more extreme opponents but provides only anecdotal evidence linking policy moderation to approval. As he says about approval, "Systematic evidence that policy moderation affects presidential popularity is, as far as I know, non-existent" (p. 185).

In Chapter Four, we showed that it is possible to test directly whether success in Congress affects perceptions of president strength. Unfortunately, there are no survey questions that ask voters whether they think the president does

---

6 It is well known that the overall distribution of opinion tends toward the center. Using the American National Election Studies from 1972–2004, respondents on average self-identified at 4.2 on the seven-point liberal–conservative spectrum (liberal = 1, conservative = 7). Moreover, 52 percent of respondents, the modal category, located themselves at 4, middle of the road or moderate. This contrasts with strong and weak Republicans, who self-locate at 4.8, and strong and weak Democrats, who locate at 3.8.

a good job representing the nation or themselves, so we cannot test directly whether presidential policy location affects perceptions of representation. But, we can test the implications of presidential policy location on presidential approval. This would give us some indirect evidence that voters value representation from presidents. Moreover, using questions from the American National Election Studies, we can construct measures for both collective and dyadic policy distance, allowing us to assess the relative importance of the two types of policy distance on voter approval of the president.

Before addressing these questions, though, we must ask whether voters can accurately locate the policy leanings of presidents. If voters cannot locate the president's policy position with a reasonable degree of accuracy, then any linkage between where voters locate the president and their approval ratings of the president will be based on noise, misperception, etc. The general lack of voter interest and knowledge of politics and public affairs (Delli Carpini and Teeter 1996) implies that voters may not be able to locate the president's policy tendencies with any accuracy. Yet, the analysis presented in this chapter demonstrates a relatively high degree of voter accuracy in locating presidents' policy positions. After assessing voters' accuracy in locating the president, I present two tests of the impact of presidential moderation-extremism on presidential approval. The first test uses aggregate quarterly approval data from 1951–2010. The second test employs individual level data from 1972–2004, using the ANES.

THE ACCURACY OF PUBLIC PERCEPTIONS OF PRESIDENTIAL POLICY LOCATION

Can voters accurately place the president in the liberal–conservative policy space? Can they make the relatively fine distinctions between very and slightly liberal (conservative) presidents? If voters cannot locate the president accurately in the policy space, then we are unlikely to find a systematic relationship between the president's location and voters' job approval ratings of the president. Any relationship that we do detect may be due to noise or public misperceptions of presidential policy location. The latter opens the possibility of president's being able to manipulate public perceptions of presidential positions, that is, convince the public that the president is moderate when he is politically extreme.[7]

---

7 For instance, presidents can use moderate rhetoric, including symbols, to create an image of moderation, while taking positions that are decidedly to the right or left of center. Through such rhetorical manipulation, presidents may even sell their position as being moderate, in the political mainstream, when in actuality it is more closely aligned with the liberal (or conservative) position. For this reason, I employ a behavioral measure of presidential policy positions, the corrected ADA scores used in Chapter Four, not a rhetorical indicator, like in Cohen (1997) or Wood (2009).

Voters may not be able to accurately place the president along the liberal–conservative policy continuum for several reasons. First, many voters do not understand what the terms "liberal" and "conservative" mean. This will undermine their ability to use these terms and thus to locate the president. Second, and related, the public on average tends to possess low levels of political knowledge and information (Delli Carpini and Keeter 1996). Even if they understand the difference between liberalism and conservatism, their lack of information may lead them to mistakenly place the president in the liberal–conservative space.

Third, news reports and criticisms of the president, especially those from the opposition party, may paint the president as being more extreme than he really is. Co-partisans and allies of the president may be inclined toward the opposite, calling "moderate" or "mainstream" a president who is actually extreme. Inasmuch as voters rely heavily on such sources for information on the president's policy location, they may make mistakes in locating the president. Moreover, the president's own public rhetoric may also affect public perceptions of his policy tendencies. A president may try to portray his opponent or critic as extreme and himself as reasonable, moderate, and closer to the mainstream, when the president's position is the more extreme one. Characteristics of voters, the information environment, and presidential rhetoric may erect barriers for the public in learning or discerning the president's actual policy posture.

We can test how accurately the public places the president along the liberal–conservative policy dimension with the ANES data, which have been asking respondents to place the president on a seven-point liberal–conservative scale since 1972.[8] For these purposes, it may not matter whether we use a roll call or a rhetorical measure of presidential policy location. Figure 5.1 plots the corrected Americans for Democratic Action (ADA) scores for the years that we have public perceptions from the ANES (1972–2004) with Wood's (2009) measure of presidential rhetorical liberalism. The two measures trend together quite closely and, for these years, correlate at a Pearson's $r = 0.87$ ($p = 0.000$), a significance level that is quite stunning given the small n (16). The only noticeable discrepancy is for 2004, when George W. Bush's public rhetoric was decidedly moderate compared with his ADA roll call positions.[9]

8 The variable is VCF9080 from the Cumulative ANES 1948–2004 data set. There are seven categories: extremely liberal, liberal, slightly liberal, moderate (or middle of the road), slightly conservative, conservative, and extremely conservative. Unfortunately, this question was not asked in 2002.

9 Wood (2009, p. 74) presents a much more extensive comparison of the several measures of presidential liberalism, using the full series available.

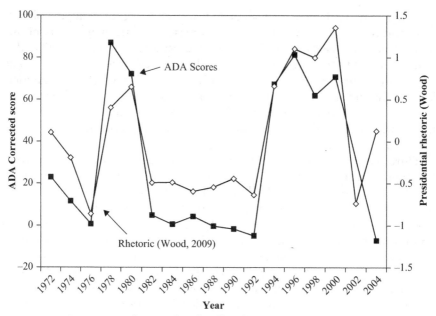

FIGURE 5.1. Comparing Rhetorical and Roll Call Measures of Presidential Liberalism, 1972–2004.

Source: Rhetorical liberalism from Wood 2009; roll call liberalism from the ADA. See Chapter Four for details.

Figure 5.2 plots average annual respondent perceptions of presidential policy liberalism and the corrected ADA scores. Due to the correction algorithm, ADA scores can vary beyond the 0–100 percent range of the original scorings. On Figure 5.2, notice that the corrected ADA scores at times take negative values. The scales of the two measures of presidential placement have been adjusted to make visual comparison easier.[10]

Voter placement of the president and the president's ADA scores tend to track each other closely. When presidents move in a liberal (or conservative) direction, voter perceptions of the president's position move in tandem. Moreover, voters seem to be able to discriminate between very liberal (or

10 ADA scores, by themselves, are not comparable from year to year. They may shift and/or stretch due to agenda composition effects; that is, the set of issues used to construct the ADA scale may change. *Shifting* means that the dividing line between liberals and conservatives may move from one Congress to another. *Stretching* refers to the variance around the issues, the degree of difference in the liberalism and conservatism of roll calls, with the difference in the liberal position being very different from the conservative position, while, on other roll calls, the difference is smaller. The corrected scores take into account shifting and stretching, while also setting one year as a base against which to compare the other years. See Anderson and Habel (2009) and Groseclose, Levitt, and Snyder (1999).

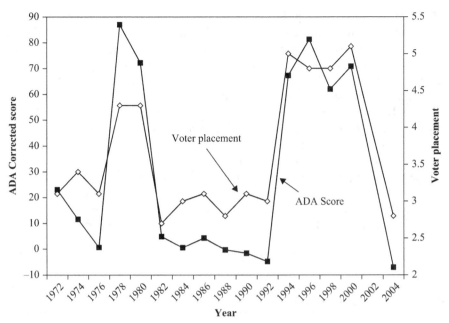

FIGURE 5.2. Aggregate Comparison of Presidential Policy Positions (Corrected ADA Scores) and Public Perceptions of Presidential Policy Positions, 1972–2000.
Source: American National Election Studies for public position and roll call liberalism from the ADA. See Chapter Four for details.

conservative) presidents from moderately liberal (conservative) executive. The aggregate correlation between voter perceptions and ADA scores is remarkably high (Pearson's r = 0.93, p = 0.000). A simple regression of voter perceptions on the ADA scores accounts for 86 percent of the variance.[11] At the aggregate level, voters appear quite accurate in their perceptions of presidential policy positioning.

Such an aggregate analysis may hide variation at the individual level. The strong aggregate correspondence may be due to large numbers of errors canceling out, with only a small number of individuals being accurate in their perceptions, the aggregation effect (Erikson et al. 2002; Page and Shapiro 1992; for alternative perspectives on aggregation see Althaus 2003; Caplan 2007).

How many respondents locate the president "correctly" at the individual level? Is the aggregate relationship between presidential positions and voter perceptions a function of a large number of random errors, which cancel out when aggregated? Or do most voters do a good job of placing the president in

---

11 Wood's (2009) rhetorical liberalism fares almost as well, with a Pearson's r = 0.90 (p = 0.000), accounting for almost 82 percent of the variance.

the liberal–conservative policy dimension? To answer this question requires a definition of what constitutes "correct" and "incorrect" placement. Let us begin with a restrictive definition of correct/incorrect placement that begins with the assumption that Democrat presidents uniformly locate on the left and Republicans on the right. Based on this definition, let us define *incorrect placement* as those who see Democratic presidents as either conservative or extremely conservative and Republicans as either liberal or extremely liberal. By the same token, let's define *correct placement* as those who see Democrats as liberal or extremely liberal and Republicans as conservative or extremely conservative. For this restrictive definition, assume that moderate, slightly liberal, and slightly conservative placements are neither correct nor incorrect. Table 5.1 presents the percentage of respondents who place the president "correctly" or "incorrectly" using this restrictive definition, by year, from the ANES 1972–2004 polls.

TABLE 5.1. *Accuracy of Public Perceptions of Presidential Policy Location, 1972–2004.*

Year	Incorrect[a]	Correct[b]	Net Correct[c]
1972	5.5	58.8	53.3
1974	7.2	49.9	42.7
1976	6.3	63.9	57.6
1978	9.7	18.0	8.3
1980	14.7	22.5	7.8
1982	8.7	62.2	53.6
1984	12.5	53.0	40.5
1986	13.0	51.0	38.0
1988	9.8	56.9	47.1
1990	9.2	41.6	32.4
1992	7.7	49.8	42.1
1994	7.1	45.3	38.2
1996	8.8	39.9	31.2
1998	9.2	37.8	28.7
2000	8.0	45.1	37.2
2004	11.8	59.6	47.8

[a] Calculated by adding the percentage who classify Democratic presidents as extremely conservative or conservative and the percentage who classify Republican presidents as extremely liberal or liberal.

[b] Calculated by adding the percentage who classify Republican presidents as extremely conservative or conservative and the percentage who classify Democratic presidents as extremely liberal or liberal.

[c] Calculated by subtracting the percentage incorrect from the percentage correct.

Source: ANES Cumulative Data File, 1972–2004.

Relatively small numbers of respondents "incorrectly" locate the president. From 1972 through 2004, the percentage of "incorrect" placements ranges from 5.4 to 13.0, averaging 9.3 percent. In contrast, the percentage of correct placements averages 47.2 percent, a figure that is brought down because of the relatively small numbers of respondents who "correctly" place Jimmy Carter in 1978 and 1980. However, about one-fifth to one-quarter of respondents classified Carter as slightly liberal, which is not unreasonable.[12]

ACTUAL PRESIDENTIAL POLICY LOCATION AND PUBLIC ESTIMATES

Instead of using this restrictive definition of presidential policy location, do the presidential ADA scores affect individual voter placement of presidents on the liberal–conservative scale? A simple bivariate regression finds a strong association between the ADA and voter perceptions of presidential liberalism ($b = 0.02$, $p = 0.000$) and accounts for about 20 percent of the variance in perceptions. The bivariate model predicts that when presidents are most opposed to the ADA (-10.4, using the corrected scores), respondent will place the president at 2.78 on the 1–7 conservative-to-liberal scale.[13] When the ADA scores are 40, respondents place the president at 3.8, near the midpoint of the seven-point scale. And when presidents are strong supporters of the ADA (90), respondents locate the president at 4.8, well into the liberal end of the spectrum. Another analysis (not shown), which regressed perceptions on presidential rhetorical liberalism (Wood 2009), essentially repeats these results. Presidential liberalism on roll calls appears to affect respondents' perceptions of presidential policy leanings.

---

12 A case can be made that these respondents are correct in classifying Carter as slightly liberal. News reports during the Carter administration generally identified him as moderate and often pointed out the difficulties that he had with Democrats in Congress, who were often painted as more liberal than the president. In addition, Ted Kennedy challenged Carter for the presidential nomination in 1980, claiming that Carter was not liberal enough for the party. And it also appears that Carter's own political rhetoric stressed his middle-of-the-road approach to policy (Cohen, 1997). But viewing Carter as a moderate is somewhat at odds with the ADA scores. Carter's rhetoric, however, is quite moderate compared with his roll call positions. Using Wood's (2009) measure of rhetorical liberalism, Carter's score is 0.33, compared with 0.71 and 0.87 for Johnson and Clinton, respectively. John F. Kennedy's liberalism score, too, is quite moderate, 0.16, which is consistent with the historical record on Kennedy: that he only moved to the left after a while in office (Stern, 1992). Perhaps Carter's rhetoric influenced public perceptions of his degree of liberalism, which led voters to think of him as more moderate than his positions on congressional roll calls. There is a slight hint of this in the aggregate data. Regressing aggregate voter perceptions on both the ADA and rhetorical liberalism scores find that both are statistically significant, with an R^2 of 0.90, which is significantly higher than the 0.86 used on the ADA scores, as reported earlier.

13 Based on the formula 2.99 (Constant) + 0.02 (Corrected ADA score).

But much more than presidential policy positions can affect public perceptions. Do the preceding findings hold up with controls for other variables that hypothetically could affect public perceptions? I use a multivariate model to test the robustness of the bivariate results. That model includes controls for age, gender, and education, as well as for whether the respondent is of the same party (co-partisan) and shares the ideological leaning of the president (co-ideology), with the idea that people may project their own partisan and ideological orientations onto the president.[14] Other variables look at respondents' interest and knowledge about the political system. Such individuals should be more accurate in their presidential placement than less interested and knowledgeable respondents. I also created an interaction variable between respondent knowledge and presidential policy positions, with the hypothesis that more knowledgeable people should be more accurate in classifying presidents.[15] Finally, the model controls for presidential election year and polarization, the latter measured as the percentage of party votes in Congress. As the parties have polarized, the differences between them have become starker. This partisan environment should make it easier to locate the policy positions of politicians, including the president. Regarding election type, we might expect greater placement accuracy during presidential election years, when more information about politics is available due to intense media coverage of the presidential election campaign.

Table 5.2 presents results of two estimations: an OLS and a multilevel model. The multilevel model is used because several variables, including presidential ADA scores, are measured annually and are not characteristics of individual respondents. Both of the estimations offer strong support for the hypothesis that "actual" presidential policy positions affect respondent perceptions of presidential policy location.[16] The only difference between the two estimations is that the multilevel model produces generally more modest t-values, and two variables found significant in the OLS model – divided

---

14　These variables are the respondent's partisanship and ideological self-identification, recoded so that a high value (7) indicates a strong partisan of the same party as the president and a 1 denotes a strong partisan of the opposition party. In the case of ideology, liberal self-identification is associated with Democratic presidents and conservatism with Republicans. Thus, a high value (7) indicates very liberal (conservative) when the president is a Democrat (Republican), and a 1 indicates a respondent identifies as a strong conservative (liberal) when the president is a Democrat (Republican). To preserve cases, missing data on the ideology variable is coded at the midpoint. There is no difference in the results with these cases included or not.

15　I use one knowledge question – whether the respondent knew which party controlled the House of Representatives – the same question that Nicholson and colleagues (2002) use.

16　Table 5.2 presents regression results, even though the dependent variable – presidential liberal–conservative placement – is an ordered nominal variable. I present the regression results because of its intuitive and ease of interpretation compared with the ordered models. Results of the ordered models can be obtained from the author.

TABLE 5.2. *Impact of Presidential Roll Call Positions (Corrected ADA Scores) on Public Perceptions of Presidential Liberalism, 1972–2004 (ANES).*

	OLS				Multilevel (Random Effects)			
	b	SE	t	p	b	SE	z	p
Education	−0.04	0.01	−5.85	0.000	−0.04	0.01	−5.82	0.000
Co-partisan	−0.09	0.01	−14.82	0.000	−0.09	0.01	−15.39	0.000
Co-ideology	0.03	0.01	3.23	0.001	0.04	0.01	4.30	0.000
Presidential election year	0.07	0.02	2.83	0.005	0.14	0.19	0.73	0.464
Divided government	0.06	0.03	1.92	0.055	0.17	0.22	0.76	0.445
Interest	−0.09	0.02	−5.69	0.000	−0.09	0.02	−5.66	0.000
Female	0.03	0.02	1.44	0.149	0.02	0.02	1.06	0.287
Age	0.00	0.00	6.84	0.000	0.00	0.00	6.50	0.000
Know party – HR	−0.44	0.03	−14.53	0.000	−0.51	0.03	−16.93	0.000
Presidential ADA score	0.01	0.00	22.73	0.000	0.01	0.00	5.15	0.000
Presidential ADA × Know party	0.01	0.00	20.96	0.000	0.02	0.00	22.89	0.000
Polarization	0.02	0.00	16.32	0.000	0.02	0.01	2.18	0.029
Constant	2.41	0.09	25.42	0.000	2.24	0.57	3.92	0.000
Random effects parameters								
sd(_cons)	—				0.34	0.08		
sd(Residual)	—				1.48	0.01		

N for both estimations = 18,638.
For OLS: R^2 = 0.26, adjusted R^2 = 0.26
For multilevel: LR test vs. linear regression: chibar2(01) = 508.09 p = 0.0000; number of groups = 15, Wald $X^2_{(12)}$ = 1122.95,
log restricted-likelihood = −33820.923, p = 0.0000.
Source: American National Election Studies and ADA for presidential liberalism. See text for details.

government and presidential election year – are no longer significant in the multilevel estimation. Otherwise, the results are nearly identical, and most importantly, presidential ADA position is significant in both.

The coefficient for presidential ADA positions is strongly positive, and the coefficient is nearly identical to that in the bivariate results. Plus, more knowledgeable respondents are more accurate in their placement of the president on the liberal–conservative continuum than less knowledgeable respondents, as shown by the interaction between knowledge and presidential positions. These results provide strong evidence that respondents use presidential behavior to locate the president on the liberal–conservative space. When the president is more liberal (conservative) based on the ADA scores, the public sees the president as more liberal (conservative). Respondents appear quite accurate in perceiving the president's policy liberalism based on actual presidential position taking.

But what affects respondent perceptions of presidential positions more, presidential roll call positions or presidential rhetoric? Earlier we found a strong, but not perfect, consistency between the two measures of presidential liberalism. To test this notion, I regress public perceptions on both presidential ADA positions and presidential liberal rhetoric, from Wood (2009). In this simple model, both types of presidential behavior are significant. The coefficient for the ADA score falls somewhat, to about 0.013 (now with a t-value of 3.09), while the coefficient for rhetoric is 0.50 (t = 2.18, p = 0.03). This suggests that voters use both types of presidential behavior to inform themselves as to presidential policy preferences.

But this conclusion changes when we add the other significant control variables from Table 5.2.[17] In the OLS estimation, presidential rhetoric is strongly significant (b = 0.37, SE = 0.04, t = 9.66, p = 0.000), but its strong significance level falls in the multilevel estimation (b = 0.43, SE = 0.24, t = 1.79, = 0.04). In contrast, the roll call measure remains the same, with the same coefficient and significance value in both the OLS and multilevel estimations. Voters appear to use both types of presidential behavior to inform themselves of presidential policy leanings but seem to rely more heavily on roll call positions than rhetoric.

Most important for the argument here, voters appear able to locate the president on the left–right political spectrum with some degree of accuracy, and they seem to be able to discriminate between very liberal (conservative) and liberal (conservative) presidents. This finding establishes an important link in our causal chain from presidential policy positions to public approval. But do presidential policy positions affect approval? The next sections turn to that question.

---

17 Gender, divided government, and presidential election year are not included.

PRESIDENTIAL POLICY EXTREMISM AND APPROVAL

An Aggregate Test

This book argues that the public demands leadership from presidents, defining *leadership* as strength and representation. Chapter Four found that success in Congress affected voters' perceptions of presidential strength. Having survey questions on voters' assessment of presidential strength allowed that test, but no such questions exist for whether voters think the president is doing a good job of representation, so we cannot directly test the hypothesis that presidential policy location affects assessments of presidential representation. But we can test whether presidential policy location affects approval ratings, an indirect test of the policy location–representation connection. This section, using aggregate data, tests the hypothesis that presidential moderation will lead to higher approval ratings.

Voters may prefer policy moderation over extremism in their presidents for several reasons. First, the public expects the president to represent and stand for the nation as a whole, and not a political faction. Voters are more likely to view presidents as doing a good job of representing the nation when presidents position in the political center, where voters also tend to locate, rather than on the right or left. Locating in the center minimizes the policy distance between the president and the largest number of voters, maximizing both collective and dyadic representation. But, voters need to accurately place presidents in the liberal–conservative policy space to reward or punish them for their policy positions. The previous section demonstrated that voters appear quite accurate in locating the president in the policy dimension.

Nicholson and colleagues (2002) offer a strong rival explanation to the policy distance idea. They hypothesize that presidential approval will be marginally, but significantly, higher during divided as opposed to united government because the public has a harder time attributing blame during divided government. Their hypothesis presents a strong rival to the policy moderation hypothesis because, as shown in Chapter Three, presidents tend to moderate their policy positions during divided but not united government, subject to the degree of party polarization in Congress. Is it divided government and blame attribution (Nicholson et al. 2002), presidential extremism, or possibly both, that affect presidential approval? This section tests these two hypotheses using aggregate data on quarterly presidential approval from 1948–2010. Because the divided government–blame attribution hypothesis of Nicholson and colleagues (2002) poses such a strong rival explanation, the analytic approach here follows their model as closely as possible.

Data

As in Nicholson and colleagues (2002), the dependent variable is quarterly presidential approval, with controls for approval lagged one-quarter, an event variable,[18] and three economic variables: quarterly unemployment, inflation, and growth in GDP. I made several minor adjustments to their estimation. First, I extended the data back to 1948 and up through 2010. Second, Nicholson and colleagues dropped the first observation for each new president. I included those cases and added a dummy variable for the first quarter of a new president. New presidents often enjoy a honeymoon with voters, resulting in higher-than-normal approval ratings in the beginning of their terms (Fox 2012).[19] The new president dummy picks up this honeymoon effect and allows us to retain all the cases in the series.

I used all the Gallup polls on presidential approval from 1948 through 2010 to create the quarterly measure.[20] To create the quarterly measure, I averaged the approval rating for all polls within the quarter. There are at least two issues with the Gallup approval poll series: missing data and "don't know" responses: (1) There are six quarters without Gallup approval polls.[21] I linearly interpolated to fill in these missing data points. (2) The percentage of "don't know" responses is higher earlier in a president's term of office than later on.[22] The percentage of "don't knows" can be quite high too, at times greater than 10 percent per quarter. To correct for the systematic bias in "don't know" responses, I created a net interpolated approval score with the formula: {(Interpolated approval)/(Interpolated approval + Interpolated disapproval)} $\times$ 100.[23] Stationarity and autocorrelation may affect time-series analysis. Either problem may lead to erroneous statistical results. Dickey-Fuller (DF) and Augmented Dickey-Fuller (ADF) tests suggest that the approval series is stationary.[24]

---

18 I use the lists of events Newman and Forcehimes (2010) and the procedures from Brace and Hinckley (1992), Gronke and Brehm (2002), and Nicholson and colleagues (2002) for events that are not included in these lists.

19 Analysis that deletes these first observations produces similar results.

20 The entire series of Gallup approval polls was accessed from the Roper Center for Public Opinion Research, http://www.ropercenter.uconn.edu/, on June 1, 2013.

21 The quarters are 1948:3, 1948:4, 1949:4, 1964:3, 1972:3, and 1976:3.

22 I regressed the "don't know" percentages on a time counter and the new president dummy. Both proved statistically significant (trend: $b = -0.04$, SE = 0.002, $t = -16.51$, $p = 0.000$; new president: $b = 10.20$, SE = 0.86, $t = 11.88$, $p = 0.000$), and accounted for 64 percent of the variance.

23 They correlate at Pearson's $r = 0.98$, $p = 0.000$.

24 The DF test statistic is -4.54 against a 1 percent critical value of -3.46 and the ADF test statistic is -4.84, with a significant one-period lag, against a 1 percent critical value of -3.46. Also, a growing number of studies contend that approval series are fractionally integrated (Clarke et al. 2005; Lebo and Cassino 2007; Newman and Forcehimes 2010). Although the quarterly approval series fractional integration parameter, d, is significant ($t = 2.21$), it is small (0.11), and is insignificant with the independent variables added to the estimation.

Results

The analysis proceeds in several steps. First, I replicate the Nicholson and colleagues model as closely as possible. The key variable of interest in their model is divided government. Then, I replace the divided government variable with the corrected ADA scores. These scores are folded at the midpoint so that high values indicate extremism and low scores indicate moderation. A third estimation includes both the divided government and presidential ADA variables. These estimations use robust regression and a lagged approval variable as a predictor variable, replicating Nicholson and colleagues.

Table 5.3 presents the results, using robust standard errors. Model 1 replicates Nicholson and colleagues (2002), using the divided government variable. In general, the results replicate Nicholson and colleagues' findings, except that GDP growth is not significant. Like Nicholson and colleagues, unemployment never reaches statistical significance. The other control variables perform as they do in Nicholson and colleagues: approval lag, the event dummy, and inflation all affect presidential approval as expected. Critically for this analysis, the divided government dummy is significant, and its coefficient indicates that president approval is about 1.9 percentage points higher for divided than united government. This is comparable to Nicholson and colleagues' estimates, which run from 1.8 percent to 2.2 percent, depending upon their specification.

Model 2 reports results for presidential extremism without divided government in the model. The other variables perform the same as before. Presidential extremism, as hypothesized, significantly affects presidential approval. As presidents become more extreme, their approval declines, indicating voter preference for moderate presidents. Each one-percentage-point increase in presidential extremism leads to a 0.07 percent decline in approval, indicating that small shifts in extremism do not register very strongly with voters, but large swings do. For instance, the least extreme president (3.1 in these data) will be about 2 percent more popular than a president of average extremism, while the least extreme president will be about 3.8 percent more popular than the most extreme president (57.1). Although these values might not appear overwhelming, they are comparable to the impact of other variables – for instance, events in which a president who has a positive event in the quarter will be about 4 percent more popular than a president who has a negative event.

Model 3 reports results including both the divided government and presidential extremism. The other variables continue to behave as in prior estimations, and the overall model performance is comparable. Divided government is still significant, but its effect falls to about 1.6 percent from the 1.9 percent found earlier. Presidential extremism falls short of statistical

TABLE 5.3. *Impact of Divided Government and Presidential Policy Extremism on Quarterly Presidential Approval, 1948–2010[a].*

	Model 1				Model 2				Model 3			
	b	SE	t	p	b	SE	t	p	b	SE	t	p
Approval (lagged)	0.84	0.03	24.99	0.000	0.83	0.04	23.39	0.000	0.83	0.04	23.08	0.000
Events	2.28	0.69	3.30	0.001	2.09	0.68	3.05	0.002	2.25	0.69	3.25	0.001
Inflation	−1.60	0.63	−2.56	0.006	−1.52	0.59	−2.56	0.006	−1.60	0.61	−2.62	0.005
Unemployment	−0.17	0.23	−0.76	0.23	0.06	0.23	0.25	0.40	−0.04	0.24	−0.16	0.43
GDP growth	0.04	0.19	0.20	0.842	0.12	0.20	0.60	0.26	0.11	0.20	0.54	0.30
New president	25.57	3.53	7.24	0.000	24.94	3.38	7.37	0.000	25.20	3.36	7.49	0.000
Divided government	1.88	0.79	2.37	0.01	—				1.56	0.86	1.82	0.04
Presidential extremism	—				−0.07	0.03	−2.12	0.02	−0.05	0.04	−1.50	0.07
Constant	9.84	3.22	3.06	0.002	12.30	3.33	3.69	0.000	11.55	3.55	3.25	0.001
R²	0.85				0.85				0.85			
N	248				248				248			

[a] Robust standard errors.
Source: See text for details.

significance, with a one-tailed p-value of 0.07, just shy of the standard 0.05 threshold. And the coefficient also falls, to −0.05, only slightly lower than estimated earlier. One reason for the weakened effects of these two variables on approval – divided government and presidential extremism – is that they are correlated. As found in Chapter Three, conditional on polarization, presidents tend to moderate during divided government and tend to be extreme during united government. In these data, divided government and presidential extremism correlate significantly, albeit modestly at −0.21 (p = 0.000). The covariation between divided government and presidential extremism makes it difficult to disentangle their separate effects on presidential approval.

Based on these results, voters tend to reward presidents during divided government, perhaps for the reasons proposed by Nicholson and colleagues (2002), but they also punish presidents for taking extreme policy positions. Unfortunately, with these aggregate data, we cannot sort through the various mechanisms through which presidential policy positions affect approval. The next section turns to individual-level data, using the pooled ANES studies from 1972–2004, which provides a method to distinguish several causal pathways from presidential policy positions to approval.

PRESIDENTIAL POLICY EXTREMISM AND APPROVAL

An Individual-Level Test

Representation requires that policy makers take into account the preferences of citizens and constituents; that is, in selecting policies, there should be a close correspondence between citizen preferences and the policy selected. Voters seem to prefer delegate style representation over trusteeship, at least for legislators. For instance, in a 1997 poll that asked respondents, "When your member of Congress casts votes on legislation, do you expect that person to represent the views of the people in your district, or do you expect that person to use strictly his or her own best judgment about what is right?", 71 percent selected the "represent the people" option compared with 20 percent who selected the "best judgment" option.[25] A second poll from 2001 asked a more discriminating question about what officials should do if there is conflict between the official and people. Again, most voters said the official should follow the public (54 percent), with 42 percent saying that the official should use his or her own best

25 Attitudes Toward Government Survey, Council for Excellence in Government. Methodology, Conducted by Hart and Teeter Research Companies, February 20–24, 1997, accessed on June 6, 2013, from the Roper Center for Public Opinion Research, http://www.ropercenter.uconn.edu/.

judgment.[26] Questions like these are rare – and even rarer for the presidency (but see Barker and Carman 2010, 2012; Carman 2007; Carman and Barker 2009). In a series of surveys, in the 2000s, Barker and Carman found that usually more than one-half of respondents prefer delegate representation over trusteeship from the president, but sizable minorities also preferred trusteeship presidents (2012, pp. 27–35).

The aggregate analysis presented earlier touched on issues of presidential representation. It found that moderate presidents enjoy higher approval than more extreme presidents. By staking out moderate positions, a president reduces the policy distance between himself and voters, who are mostly moderate. Yet, the aggregate analysis could only distinguish two reasons for why moderate presidents enjoy higher approval among voters. First, it could be because moderate presidents are closer on average to the preferences of voters as individuals – that is, dyadic representation. But second, voters may also like moderate presidents because they are thought to do a better job of representing the nation as a whole – that is, collective representation. This section turns to individual-level data, the cumulate ANES 1972–2004 data file, to sort out these varying pathways from policy distance to approval. Again, as earlier, Nicholson and colleagues (2002) provide a strong rival hypothesis – that divided government affects job approval. A second limitation of the aggregate analysis was the inability to disentangle the effects of divided government from presidential policy moderation. As found in Chapter Three, conditional on party polarization, presidents tend to be more moderate during divided than united government.

Measuring Policy Distance

There are three ways of conceptualizing, and thus, measuring policy distance. The policy extremism measure based on the ADA roll calls can be thought of in policy distance terms. Extreme presidents will be located farther from voters than moderate presidents because voters, and especially the median voter, tend to locate near the center. But there are issues with considering this as a measure of policy distance. Most importantly, we do not have a measure of public opinion on a comparable measure to compare the president's location with the median or average voter's. If the location of the average or median

---

26 The question reads, "I am going to read you two statements. Please tell me which comes closer to your views, even if neither is exactly right. The first statement is, elected and government officials should use their knowledge and judgment to make decisions about what is the best policy to pursue, even if this goes against what the majority of the public wants. The second statement is, elected and government officials should follow what the majority wants, even if it goes against the officials' knowledge and judgment. Which comes closer to your views?" Role of Polls in Policymaking Survey, Survey by Henry J. Kaiser Family Foundation, Conducted by Princeton Survey Research Associates, January 3–March 26, 2001, accessed on June 6, 2013, from the Roper Center for Public Opinion Research, http://www.ropercenter.uconn.edu/.

voter changes, then presidential extremism may over- or understate the degree of policy distance between the president and voters. For instance, Stimson's (1999) public mood scale indicates that sometimes the public veers to the left and at other times to the right. A roll call-based measure of presidential extremism/moderation cannot pick up changes in distance between the president and voters when the central tendency of voters shifts to the right or left.

Still, the ADA measure has it usefulness for this research. Presidential roll call positions seem to affect the president's ideological image, that is, whether voters consider the president to be liberal, moderate, or conservative. Inasmuch as voters punish presidents for taking extreme versus moderate positions, then we might find lower approval ratings for presidents who situate on the ideological poles rather than closer to the center, irrespective of the location of average voters. To avoid terminological confusion, I call the folded ADA roll call variable *presidential extremism.*

In contrast, two variables asked on ANES studies from 1972–2004 will help us define and measure policy distance more precisely. The ANES asked respondents their own and the president's location on the seven-point liberal-to-conservative dimension, from very conservative to very liberal.[27] Collective policy distance can be thought of as the distance between the positions the president takes and position of the average or median voter. To measure collective policy distance, I take the absolute difference between the average annual placement of the president and the average annual respondent placement on the seven-point ideology scale:

$$\text{Collective policy distance} = \text{abs}\,(\overline{X}R_j - \overline{X}P_j)$$

where abs is absolute value, the subscript j is for the year of the survey, $\overline{X}R$ is the average annual respondent ideological self-placement, and $\overline{X}P$ is the average annual respondent placement of the president on the seven-point ideological scale. This quantity is meant to measure the policy distance between the president and voters on average in a year.

27 The seven categories are extremely liberal, liberal, slightly liberal, moderate or middle of the road, slightly conservative, conservative, or extremely conservative. There are some issues over the measurement of ideological identification or preferences in the mass public. Since Free and Cantril (1967), the literature has noted the distinction between symbolic and operational ideology. The seven-point liberal–conservative self-identification scale used here is an example of *symbolic ideology*, while *operational ideology* refers to positions on specific issues. Ellis and Stimson (2012) detail the differences between symbolic and operational ideology, finding that voters lean conservative on symbolic ideology but liberal on operational ideology. Ellis (2012) also demonstrates that operational ideology is more predictive of election outcomes than symbolic ideology. Plus, it is well known that many voters do not understand or use correctly the terms "liberal" or "conservative" (Jacoby 2002; Knight 2006). However, there are advantages to using liberal–conservative self-identification in this research: (1) We have a common measure for both the president and the public. (2) That symbolic ideology is less predictive of election outcomes than operational ideology puts the variables used here to a strong test because it biases against finding significant results.

Dyadic policy distance can be conceptualized as the distance from the individual voter's policy location to the president's policy location. Because, at the individual level, voters may project from their preferences to where they locate the president, I follow Wlezien and Carman (2001) in constructing the dyadic policy distance measure. They argue that we can purge these projection (endogeneity) effects in placing the president by using the average annual respondent placement of the president.

Dyadic policy distance, thus, is intended to capture how far the president is from each individual voter:

$$\text{Dyadic policy distance} = \text{abs} \, (r_{ij} - \overline{X}P_j)$$

where the subscript i denotes individual respondents, subscript j is for the year of the survey, r is each respondent's ideological self-identification, and abs and $\overline{X}P$ are as previously defined, absolute values and the mean presidential placement for each year of the ANES.

Figure 5.3 plots these three measures of policy distance, aggregated by year, from 1972–2004. Casual inspection of the figure suggests some differences across the three ways of thinking about policy distance. The collective and dyadic policy distance measures, which employ the ANES data, are highly correlated at the annual aggregate level (Pearson's r = 0.98, p = 0.000), while the aggregate correlation between presidential extremism and the other two measures is only 0.08 (p = 0.77), essentially unrelated.

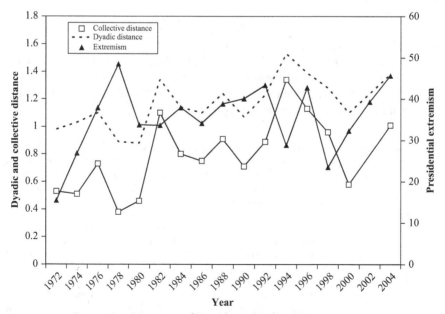

FIGURE 5.3. Comparing Measures of Presidential Policy Distance.
Source: ANES and Presidential ADA roll call positions. See text for details.

Baseline Analysis

As earlier, I use Nicholson and colleagues (2002) as a baseline and because their theory of blame attribution provides a strong rival explanation to the policy distance perspective offered here. Their individual-level model includes controls for events, whether the respondent is of the same party and ideological leaning as the president, economic prospections and retrospections, a midterm dummy, whether the respondent can correctly identify the party controlling the House of Representative, and a divided government dummy.

The dependent variable is the dichotomous approve–disapprove question, which has been asked on the ANES since 1972. Like Nicholson and colleagues, the analysis uses probit. Table 5.4 presents results replicating Nicholson and colleagues, but with 1996 through 2004 added.[28] (The Nicholson and colleagues analysis ended with 1994.) These results, with only minor differences in the size of coefficients and significance levels, nearly perfectly replicate their findings. The only notable difference is that the midterm election variable is no longer associated with approval. Respondents are more likely to approve of the president when they share party and ideological leanings, when they have optimistic attitudes about the economy, and when there are positive as opposed to negative events. We must be cautious in interpreting the economic perceptions variables because of their potential endogeneity with approval (Erikson 2004; Kramer 1983).[29] Replicating Nicholson and

28 A logit estimation produces the same results. Moreover, for this and all other individual-level analyses, I also ran a multilevel model, using xtprobit in STATA 11.0. The rho statistic, which provides the amount of variance accounted for by the panel variable, year, was very small in all estimations, about 3 percent. From a practical standpoint, this suggests that the multilevel model does not add much; hence, I do not present or stress the multilevel results. Still, rho is statistically significant, but with such large n's achieving statistical significance is easy.

29 There are several important critiques of the endogeneity problem – that approval (or vote intention) affects perceptions of the economy. Lewis-Beck and colleagues (2013) find that actual economic conditions strongly affect individual level economic perceptions, and Stevenson and Duch (2013) argue that, under some circumstance, it is reasonable to expect voters to have differing perceptions of the economy. Still, to guard against problems of using the economic perceptions variables in the analysis, I performed several additional analyses. First, dropping the economic perceptions variables from the estimated models does not substantively affect the other variables in the estimation. I also created an aggregate measure of economic attitudes, as Erikson (2004) recommends, by taking an average annual score for both of the economic attitudes. Because they are highly correlated at the aggregate level, I could not enter them both into the estimation at the same time. They did prove positive and significant when entered singly, and their inclusion did not alter any of the results reported in Table 5.4. In addition, if I dropped the individual-level economic attitudes variables and ran the estimation with only one of the aggregate measures, the behavior of the other variables remained unchanged. I also ran estimations using the annual Misery Index for the year of the survey. Unlike Nicholson and colleagues (2002), who did not find the Misery Index to be significant, it did not matter whether there was another economic variable included or not.

colleagues, respondents are more likely to approve of the president during divided government – even more so when they know which party controls the House.

Because probit coefficients are not intuitively interpretable, the table also includes probability effects. Based on these probabilities, during divided government, respondents are 0.18 (or 18 percent) more likely to approve of the president than during united government. This effect is slightly more than twice that found in Nicholson and colleagues (2002). In addition, respondents who can correctly identify the party controlling the House are another 8 percent more likely to approve of the president during divided government. The approval boost during divided government of knowledge in these results is approximately the same that Nicholson and colleagues (2002) found.[30]

TABLE 5.4. *The Impact of Divided Government on Presidential Approval, a Replication, 1972–2004[a] (Probit Results).*

	b	SE	z	p	Effect[b]
Divided	0.46	0.04	11.43	0.000	0.18
Co-partisan	0.31	0.01	56.39	0.000	0.12
Co-ideology	0.18	0.01	19.85	0.000	0.07
Economic retrospections	0.19	0.01	15.64	0.000	0.07
Economic prospections	0.14	0.02	8.94	0.000	0.05
Events	0.31	0.03	12.47	0.000	0.11
Midterm	0.02	0.03	0.67	0.501	0.01
Know party controlling House	−0.22	0.04	−5.59	0.000	0.08
Divided × Know party	0.22	0.05	4.72	0.000	0.08
Constant	−2.65	0.06	−41.16	0.000	
N	20502				
Pseudo-R^2	0.23				
Percent correctly classified (1 = 62.2%, 0 = 37.8%)	74.4%				

[a] Replication of Nicholson, Segura, and Woods (2002).
[b] Probability change for a one-unit shift in variable or discrete change from 0 to 1 if a dummy variable.
Source: ANES 1972–2004. See text for details.

---

30 My results are more in line with Newman and Lambert (2012, p. 382), who update the Nicholson and colleagues model through 2008.

IMPACT OF POLICY DISTANCE ON APPROVAL

Does policy distance affect approval? Since we have three measures of policy distance, I deal with each in turn—first presidential extremism, then dyadic distance, then collective distance. Then I include all three measures into the same equation.

It is also likely that the linkage between presidential policy distance and approval will be stronger for knowledgeable voters than those with less knowledge.[31] Political knowledge has been found to affect participation, voting decisions, and blame attribution (Delli Carpini and Keeter 1996; Gomez and Wilson 2001; Lau, Anderson, and Redlawsk 2008; Nicholson et al. 2002). Before a voter can blame or reward a president for the policy positions that the president takes, the voter must have some sense of those positions and the relationship between the president's positions and the voter's. Knowledgeable voters are more likely to have that information than less knowledgeable voters. Also, knowledgeable voters may have a more sophisticated or realistic understanding of how the American political system operates. Thus, I hypothesize that knowledgeable citizens will be better able to apply policy distance criteria in evaluating the president for these two reasons. Although there is some debate over how to measure political knowledge,[32] for comparability with Nicholson and colleagues (2002), I use whether the voter knows which party controls the House, as earlier. For each measure of policy distance, there is an interaction term: the multiplication of the dummy for knowledge with the individual policy distance measures.

Table 5.5 presents the results of the different measures of policy distance and their interactions with political knowledge on presidential approval. The addition of these policy distance measures does not affect the statistical performance of the baseline variables from Table 5.4, other than minor changes in the coefficients.

Turning to the distance variables, presidential extremism has no direct effect on approval. But the linkage between presidential extremism and approval tightens for knowledgeable voters. There are two issues in interpreting the results of Table 5.5: (1) Probit coefficients are not intuitive; thus, the Effects columns present the probabilities associated with changes in the values of the independent variables. (2) With such a large n, almost any variable can

---

31 Various terms are used to distinguish voters on their knowledge level. "The concepts variously referred to as political sophistication, political awareness, political expertise, and political knowledge rate among the most important individual characteristics for understanding and explaining mass public opinion and political behavior" (Highton 2009, p. 1564).

32 For example, factual knowledge, media exposure, and education have all been offered to distinguish voters on political knowledge (see Delli Carpini and Keeter 1996; Luskin and Bullock 2011; and Mondak 2001).

TABLE 5.5. *Impact of Various Measures of Presidential Policy Distance on Presidential Approval, 1972–2004 (Probit Results).*

Variable	Presidential Extremism					Collective Distance					Dyadic Distance				
	b	SE	z	p	Effect[a]	b	SE	z	p	Effect[a]	b	SE	z	p	Effect[a]
Divided	0.47	0.04	11.14	0.000	0.18	0.48	0.04	11.80	0.000	0.19	0.48	0.04	11.84	0.000	0.19
Co-partisan	0.31	0.01	56.39	0.000	0.12	0.31	0.01	56.33	0.000	0.12	0.30	0.01	55.35	0.000	0.11
Co-ideology	0.18	0.01	19.86	0.000	0.07	0.18	0.01	19.61	0.000	0.07	0.10	0.01	8.39	0.000	0.04
Economic retrospections	0.19	0.01	15.6	0.000	0.07	0.19	0.01	15.68	0.000	0.07	0.19	0.01	15.66	0.000	0.07
Economic prospections	0.14	0.02	8.84	0.000	0.05	0.15	0.02	9.36	0.000	0.06	0.15	0.02	9.42	0.000	0.06
Events	0.31	0.03	12.27	0.000	0.12	0.31	0.03	12.18	0.000	0.12	0.31	0.03	12.25	0.000	0.12
Midterm	0.02	0.03	0.59	0.557	0.01	0.04	0.03	1.30	0.195	0.01	0.03	0.03	0.95	0.340	0.01
Know party	−0.01	0.12	−0.12	0.907	0.01	−0.21	0.04	−5.40	0.000	0.08	−0.10	0.05	−2.08	0.038	0.04
Divided × Know party	0.20	0.05	4.27	0.000	0.08	0.21	0.05	4.64	0.000	0.08	0.22	0.05	4.75	0.000	0.08
Presidential extremism	0.00	0.00	1.05	0.292	0.001	—					—				
Presidential extremism × Know party	−0.01	0.00	−1.89	0.030	0.002	—					—				
Collective distance	—					−0.21	0.04	−5.63	0.000	0.08	—				
Dyadic distance	—					—					−0.12	0.02	−5.34	0.000	0.04
Dyadic × Know party	—					—					−0.09	0.02	−3.56	0.000	0.03
Constant	−2.74	0.12	−23.77	0.000		−2.50	0.07	−36.07	0.000		−2.20	0.08	−28.09	0.000	
N	20502					20502					20502				
R²	0.23					0.23					0.24				
Percent correctly predicted	74.3					74.5					74.6				

[a] Probability change for a one-unit shift in variable or discrete change from 0 to 1 if a dummy variable.

Source: ANES 1972–2004. See text for details.

attain statistical significance at conventional levels. Thus, it is important to discuss a variable's substantive impact, which can be assessed by estimating its magnitude of effect. Comparing the probability of approval for the most and the least extreme president tells the maximum effect on presidential approval. The minimum, mean, and maximum values for presidential extremism are 15.5, 36.4, and 48.5, respectively. There is no difference in the effect of extremism on approval for less knowledgeable voters. But knowledgeable voters will have a 3 percent lower probability of approving of the president when the president is of average extremism and 5 percent when the president is at his most extreme than when least extreme. This is a substantively important effect.

Turning to collective policy distance, results indicate no significant interaction effect, so the table only presents the direct effects. Again, we find support for the hypothesis that collective policy distance affects approval, with approval more likely when policy distance narrows. In these data, collective distance varies from a low of 0.38 to a high of 1.34, with mean of 0.8 (recall this variable can range only from 0 to 3). The impact here is slightly greater than that for presidential extremism. With all variables held at their mean, the overall probability of a respondent approving of the president is 0.60. For the most distant presidents, respondent probability of approval is 0.59, but increases to 0.63 for mean distance presidents and 0.66 for least distant presidents. There is a 7 percent probability shift in approval from least to most collectively distant presidents. Again, this is a substantively meaningful amount.

Finally, let's turn to the effects of dyadic policy distance on approval. Not only does dyadic distance have a direct effect on approval, but the effect strengthens for knowledgeable voters. The effects of dyadic distance on approval are stunning. Dyadic distance varies from essentially 0 (0.01) to a maximum of 4.3, with a mean of 1.17.[33] Figure 5.4 displays the effects of dyadic policy distance on presidential approval for those who know and don't know the party controlling the House. For both types of voters, as dyadic policy distance narrows, the probability of approving of the president rises, but it does so more steeply for those who know the party controlling the House. The average probability of approving of the president is 0.60. For those without knowledge of the party controlling the House, at the greatest dyadic distance, the probability of approving is 0.49, but it rises to 0.69 when dyadic distance is at its smallest value, a probability increase of 20 percent. For those who know the party controlling the House, the probability of approval is much lower than for the unknowledgeable when dyadic distance is at its maximum, 0.39, but it rises steeply to 0.62 when dyadic distance is at its average and 0.71 when dyadic distance is minimized.

Each of the three measures of policy distance separately predicts presidential approval, but how well do they hold up with controls for each other? The

---

33 This variable can range from 0 to 6.

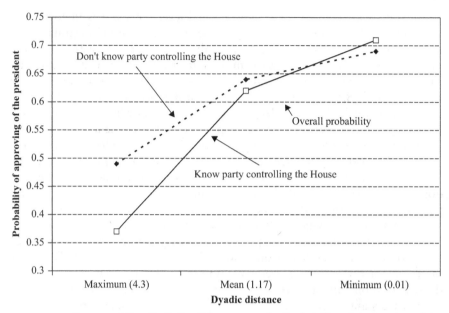

FIGURE 5.4. Impact of Dyadic Policy Distance on the Probability of Approving of the President.

Source: ANES 1972–2004, based on results on Table 7.5, Dyadic Distance model. See text for details.

column labeled "Full Policy Distance Model" in Table 5.6 presents results of this estimation. The forms of policy distance and their interactions that were significant separately continue to be so with these controls. Moreover, the probability effects are nearly identical in all cases except for collective distance, whose probability effect drops from 0.08 to 0.05 for each one-unit shift in distance. Because collective policy difference ranges from 0.38 to 1.34, a voter will have about a 5 percent greater probability of approving of the president when collective policy distance is at its minimum versus its maximum.

These findings present strong evidence that the public takes into account presidential policy positions when rating the president's job performance. No matter how we measure presidential policy distance – extremism, collective distance, or dyadic distance – voters prefer presidents who do a good job of representing them – that is, who minimize the policy distance between the president and voters. Important, too, in rating presidents, voters care not only about personal representation from the president – that is, whether the president and the voter hold similar policy positions – but also the president's fealty to representing the nation at large. We see this in the two collective measures of policy distance, extremism and collective distance, both of which have significant effects on approval.

TABLE 5.6. *Impact of All Policy Distance Measures and Presidential Success on Presidential Approval, 1972–2004 (Probit Results).*

Variable	Full Policy Distance Model					Full Policy Distance Model Plus Success				
	b	SE	z	p	Effect[a]	b	SE	z	p	Effect[a]
Divided	0.50	0.04	11.65	0.000	0.19	0.47	0.06	7.66	0.000	0.18
Co-partisan	0.30	0.01	55.36	0.000	0.11	0.30	0.01	55.48	0.000	0.12
Co-ideology	0.10	0.01	8.72	0.000	0.04	0.10	0.01	8.75	0.000	0.04
Economic retrospections	0.19	0.01	15.63	0.000	0.07	0.19	0.01	15.48	0.000	0.07
Economic prospections	0.15	0.02	9.51	0.000	0.06	0.15	0.02	9.52	0.000	0.06
Events	0.30	0.03	11.79	0.000	0.11	0.28	0.03	10.82	0.000	0.11
Midterm	0.03	0.03	1.21	0.225	0.01	0.04	0.03	1.37	0.169	0.01
Know party	0.14	0.12	1.15	0.249	0.05	-1.63	0.20	-8.08	0.000	0.53
Divided × Know party	0.20	0.05	4.28	0.000	0.07	0.72	0.08	9.23	0.000	0.26
Presidential extremism	0.00	0.00	0.89	0.374	0.001	0.003	0.002	1.73	0.04	0.001
Presidential extremism × Know party	-0.01	0.00	-2.15	0.010	0.002	—				
Collective distance	-0.14	0.04	-3.39	0.001	0.05	-0.17	0.04	-4.24	0.000	0.06
Dyadic distance	-0.11	0.02	-4.67	0.000	0.04	-0.10	0.02	-4.50	0.000	0.04
Dyadic distance × Know party	-0.09	0.03	-3.65	0.000	0.03	-0.10	0.03	-3.93	0.000	0.04
Success	—					-0.001	0.002	-0.36	0.72	0.0003
Success × Know party	—					0.02	0.002	7.81	0.000	0.007
Constant	-2.22	0.13	-17.54	0.000		-2.17	0.19	-11.44	0.000	
N	20502					20502				
Pseudo-R²	0.24					0.24				
Percent correctly predicted	74.7					74.7				

[a] Probability change for a one-unit shift in variable or discrete change from 0 to 1 if a dummy variable.
Source: ANES 1972–2004. See text for details.

Moreover, these results hold with controls for other variables that affect approval, especially Nicholson and colleagues' (2002) rival explanation that is rooted in blame attribution. As they argue, blame attribution is harder for voters during divided than united government. Their rival explanation is important because results presented in Chapter Three demonstrate that presidents tend to moderate during divided government, conditional on the degree of party polarization. The co-variation between divided government (and blame) and presidential moderation made it difficult to distinguish the separate effects of these two mechanisms on presidential approval in the aggregate analysis. But the individual-level analysis here shows that both mechanisms operate and that both appear to be substantively significant for understanding public attitudes toward the president.

SUCCESS, POLICY MODERATION, AND APPROVAL

Voters expect leadership from presidents. As argued here, voters define presidential leadership in strength and representational terms. *Success* is a handy and easy way for voters to assess a president's strength of leadership, while *policy distance* informs them of the quality of presidential representation. Thus far, we have found that voters are more likely to view presidents as strong when they are successful in their relations with Congress. In addition, we found that policy distance – no matter if we conceptualize it as extremism, collective policy distance, or dyadic policy distance – affects voter approval of the president.

We have not yet compared the relative importance of presidential strength and representation to voters. To a degree, with the data at hand, we cannot perform a comprehensive comparison of the relative importance of these two dimensions of presidential leadership to voters. First, we have only one measure of strength to use here: success on congressional roll calls.[34] Presidents

---

34 For this analysis, we cannot employ voter perceptions of presidential strength from the ANES, as done in the previous chapter. Those perceptions are more direct measures of public perceptions of presidential leadership strength than the congressional success measures, making them ideal measures in one regard. But as found earlier, approval and strength perceptions are endogenous. While we could instrument approval to determine its effects on strength perceptions in the last chapter, there is no instrument to use to model the effects of strength perceptions on approval. An alternative approach would be to construct average annual perceptions measures (Erikson 2004), but the strength perceptions variable was first asked in 1980, and was not asked in 2002, leaving only eleven years in the data set. We already have a large number of variables measured in annual units. The combination of those annual variables plus the reduction in years creates a situation of each variable picking up the effects of one year on approval. Thus, for this analysis, I have opted to only use congressional success. The effects of success on approval prove quite impressive; we can speculate that strength perceptions effects on approval will be equally strong if not stronger.

can be successful in other domains, for instance, negotiations with foreign leaders or disputes with other policy makers. And success in Congress may be only one aspect of success that affects whether voters view a president as strong or weak. The fact that we possess three measures of policy distance here stacks the deck in favor of finding presidential representation to be more important than strength. Still, these data allow us to test whether both success and policy distance affect voter approval of the president.

We could perform both aggregate- and individual-level analyses, as I have been doing throughout. However, I will only show the individual-level analysis because there are thorny issues of endogeneity among presidential success in Congress, aggregate approval, and presidential policy extremism (Cohen 2013). Also, an aggregate analysis precludes using the collective or dyadic measures of presidential policy distance from the ANES data. Although an individual-level analysis limits us to one measure of presidential success, we do not have to worry about it being endogenous with approval. The roll call votes that are used to construct the aggregate measure of success were held before the ANES went into the field. And, as argued earlier, knowledgeable voters may be more likely to link presidential success to approval, primarily because they are more likely to know whether the president has been successful or not with Congress. Thus, the analysis includes an interaction between knowledge of the party controlling the House and success.

The column labeled "Full Policy Distance Model Plus Success" in Table 5.6 presents the results of adding aggregate success to the estimation that includes all three measures of policy distance.[35] As hypothesized, success with Congress is positively and statistically significantly related to approval, but only for knowledgeable voters. The coefficient for the interaction between knowledge and success is statistically significant, while the term for success is not. In fact, the probability effect for success by itself is essentially 0. The probability effect for knowledgeable voters is 0.007, that is, a 1 percent shift in success is associated with a 0.007 probability increase in approving of the president. Clearly a 1 percent shift is not very noticeable to voters, or probably even presidents and members of Congress, but over the full range of presidential success, the interaction between knowledge and success becomes substantively meaningful.

---

35 I also performed a multilevel estimation using xtprobit in STATA 11.0. Again, the rho statistic, while significant, was substantively tiny at 0.03, leading me against the multilevel approach. Although most variables performed similarly in the probit and multilevel probit estimations, two of interest here – presidential extremism and collective policy distance – fell well short of significance. This is a function of both of these variables being measured at the annual level, like the panel variable in the multilevel model, and the fact that there are other variables also measured at the annual level.

In these data, success varies from 43 to 88, with a mean of 62. Figure 5.5 plots the probability of approval for knowledgeable and unknowledgeable voters at difference levels of presidential success with all other variables held at their means. Voter approval does not respond to presidential success when voters do not know which party controls the House, as evident by the flat line, which hovers very close to the overall predicted probability of approval at 0.6. It is almost as if these voters are completely unaware of presidential success, perhaps because they pay so little attention to news about presidential–congressional relations. In contrast, knowledgeable voters' probability of approval is highly responsive to presidential success. A knowledgeable voter is about 19 percent more likely to approve of the most successful president than a president of average success and nearly 16 percent less likely to approve of the least successful president compared to a president of average success. There is a difference of 35 percent in the probability of approval for knowledgeable voters between the least and most successful presidents.

Moreover, the figure indicates that when success is low, knowledgeable voters are inclined to disapprove of the president on average. Only when success hits the 50 percent mark do knowledgeable voters begin to become more

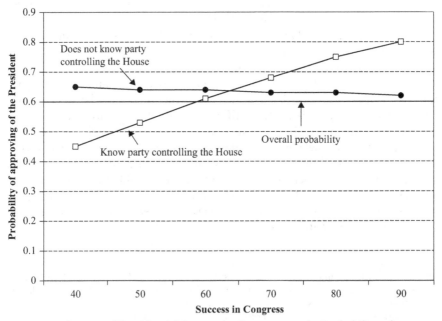

FIGURE 5.5. Impact of Presidential Success in Congress on the Probability of Approving of the President.

Source: ANES 1972–2004, based on results on Table 5.6, Full Policy Distance Model Plus Success. See text for details.

disposed to approving than disapproving of the president. At very high levels of success, knowledgeable voters are almost certain to approve of the president's job performance – when success is near the maximum, the probability of approval is almost 80 percent. Presidents reap large approval rewards when they win frequently on roll calls, but they are also likely to lose voter support when Congress defeats them routinely.

To put these results into context, the impact of success in Congress is comparable in magnitude to that for dyadic distance, the strongest of the policy distance factors on approval. The probability shift in approval from the highest to lowest success levels approximates 34 percent, which is about the same amount when comparing the least to the highest dyadic policy distance, about 32 percent. Both representation and success have substantively consequential effects on voter approval of the president.

CONCLUSION

The topic of this chapter has been presidential representation. Like strength and success, voters want their president to be a good representative. But what do voters mean by presidential representation? Voters can think of presidential representation in individual, dyadic terms, that is, how well the president represents them as individuals: Are the policies that the president pursues close to or distant from those of the voter as an individual? But unlike individual legislators, voters also hold the president responsible to and for the nation as a whole. Thus, in addition to dyadic representation, voters may judge the president on collective, national representation.

This chapter looked at the implications of both dyadic and collective representation on presidential approval. Using both aggregate- and individual-level data, the analysis found that when presidential representation is better in both dyadic and collective terms – that is, when the policy distance between voters and the president is small rather than great – presidents receive higher approval ratings from voters. Plus, presidential approval is higher when presidents are moderate as opposed to extreme in the roll call positions they take. These findings hold with controls for other factors often found to be important predictors of presidential approval. This chapter also compared the effects of presidential success and representation on approval. In addition to representation, success in Congress also affected approval. Presidents with higher success levels also received more approving job ratings from voters.

The impact of success on approval has important implications not only for this study, but also for studies of presidential success in Congress. As reviewed previously, most studies view approval as an exogenous resource that may improve the prospects of presidential success in Congress.[36] That success also

36 The literature is large. See the studies cited earlier.

appears to affect approval means that approval and success may be endogenous to each other. If this is the case, then the theory of the impact of approval on success, and the models employed, are misspecified and require revision (Cohen 2013). The relationship between approval and success in Congress appears more complex than the bulk of the literature suggests.

6

Presidential Leadership and Presidential Elections

This chapter turns to the third question raised by the theory of public perceptions of presidential leadership: the implications of those perceptions for the presidency and the political system. The previous chapter touched on the question of implications for the presidency, showing that presidential strength and representation influence job approval ratings. This chapter turns to the implications of presidential leadership for elections.

Because those leadership perceptions affect job approval ratings, it is not much of a stretch to also suggest that they will affect elections when a president is running for reelection. But do those perceptions toward an outgoing president affect the electoral results for his successor? The theory of public perceptions of presidential leadership predicts that those perceptions will affect nonincumbent presidential elections because attitudes toward the president are important to many voters and voters generalize their attitudes from the sitting president to other elements of the political system.

DETERMINANTS OF PRESIDENTIAL ELECTIONS

The vast literature on presidential elections has looked at several sets of factors to explain who wins such contests. These factors include partisanship, candidate traits, the issue positions of candidates, and campaign events and processes (Lewis-Beck et al. 2009). For current purposes, there are several relevant subtopics: approval effects, succession effects, and party reputations. These literatures present varying expectations about the conditions under which presidential leadership may affect voting in presidential elections.

Since Sigelman's (1979) seminal article, presidential approval has been a mainstay in studies of presidential elections. Sigelman's paper spawned two types of studies: aggregate-forecasting and individual-level vote analyses. For both sets of studies, presidential approval is now an obligatory variable.

The effects of approval on presidential elections have been documented in study upon study, the only debate being that over the degree and conditionality of impact.[1]

Although vaguely worded, the approval question conveys a sense of how voters rate the performance of the president in office and is generally thought of as a type of retrospective evaluation that voters use in deciding who to vote for (Campbell, Dettrey, and Hongxing 2010). Compared with prospective voting, the retrospective voting calculus does not impose heavy demands on voters. For *prospective voting*, voters need to be able to compare the two candidates for office, as well as comparatively predict how well they will perform in office.[2] Instead, *retrospective voting* only requires the voter to assess whether he or she has done well or poorly with the incumbent in office. The decision rule, crudely put, is that if the voter has done well, vote again for the incumbent (or the incumbent's party), but if the voter has not done well, vote against the incumbent (or the incumbent's party). From this perspective, presidential approval becomes a useful summary, retrospective evaluation of perhaps the most important incumbent in office, the president.

Campbell and colleagues (2010) argue that retrospective standards, like presidential approval, will be most strongly felt when the incumbent president is running for reelection:

"[T]he theory of conditional retrospective voting suggests that accountability for governmental performance is partly a matter of party responsibility and partly a matter of personal responsibility associated with the president. When an incumbent is running, both personal and party responsibility apply. When the incumbent is not running, only party responsibility applies to the vote, and voters must look to information about the particular candidates to determine who is more likely to govern effectively." (p. 1084)

Using a variety of tests at both the aggregate and individual levels, Campbell and colleagues find support for their conditional retrospective theory (also Weisberg 2002). Approval always has a stronger impact in incumbent than open-seat presidential elections. In fact, in Campbell and colleagues' aggregate analyses, approval never reaches statistical significance in open-seat contests but does in their individual level analyses.[3]

Mattei and Weisberg (1994) look at succession effects in presidential voting – that is, the effect of the previous administration on electoral

---

1 Both literatures are quite large. Forecasting models have become a standard feature with each new presidential election in the journal, *PS: Political Science & Politics*; the latest is the symposium therein in the January 2013 issue. A good review of the forecasting literature can be found in Holbrook, 2010.

2 Yet Lewis-Beck (1988) argues, for instance, that retrospective evaluations inform prospective ones.

3 As they point out (Campbell et al. 2010, p. 1093), the differences might be a function of different sets of elections. Their aggregate analysis used all presidential elections from 1952–2008, while their individual-level analysis, because of question availability on the ANES, could only use presidential elections from 1972–2000.

performance when the vice president is the party's nominee. They argue that "Vice-presidents are a special type of candidate. Because of the nature of their job and institutional role, vice-presidents are very likely to be identified with the administration in which they worked and with the president whom they served. Therefore, the perceptions the public has of a vice-president are likely, at least in part, to be derived from perceptions of that president" (p. 496). For the elections they study, they find that the approval of the sitting president has a strong effect on the vote when the vice president is running (e.g., 1968, 1988). Further, evaluations of Richard Nixon affected the vote decision for Gerald Ford in 1976. Ford's status in 1976 is somewhat ambiguous – he was appointed by Nixon to be vice president when Spiro Agnew stepped down, then succeeded Nixon into the Oval Office when Nixon resigned in August 1974 because of the Watergate scandal.

These studies have implications for whether presidential leadership perceptions will also affect election results. First, as shown earlier, presidential success and representation, aspects of leadership to voters, influence presidential approval. One possibility is that these leadership attributes will only affect election outcomes indirectly, through their effects on approval. But, Lebo and O'Geen (2011) find that presidential success affects the number of seats the president's party wins in the upcoming election. Moreover, in estimations that include both presidential success and approval, it is success, not approval, that affects congressional election outcomes (Lebo and O'Geen 2011, p. 13). In addition, Zaller (1998) presents evidence that presidential moderation, related to our notion of presidential representation, influences election outcomes.[4]

The following analysis considers all the leadership variables used thus far, including presidential success and extremism in Congress, as well as the public perceptions variables (presidential strength, collective and dyadic policy distance). Although we would expect the perceptions variables to have stronger effects on voting than the Congress-based variables, there are two reasons for employing the Congress variables: (1) They exist for a longer time period, from 1956 on, than the perceptions variables, which ANES only began collecting in 1972.[5] (2) Using the Congress-based variables allows us to test whether relations with Congress directly affect election outcomes, as Lebo and O'Geen (2011) suggest.

Finally, the analysis also compares the impact of these leadership variables with approval and asks whether the leadership variables are stronger

---

4 Zaller's (1998) model uses elections from 1948–96, with three independent variables: presidential candidate moderation, income growth, and war. He does not include an approval variable. There are two other issues: (1) He is not particularly clear as to the coding rules for candidate moderation, which compares the relative position of the vying candidates. (2) He codes 1952 and 1968 as war years, but not 1972, although large numbers of U.S. troops were in Vietnam and fighting there in 1972.

5 Actually, the extremism variable exists for 1948 and 1952 also, but the success data start with 1953, too late to include the 1952 election.

for incumbent versus nonincumbent elections. Approval is a general summary variable, where the leadership variables are more specific in orientation. Does approval contain all the information of the leadership variables or not? Dealing with presidential incumbency effects on successor candidates, like vice presidents, may prove more daunting, as nine of the thirteen elections from 1956–2004 had incumbents running and only four were nonincumbent presidential elections.[6] The analysis turns first to an aggregate demonstration of the relationship between relations with Congress and presidential elections, followed by an analysis of individual-level voting from the ANES studies.

RELATIONS WITH CONGRESS AND PRESIDENTIAL ELECTIONS

An Initial Aggregate Test

The analysis starts with an aggregate test of whether presidential success and policy extremism in Congress are associated with presidential election outcomes. This analysis, which uses election results from 1956–2008, suffers from all the problems associated with forecasting presidential elections – the small n, here, 14.[7] Figures 6.1 and 6.2 plot success and extremism for the year of the presidential election against the percentage of the two-party vote that the incumbent party received. The incumbent party's vote share increases both with presidential success in Congress (Pearson's r = 0.41, p = 0.08) and with how extreme the president is in his roll call positions (Pearson's r = −0.30, p = 0.15). But, these relationships fall short of statistical significance. In contrast, the correlation between approval and vote share is healthy and highly significant (Pearson's r = 0.75, p = 0.001). And, when we control for approval, the impact of success and extremism wash out. At least at the aggregate level, the approval variable contains all the information from the success and extremism variables. Presidential relations with Congress may only affect election outcomes indirectly, insofar as those relations affect job approval.[8]

---

6 Despite their abbreviated terms, I consider Johnson in 1964 and Ford in 1976 as incumbents.
7 See Sidman, Mak, and Lebo (2008) for an attempt to deal with this limitation. Other studies have used state-level election returns as a way to deal with the small n problem (Holbrook and DeSart 1999; Soumbatiants, Chappell, and Johnson 2006).
8 For these fourteen elections (1956–2008), success and extremism together account for nearly 50 percent of the variance in approval during September of the election year, and both are statistically significant. They remain significant with the addition of economic misery, whose addition increases the R^2 to 69 percent and a dummy variable for war boosts the R^2 to 92 percent. The adjusted R^2 is 89 percent, and success and extremism still retain their significance. The following years are coded as war years: 1968, 1972, 2004, and 2008. Here are the results of this regression b (SE): Approval = 51.74 (7.21) Constant + 0.49 (0.09) Success + −0.23 (0.08) Extremism + −1.85 (0.32) Misery Index + −13.51 (2.69) War. All variables are significant at p = 0.01 or better.

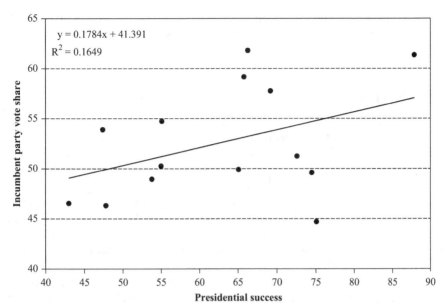

FIGURE 6.1. Relationship between Presidential Success in Congress and Incumbent Party Vote Share in the Presidential Election, 1956–2008.
Source: See text for details.

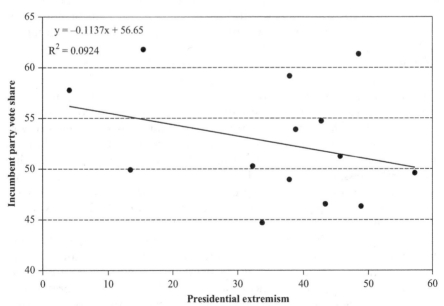

FIGURE 6.2. Relationship between Presidential Roll Call Extremism and Incumbent Party Vote Share in the Presidential Election, 1956–2008.
Source: Roll call extremism from the corrected ADA scores. See text for details.

But this analysis is limited not only by the small n, but the lack of direct measures of public perceptions of presidential leadership.

PRESIDENTIAL LEADERSHIP AND PRESIDENTIAL CANDIDATES

Individual-Level Analysis

The pairing of the candidates in an election may have important implications for voter choice and the eventual outcome. If voters, for instance, like one candidate over the other, the comparatively well-liked candidate possesses an advantage that may lead to victory. At times, such an advantage may spur a minority party candidate toward victory, despite the other party having a much larger number of identifiers and even being closer to the public on the important issues. Dwight Eisenhower's victories over Adlai Stevenson in 1952 and 1956 are cases in point. Consequently, the sources of attitudes toward the candidates have been a major focus of presidential election studies (e.g., Hayes 2005, 2009; Wattenberg 1991).

This analysis departs from the existing literature by asking whether presidential leadership traits affect attitudes toward the candidates, a topic that has received little attention except for the effects of presidential approval (Campbell et al. 2010; Mattei and Weisberg 1994). Although it makes sense that a president's leadership traits should affect voter attitudes toward him for his own reelection, it is not clear that those leadership traits can be transferred to his successor, whether a sitting vice president or not. Voter attitudes toward presidents tend to be highly personalized, crediting or blaming presidents for accomplishments or flops because of the president's behaviors, talents, and/or personalities (Campbell and Gillies 2009; King 2002; Lowi 1985), even though, as shown earlier, political conditions in Congress, such as party control and polarization, have a strong impact on presidential success and position taking. If a president's accomplishments are a function of his own personal endeavors and traits in the eyes of voters, the leadership qualities associated with the incumbent may not shine on his successor. There is a second reason to look at the impact of leadership on voters' assessments of candidates. Inasmuch as comparative candidate traits influence voting behavior, presidential leadership traits may not have a direct effect on voting once we control for voters' comparative assessments of the candidates.

The analysis proceeds in two steps. First, I look at the impact of presidential success and extremism on candidate assessments, which allows me to employ all the presidential elections in the ANES cumulative data file from 1956–2004. The second stage incorporates voters' perceptions of presidential strength and policy distance, which restricts the analysis to 1972–2004, when ANES asked the relevant questions.

PRESIDENTIAL LEADERSHIP AND CANDIDATE LIKES–DISLIKES, 1956–2004

The dependent variable is the difference in the number of likes and dislikes by the voter for the two presidential candidates.[9] Respondents are allowed to identify up to 10 likes or dislikes per candidate. Subtracting net likes for one candidate from the other produces a scale that can range from +10 to –10. Then this comparative like–dislike score is adjusted to measure net likes for the incumbent party candidate; that is, positive scores indicate more net likes for the incumbent versus the challenger and negative scores, more dislikes.

The estimation also includes party identification, rescaled so high values are for strong partisans of the incumbent president's party, several demographic controls (black, age, female, and education), a dummy for whether the incumbent is running for reelection, a dummy variable for divided government, and economic variables.[10] The longer series uses the annual Misery Index of the year of the election, while the shorter series includes personal prospective family finances.[11] Finally, the analysis includes interactions of incumbency status with approval, success, and extremism.

Table 6.1 presents results of the two estimations. OLS results are shown for both estimations.[12] The demographic controls, other than race and the Misery Index, never reach statistical significance. As expected, co-partisanship had the greatest effect of any variable. Voters much more strongly like candidates of their party than the opposition. Based on the regression results, a strong co-partisan will have seven more net likes for a candidate of the respondent's party than a candidate of the opposition party.

Turning to the variables that are interacted with incumbency, both estimations find that approval effects are stronger for incumbents than nonincumbents. The interaction with presidential extremism always pointed in the wrong direction; thus, it is dropped from the presentation. In fact, for

---

9 The variables are VCF0403 and VCF0407 for the Democratic and Republican candidates, respectively. These variables are based on two questions per candidate, one each asking the respondent to name what she or he likes about the candidate and the second asking about dislikes. VCF0403 and VCF0407 subtract the number of dislikes from likes. This results in variables that can range from +5 to –5.

10 Because approval is higher during divided government and divided government affects success levels, it makes sense to add divided government into the estimation. I also found that the results, especially for success, make more sense with the divided government variable in the estimation.

11 VCF0881. This economic question has been asked for almost all the elections since 1956. The personal economic retrospection question has only been asked since 1960, and the sociotropic economic questions have been on the ANES only since 1980.

12 I also ran a multilevel model random effects model, with year identified as the random effect, but the Breusch and Pagan Lagrange Multiplier test for random effects was insignificant, indicating no difference between the OLS and the random effects model.

TABLE 6.1. *Impact of Success in Congress and Presidential Extremism on Comparative Candidate Likes–Dislikes, 1956–2004 (ANES).*

Variable	Model 1				Model 2			
	b	SE	t	p	b	SE	t	p
Co-partisanship	1.108	0.010	107.80	0.000	1.111	0.011	103.15	0.000
Incumbent	−6.699	0.859	−7.80	0.000	−6.678	0.925	−7.22	0.000
Approval (September)	−0.052	0.012	−4.33	0.000	−0.053	0.013	−4.02	0.000
Presidential extremism	−0.035	0.002	−16.10	0.000	−0.036	0.002	−15.18	0.000
Black	−0.217	0.069	−3.13	0.002	−0.275	0.074	−3.74	0.000
Age	0.001	0.001	0.93	0.354	0.005	0.001	3.54	0.000
Misery Index	−0.053	0.013	−4.03	0.000	−0.044	0.014	−3.13	0.002
Education	0.000	0.013	0.02	0.980	−0.010	0.014	−0.73	0.465
Female	0.013	0.043	0.29	0.770	0.020	0.045	0.44	0.658
Success	−0.024	0.005	−4.50	0.000	−0.023	0.006	−4.10	0.000
Divided	0.708	0.107	6.62	0.000	0.746	0.119	6.27	0.000
Personal economic prospections	—				0.363	0.037	9.68	0.000
Incumbent × Approval	0.071	0.010	7.33	0.000	0.071	0.010	6.78	0.000
Incumbent × Success	0.055	0.008	6.73	0.000	0.055	0.009	6.32	0.000
Constant	0.851	0.903	0.94	0.346	−0.221	0.971	−0.23	0.820
N	22055				20038			
R^2/adjusted R^2	0.38	0.38			0.37	0.37		

Source: ANES Cumulative Data File, 1956–2004. See text for details.

nonincumbents, approval is not a significant influence on net candidate likes. For incumbent presidents, however, approval has positive effects on how much voters like them compared with their opponents. Depending on the incumbent president's approval level, this can either help or hurt. For instance, a president of approximately average approval (50 percent) will have about 1.4 more likes than a president of low September approval (30 percent). Presidents with very high approval levels in September (80 percent) can expect 3.5 more net likes than low-approval presidents.

Presidential success with Congress also appears to affect net candidate likes for incumbent presidents. The coefficient for success itself is negative – that is, it points in the wrong direction – which is not unusual in models with interaction terms. To determine the effect of an interaction, we must combine the effects of the constituent terms (here, incumbency and success), with the interaction terms. Thus, a president of average success (65) will have about 0.8 more net likes than a president of low success (43), while the most successful president (88) will garner about 1.5 more net likes than the least successful president.

In contrast, presidential extremism affects candidate net likes similarly for incumbent and nonincumbent candidates. The most extreme presidents in these data (57) will receive about −0.8 net likes than a president of average extremism, and the least extreme president (3) will reap nearly 1.9 more net likes than the most extreme president. For both success and extremism, these appear to be substantively meaningful effects, about 7.5 percent of the possible range in net likes when comparing the least and most successful (incumbent) presidential candidates and almost 10 percent of the possible range when comparing the most and least extreme presidents.

These results suggest that attributes of presidential – congressional relations that influence public thinking about presidential leadership (see Chapter Five) – for example, success and policy positions – directly affect voter comparative attitudes about presidential candidates. Moreover, these congressionally based factors affect voter attitudes above and beyond the effect of aggregate approval. Substantively, the effects of success and presidential extremism appear meaningful, too. But, as we have seen, not all voters are aware of the tenor of presidential relations with Congress, and direct measures of public perceptions of presidential leadership appeared more powerful, at least in their effects on approval, as documented in Chapter Five. Thus, these results may understate the effect of presidential leadership on voter attitudes toward the presidential candidates. The next section addresses that question.

PERCEPTIONS OF PRESIDENTIAL LEADERSHIP AND ATTITUDES TOWARD CANDIDATES

The primary limitation of the preceding analysis was the inability to use voter perceptions of presidential leadership: strength and representation. Including the perceptions variables into the estimation comes with its own costs, the restriction of the analysis to 1980–2004. Perceptions of presidential strength were first asked on the ANES in 1980. In addition, from 1980 to 2004 there are only two nonincumbent elections, 1988 and 2000. With only two nonincumbent elections, it may be difficult if not impossible to test for incumbency interactions with the presidential leadership perceptions variables.

Table 6.2 presents the results of the candidate net likes estimation with the three presidential perceptions variables included: strength, collective policy distance, and dyadic policy distance.[13] Instead of aggregate September

13 OLS results are shown. I also ran a multilevel model, but the Breusch and Pagan Lagrange Multiplier test for random effects was insignificant.

TABLE 6.2. *Impact of Presidential Leadership Qualities on Comparative Candidate Likes–Dislikes, 1980–2004 (ANES).*

Variable	b	SE	t	p
Co-partisanship	0.299	0.024	12.37	0.000
Co-ideology	0.181	0.046	3.93	0.000
Incumbent	−0.358	0.111	−3.22	0.001
Personal economic retrospections	0.115	0.052	2.23	0.026
Personal economic prospections	0.165	0.068	2.44	0.015
Approval	1.121	0.110	10.21	0.000
Black	−0.016	0.126	−0.12	0.902
Age	0.007	0.002	2.77	0.006
Education	−0.022	0.025	−0.89	0.372
Female	−0.100	0.081	−1.24	0.214
Divided	0.255	0.151	1.69	0.091
Collective distance	−0.273	0.174	−1.57	0.117
Dyadic distance	0.017	0.063	0.27	0.791
Strong leader	0.358	0.057	6.34	0.000
Success	0.021	0.006	3.76	0.000
Constant	−4.994	0.527	−9.47	0.000
N	9380			
R^2/adjusted R^2	0.12	0.12		

Source: ANES Cumulative Data File, 1956–2004. See text for details.

approval, as used earlier, I now use individual-level voter approval. Also, the analysis uses personal economic perceptions, retrospective and prospective, instead of the Misery Index. The estimation also includes ideological identification, scaled so that high values are consistent with the proper party (e.g., conservatives associated with Republicans). Otherwise, the analysis includes all of the variables from Table 6.1.

First, none of the interactions with incumbency proved to be significant. This may be a function of only two nonincumbent presidential elections from 1972–2004. Second, presidential extremism (based on the corrected ADA roll calls) did not reach statistical significance.[14] Other than gender, race, and education, all of the other control variables are statistically significant and properly signed.

14 In some trials, it had the wrong sign, a function of its correlation with success and the limited number of elections, 8.

As expected, approval of the president strongly affects net candidate likes. Respondents who approve of the president's job give the candidate of the incumbent party 1.1 more net likes than the opposition party candidate. On the +10 to –10 scale, this is a substantively meaningful effect. Repeating the preceding findings, presidential success with Congress also influences voters' comparative assessments of the candidates, and the magnitude of impact compares favorably with the effect of approval. The incumbent party candidate will receive 1.2 more likes with the most successful president (96 percent) than the least (36).

But perceptions of presidential leadership qualities also affect comparative candidate assessments, even with controls for approval and success. Voters who view the president as strong are more likely to like the incumbent party candidate. The incumbent party candidate will receive 1.4 more net likes when voters view the president as strongest compared to weakest, an effect slightly larger than that for approval. Of the two representation variables, dyadic distance is not significant, while collective distance falls just short of statistical significance at 0.06. The coefficient suggests that the president closest to the respondent will receive about 1.1 more net likes than a president viewed as farthest from the respondent. We need to be cautious in accepting this effect because collective distance may not be statistically significant.

Thus, of the perceptions variables, only strength emerged as an unambiguously statistically significant and substantively meaningful variable. The importance of this analysis is that more than just approval of the president affects voters' comparisons of the candidates for the presidency. Presidential success with Congress and perceptions of strength also enter into voters' likes and dislikes of the incumbent party's candidate. And while representation (policy distance) did not appear to affect those attitudes, the earlier analysis – using a longer time frame and actual presidential policy positions – found voters rate the incumbent party's candidate higher when the incumbent president was moderate rather than extreme. But what are the implications of these results for the presidential vote decision? Do presidential leadership qualities have a direct impact on the vote decision with controls for approval and comparative candidate assessments? The next section addresses this question.

PRESIDENTIAL LEADERSHIP AND VOTING BEHAVIOR, 1956–2004

This analysis of presidential leadership on the vote choice parallels that for candidate likes. First, for the full set of presidential elections from the ANES, 1956–2004, I use the congressional measures (presidential success and extremism) and the September job approval number. The equations use the same variables as for the candidate net likes estimations, but now the candidate net likes index also serves as an independent variable on vote choice. Presidential leadership characteristics, then, may affect the vote choice directly or indirectly through approval and/or candidate net likes. Because the dependent

TABLE 6.3. *Impact of Success in Congress and Presidential Extremism on the Probability of Voting for the Incumbent Party's Presidential Candidate, 1956–2004 (Probit Results).*

Variable	Model 1				Model 2			
	b	SE	z	p	b	SE	z	p
Candidate likes	0.311	0.006	48.67	0.000	0.312	0.007	46.65	0.000
Co-partisanship	0.358	0.009	39.61	0.000	0.360	0.009	38.29	0.000
Incumbent	−2.020	0.654	−3.09	0.002	−2.538	0.694	−3.66	0.000
Approval (September)	−0.026	0.009	−2.88	0.004	−0.035	0.010	−3.53	0.000
Presidential extremism	−0.005	0.002	−3.19	0.001	−0.007	0.002	−4.06	0.000
Black	−0.125	0.059	−2.10	0.036	−0.121	0.062	−1.95	0.051
Age	0.000	0.001	−0.33	0.738	0.000	0.001	0.30	0.765
Misery Index	−0.026	0.010	−2.57	0.010	−0.030	0.011	−2.83	0.005
Education	−0.005	0.010	−0.53	0.594	−0.004	0.011	−0.39	0.697
Female	0.055	0.033	1.67	0.096	0.066	0.035	1.91	0.056
Success	−0.006	0.004	−1.58	0.115	−0.007	0.004	−1.78	0.076
Divided	0.437	0.078	5.58	0.000	0.501	0.086	5.83	0.000
Personal economic prospections	—				0.091	0.029	3.15	0.002
Incumbent × Approval	0.029	0.007	3.88	0.000	0.034	0.008	4.35	0.000
Incumbent × Success	0.012	0.006	1.98	0.048	0.017	0.007	2.53	0.011
Constant	0.435	0.690	0.63	0.529	0.736	0.731	1.01	0.314
N	13872				12919			
Pseudo-R^2	0.62				0.62			

Source: ANES Cumulative Data File, 1956–2004. See text for details.

variable is binary – vote for the incumbent party (1) or the opposition party (0) – I use probit.[15] Table 6.3 presents the results. Again, most of the controls, other than age and education, display significant effects on vote choice with the expected signs. Notably, however, incumbency and September approval have negative signs, but sign reversals are common in models that employ interactions. Both of these variables are components of one or more of the interaction effects.

15 Again, I also ran multilevel models, but in each case, no difference was found between the plain and the multilevel probits, and the random effects on years never accounted for much of the variance in vote behavior.

Turning to the effects of approval, the interaction with incumbency is positive, suggesting that approval has stronger effects on vote choice when the presidential candidate is also the incumbent. But notice that the size of the coefficient is nearly identical to that for the noninteracted approval term. If we drop the approval–incumbency interaction from the estimation, approval is no longer significant. Because the coefficients for the noninteracted and interacted approval variables are similar in magnitude, they cancel out each other's effect. From this, it is unclear that there is an interaction effect of incumbency with the aggregate September approval level.

The two presidential–congressional variables are also significant predictors of the vote choice. Presidential policy extremism does not exhibit any significant interactions with incumbency. No matter whether the candidate of the president's party is an incumbent or not, policy extremism affects vote choice. The probability of voting for the incumbent party's candidate increases by 8 percent if the president is moderate (33) as opposed to most extreme (57), and the probability increases another 7 percent when comparing average presidents to least extreme ones (3). There is a 15 percent higher probability of voting for the incumbent party candidate when the sitting president is least extreme compared with most extreme. These effects of policy extremism are ample and meaningful.

Where extremism was not mediated through incumbency, success with Congress is. There is a very small, trivial, negative effect of success on voting for nonincumbent candidates. But the impact of success becomes clearly statistically significant and positive when the candidate for office is also the sitting president. For instance, the probability of a voter casting a ballot for a president of average success (65 percent) is about 9 percent higher than that of the least successful president (40 percent), and the probability increases another 10 percent when we compare the average and most successful (88 percent) presidents. There is a 19 percent difference in the probability of voting for the incumbent party's candidate when comparing the most and least successful presidents, a large substantive effect on the vote choice.

Voters reward the incumbent party with votes when the incumbent president was *moderate and successful*. But recall from Chapter Three that there may be a trade-off between policy moderation and success. Further, success and extremism affect both approval and candidate net likes. In this estimation, approval does not significantly affect vote choice, but candidate likes clearly do.[16] The results of success and extremism in Table 6.3, which report direct effects on vote choice, may understate the full effect of these variables because success and extremism affect candidate net likes and candidate net

16 There is approximately an 80 percent higher probability of voting for the incumbent party candidate when the voter most likes the candidate (+10) versus most dislikes the candidate (−10). A one-standard-deviation shift in net likes (4) corresponds with about a 16 percent probability shift.

likes affect vote choice. The most important message from these results is the effect of relations with Congress on the electoral prospects of the incumbent party's candidate for the presidency.

PERCEPTIONS OF PRESIDENTIAL LEADERSHIP AND VOTING BEHAVIOR

The preceding discussion suggests that relations with Congress directly and indirectly affect voting for the incumbent party's presidential candidate. Do perceptions of the sitting president's leadership qualities – strength and representation (policy distance) – also affect vote choice? This analysis uses the 1980–2004 data, which enables us to include perceptions of presidential leadership as independent variables, but like the earlier analysis for candidate net likes, no interactions effects with incumbency were unearthed, which is probably a function of few nonincumbent elections. Also as described earlier, the estimation substitutes individual-level voter approval for aggregate September approval and includes measures for personal economic perceptions (retrospective and prospective) as well as ideological identification.

Table 6.4 presents the probit results.[17] With the constraints on the number of contests, the presidential extremism variable did not reach significance, nor were there any interaction effects with incumbency. In addition, approval has only a modest substantive effect on vote choice once we control for presidential leadership effects. Although the coefficient attains statistical significance, substantively it has only a small effect on vote choice, about a 2 percent probability difference between those who approve versus those who disapprove of the president. Lebo and O'Geen (2011) found that approval failed to affect congressional elections once controlling for presidential success. Here, we find a weak effect of approval for voters in presidential elections.

At the same time that approval does not appear to strongly affect vote choice, presidential leadership effects do. First, success with Congress is statistically significant, and the impact of success appears to be substantively meaningful. The probability of voting for the incumbent party candidate is about 6 percent and 15 percent lower, respectively, when the incumbent president is least successful compared to average or most successful presidents. Perceptions of presidential strength also affect vote choice, even with controls for success with Congress. Voters who think the incumbent is very strong are about 4 percent more likely to vote for the incumbent party's candidate than voters who view him as very weak. Presidential representation also affects vote choice, but here, collective distance is significant and dyadic distance is not. Substantively, while the impact of collective distance is noticeable, it is not overly large, with about a 3.5 percent increased

17 Again, a multilevel estimation did not differ from these results, and the random coefficient in the multilevel model was also insignificant.

TABLE 6.4. *Impact of Presidential Leadership Variables on the Probability of Voting for the Incumbent Party's Presidential Candidate, 1980–2004 (Probit Results).*

Variable	b	SE	z	p	Effects[a]
Candidate likes	0.399	0.010	40.63	0.000	0.07
Co-partisanship	0.093	0.014	6.42	0.000	0.02
Co-ideology	0.026	0.030	0.86	0.390	0.004
Incumbent	0.147	0.068	2.15	0.031	0.02
Personal economic retrospections	−0.011	0.032	−0.35	0.724	−0.002
Personal economic prospections	0.042	0.042	1.00	0.318	0.007
Approval	0.115	0.064	1.79	0.073	0.02
Black	−0.222	0.079	−2.83	0.005	−0.04
Age	0.002	0.002	1.28	0.199	0.0003
Education	−0.006	0.016	−0.38	0.703	−0.001
Female	−0.004	0.050	−0.08	0.938	0.001
Divided	0.529	0.095	5.58	0.000	0.087
Collective distance	0.230	0.106	2.17	0.030	0.038
Dyadic distance	0.036	0.040	0.90	0.367	0.006
Strong leader	0.090	0.035	2.60	0.009	0.015
Success	0.015	0.004	4.19	0.000	0.002
Constant	−2.289	0.336	−6.82	0.000	
N	5741				
Pseudo-R^2	0.58				

[a] Probability of a one-unit change or 0 to 1 for dummy variables.
Source: ANES Cumulative Data File, 1956–2004. See text for details.

probability for presidents whose perceived collective distance from voters is at the minimum level compared to the maximum. Still, in tight contests, this may be the margin that enables the candidate to win.

Again, the leadership qualities of the sitting president have direct effects on vote choice for the incumbent party's candidate. In general, it appears that success and strength have greater impact on the vote choice than representation, but the preceding analysis that used all elections from 1956–2004 found strong effects of presidential moderation/extremism. The limited number of elections precluded our inclusion of this aggregate measure along with success, and in separate analyses, success always appeared to be the stronger variable. Still, these direct effects understate the full effects of presidential leadership on vote choice because the earlier analyses in this chapter found that leadership variables strongly affect candidate net likes, and candidate net likes have very strong effects on vote choice.

CONCLUSION

This chapter asked the question of whether presidential leadership qualities affect voting in presidential elections. All the analyses found that leadership qualities measured either as relations with Congress and/or as perceptions affected voters' ballot decisions either directly or indirectly through candidate net likes. Most surprising, however, is that once these leadership qualities are entered into models of the vote choice, approval of the president either weakens demonstrably or becomes statistically insignificant. Job approval has been an identified factor affecting all types of elections – obviously presidential, but also congressional (e.g., Canes-Wrone, Brady, and Cogan 2002; Carson et al. 2010) and lower-level elections, such as gubernatorial (Brown 2010) and state legislative races (Klarner 2010). But Lebo and O'Geen (2011) also found that once controlling for success in Congress, presidential job approval no longer affected congressional elections. The analysis here found a parallel effect.

Lebo and O'Geen (2011) argue that presidents will be important for congressional elections because of the primacy of the president to the public, and thus, party brands, at least to voters, are essentially presidential brands. Their point is well taken and consistent with the perspective and results reported here. Yet, the president-party brand idea does not tell us why success – but not approval – affects congressional (and perhaps other) elections.

Differences in what the job approval question and leadership qualities measure may provide an answer. Although the job approval question asks voters whether they approve or disapprove of the job the president is doing, volumes of research have documented that many factors beyond the president's control influence those performance ratings, such as the economy. In contrast, factors more under presidential control, such as public appearances, have inconsistent and/or fleeting, if any, effect on public assessments of presidential job performance. Some of this arises because voters hold presidents responsible for the "state of the union" coupled with naïvety about the tools and capabilities presidents have to shape it. In a sense, the job approval question expresses generalized contentment or discontent with the state of the world and channels the emotions aroused from that (dis)content toward the most visible political actor.

The presidential leadership qualities, focused on here, are more pointed and specific than the job approval question. Approval, perceptions of strength, and perceptions of policy distance are related as shown in the previous two chapters. Still, voters may perceive a president as strong yet disapprove of his job performance, as may have been the case for many Democrats toward Ronald Reagan. The leadership quality variables used here convey different, albeit overlapping, information with approval. And for some outcomes, such as congressional and presidential elections, they may be superior explanatory variables to approval because they are more specific and appear statistically more important. The advantage of presidential approval is the volume of data we have on that attitude – literally thousands of surveys have asked respondents variations on that question for an extended period of time, and more recently, with great frequency, almost every day. Thus, two of the messages of this research are that scholars of public opinion and the presidency should not focus exclusively on approval but shift some attention to presidential leadership qualities and that we need more data on these other ways that voters think about presidents.

7

Perceptions of Presidential Leadership, Trust in Government, and Attitudes toward Congress

The previous two chapters explored the implications of presidential leadership on presidential approval and elections. Results of the analyses in those chapters found that both of the dimensions of presidential leadership – strength and representation – affected voters' job approval ratings and election decisions. It is probably not too surprising that presidential leadership qualities will affect presidential job approval and voting in presidential elections, although, somewhat unexpectedly, the presidential leadership variables displaced and/or significantly weakened approval as a predictor of voting behavior.

This chapter continues with the question of the implications of presidential leadership, looking at its effects beyond the presidency – in particular, the effect on trust in government and attitudes toward Congress. An assumption of this study is that public perceptions of presidential leadership are fundamental, that voters tend to generalize their perceptions about the president beyond the presidency, onto the larger political system. It is necessary, however, to test that assumption.

This chapter proceeds as follows. The first part of this chapter looks at trust in government, while the second half looks at attitudes toward Congress, employing the previously developed analytical strategies. Foreshadowing the results, perceptions of presidential leadership strongly influence trust in government and attitudes toward Congress. When the president is considered strong and representative, voters are more trusting of government, they like Congress better, and they even like their own representative better.

POLITICAL TRUST: MEANING AND CONTROVERSIES

Political trust is a general evaluation of voters' feelings toward government. It is distinguishable from the policy preferences that voters hold and attitudes toward incumbents or government policies. In representative political systems, trust of those in power is consequential because citizens do not directly make public policies but elect others to do so for them. Political trust links the citizen to the larger political system and has been found to have important consequences for citizens and the political system. Research suggests that trust in government may affect political participation, electoral support for incumbents in office, compliance with laws once enacted, and whether government can implement policy reform (Hetherington 2004).[1]

Although the ANES began measuring voters' political trust in 1958, research on why some people are trusting and others less so only emerged in the mid-1970s, when the aggregate level of trust began to plummet. Figure 7.1 plots the ANES Political Trust Index, from 1958, when it was first measured, to 2008. The index, described more fully later, ranges from 0 to 100, with high values indicating more trust. As is clearly evident, political trust peaked in 1966, with a value topping 60. From then to 1974, the trust index fell sharply and steeply, to 29 in 1974.

The precipitous drop in trust called for an explanation, especially given the then-existing perspective on trust in the United States. Prior to the decline of

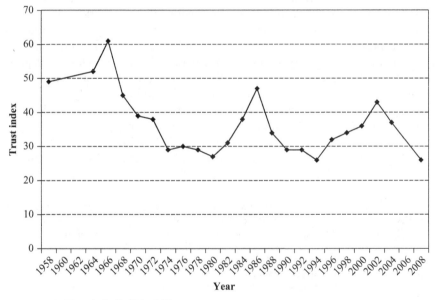

FIGURE 7.1. Trends in Political Trust, 1953–2008.
Source: From the ANES, Guide to Public Opinion and Electoral Behavior, Table 5A.5, accessed on June 18, 2013, at http://www.electionstudies.org/nesguide/gd-index.htm.

1 Levi and Stoker (2000) provide a useful overview of many of the empirical findings regarding the implications of political trust.

the late 1960s–early 1970s, it was almost an article of faith that the American political system and institutions were resilient and voters held the system in high regard. Thus, trust should be relatively high and stable. For instance, Almond and Verba's (1963) early study showed that Americans were quite proud of their political system compared with voters in Mexico or Italy.

The debate between Arthur Miller (1974) and Jack Citrin (1974) on the sources of the decline in trust shaped much of the research on the topic. Miller and Citrin divided over whether trust was an indicator of diffuse or specific support, borrowing from Easton's (1965) distinction. *Diffuse support* refers to general system–level properties, how well the political system is functioning, while *specific support* refers to the incumbents in office.

Miller claimed that trust was a measure of diffuse support, arguing that the decline in trust could be attributed to the centrist nature of the political system at the time. This political centrism either led to compromised policies or the inability of the political system to produce policy that responded to voters' concerns. Thus, voters who stood on the left or right of the political spectrum would be the least trusting because the centrism of the political system seemed unable to respond to growing challenges and discontent coming from people located on the left or right.[2]

In contrast, Citrin argued that the decline in trust reflected more on (dis)enchantment with those in power, especially the sitting president and government policies, like the Vietnam War, and thus, had little to do with the performance of the political system in general.[3] With the inclusion of presidential approval questions on the ANES beginning in 1972, Citrin and Green (1986) marshaled evidence in support of the incumbent-based, specific support hypothesis. They noticed a rise in trust in the mid-1980s, which they attributed to Ronald Reagan and his effectiveness and popularity.[4] In subsequent research, Citrin and Luks (2001) provided additional support linking presidential approval to trust. But Citrin and Luks (2001) also suggested that

---

2 As the political system has polarized and the parties have become more ideologically and policy extreme, the "frustrated ideologue" thesis of Miller has given way to the "frustrated middle" thesis, which contends that moderates and others located between the parties will be most distrustful because their views are least well represented by the parties when making policy (Dionne 1991; King 2003). Hibbing and Smith (2004), however, are unable to find support for the frustrated middle hypothesis.

3 As national politics has polarized, Craig (1993) flips Miller's argument around, suggesting that moderate and middle-of-the-road voters are now more likely to be distrusting, with the more ideologically positioned demonstrating higher trust when their party, with its compatible and amicable policies, is in power.

4 As an aside, it is interesting to note that prior to Reagan's presidency, Paul Light (1982) termed the presidencies from Kennedy to Carter as "no-win presidencies," an indication of the difficulty of governing during the third quarter of the twentieth century, a perspective in line with Miller's diffuse support hypothesis.

"the debate between Miller and Citrin probably posed too stark a distinction between support for the political system and trust in the government of the day. It is not simply that these attitudes are empirically interrelated . . . [B]oth concepts have multiple referents" including both the president and Congress, and calls to reform the system may indicate disenchantment with attributes of the system and those in office (pp. 11–12).[5]

Our empirical understanding of political trust owes much to the questions used in the ANES to measure it.[6] With minor wording changes since 1958, the ANES has employed the following four items to measure the degree of respondents' political trust:[7]

- How much of the time do you think you can trust the government in Washington to do what is right – just about always, most of the time, or only some of the time? (VCF0604)
- Would you say the government is pretty much run by a few big interests looking out for themselves or that it is run for the benefit of all the people? (VCR0605)
- Do you think that people in the government waste a lot of the money we pay in taxes, waste some of it, or don't waste very much of it? (VCF0606)
- Do you think that quite a few of the people running the government are crooked, not very many are, or do you think hardly any of them are crooked? (VCF0608)

These questions are then combined into an index, which ranges from 0, indicating a complete lack of trust, to 100 for a person who is completely trusting.[8]

---

5 As a consequence, it is difficult to disentangle in measures, such as presidential approval, the relative contribution of process factors (Miller's arguments) from incumbent factors (Citrin's position). See Keele (2005) on this point.

6 ANES's measurement of trust also affects the ability to resolve the debate between Miller and Citrin. The questions tend to refer to those "running government," which directs respondents to think about incumbents, and there are no general questions about system performance independent of those in office. For a thoughtful critique of the ANES measure of trust see Cook and Gronke (2005).

7 From the ANES Cumulative Data file, these are variables VCF0604, VCF0605, VCF0606, and VCF0608.

8 ANES uses a somewhat complex formula for combining these items to create the political trust index: Variable 604 is recoded: none of the time = 0, some of the time = 33, most of the time = 67, just about always = 100. Variable V605 is recoded: few big interests = 0, benefit of all = 100. Variable 606 is recoded: a lot = 0, some = 50, not much = 100. Variable 608 is recoded: quite a lot = 0, not many = 50, hardly any = 100. These new scores are then totaled (don't know is not scored) and the sum is divided by the number of valid responses. The result is then rounded to the nearest integer.

THE SEPARATION OF POWERS, THE PRESIDENCY, AND POLITICAL TRUST

Legislation is the primary policy instrument that the federal government uses to address public problems. For the most part, enacting legislation requires the cooperation of the president and Congress – Congress must produce a bill that the president is willing to sign.[9] The process and outcomes of the legislative process, especially how it reflects on the president, may have implications on trust in government. A government that does not enact legislation on issues of public concern, for whatever reason, will look ineffective, perhaps unresponsive, to voters and their concerns and may shake voters' confidence that government is capable or willing to address their concerns. The ability of government to produce public policy thus should have implications for trust in government.

By design and the intention of the founders, it is difficult to enact legislation in our Madisonian system of separation of powers and checks and balances. The founders did not intend it to be easy for government to legislate, designing the system to stymie minorities and factions from controlling government. But frustrating minority control of government also makes it more difficult for the majority party to produce legislation and policy.

Due to the often imposing barriers to interbranch cooperation, the legislative enactment of a president's policy proposal is often widely heralded. The news media give more coverage to whether a bill has been passed or defeated than to the long and often torturous legislative process leading toward the final resolution (Miller 1977, 1978). Consequently, the president and Congress tend to receive positive news coverage when a bill is passed and enacted but will be criticized when no policy of consequence emerges, such as when important legislation does not reach the floor or is defeated on the floor.

In this process, presidents may receive outsized credit or blame for legislative production or its lack. Presidential success with Congress not only marks the ability of government to enact legislation and signifies cooperation between the branches, but, for many voters, attests to the president's legislative leadership capabilities. When the president is more successful with Congress, voters should feel more trusting of government than when presidential success rates fall.

But voter trust may also be a function of the content of policy, whether it reflects voters' policy preferences or not. Voters may become distrustful when they do not feel that their preferences have been taken into account in making policy. Miller's (1974) idea that government was too centrist in the

---

9 The only exceptions are when enough members of Congress in both chambers are willing to override a presidential veto, which is a rare occurrence, and when presidents try to make policy through unilateral devices, such as executive orders.

1960s and 1970s can be viewed from this representation lens. Similarly, the more modern version – the frustrated middle hypothesis (Dionne 1991) – is also about representation. For instance, Jacobs and Shapiro (2000) argue that the declining responsiveness of government to centrist opinion, where most voters are located, is an important factor accounting for the decline in trust (pp. 319–20). Keele (2005) presents some evidence supportive of the representational perspective: When control of the government branches aligns with voters' partisanship, their trust levels rise, but when control shifts to the opposition party, trust falls. Although Keele looks at party control of both chambers of Congress and the presidency, my contention is that the president is especially important for perceptions of representation. This derives, again, from the centrality of presidents for most voters.

However, as noted in Chapter Three, there is a trade-off between presidential success and representation. The factors that breed success, especially party control, also lead presidents to take more extreme policy positions, to act as the representative of his party more than of the nation. This chapter tests the presidential leadership–political trust hypotheses, testing first the hypothesis that success should be associated with higher trust and that extremism should be associated with lower levels of trust. Then the analysis turns to the perceptual measures of presidential leadership. When voters perceive the president as strong, they should also exhibit higher levels of trust. Plus, when dyadic and collective policy distance between the president and voters is minimized, trust in government should also be higher.

This presidential leadership perspective integrates the positions of Miller and Citrin on the sources of political trust. Representation resembles Miller's point, while presidential success and strength relate more toward Citrin's. As Keele says in reviewing the debate between Miller and Citrin:

"[W]e do not know if authorities matter *relative* to how citizens judge the responsiveness of the political process. This was, in fact, Miller's point about evaluations of authorities and trust. He argued that while some distrust existed due to how citizens evaluated incumbent authorities, 'other forms of discontent predominate.' Particularly, he saw citizens as disenchanted with a political process they viewed as unresponsive and broken regardless of who was elected." (2005, p. 874)

Where Keele (2005) tested for the effects of changing party control of Congress and the presidency on trust, arguing that such changes affected feelings of being represented, the analysis here changes the focus to the presidency and looks at a variety of ways of measuring presidential representation, as in the previous chapters. Furthermore, while Keele controlled for demographics and presidential approval, my analysis adds the other side of presidential leadership: success with Congress and perceptions of presidential strength. Do both dimensions of presidential leadership – representation and strength – affect trust in government?

SUCCESS, EXTREMISM, AND POLITICAL TRUST

An Aggregate Analysis

This section begins with an aggregate analysis of the effects of success and extremism on political trust, comparing these two measures with presidential approval. For this analysis, I use the aggregate trust levels the ANES asked respondents about, intermittently, from 1958–2008 (see Figure 7.1). The ANES only polled respondents every even year, in presidential and midterm elections years. After 1958, the political trust questions were not asked again until 1964. Thereafter, we have a trust measure for every two years, except for 2006, when ANES did not field a survey. Across these years there are twenty-three aggregate trust readings, not a large number, but enough for some basic statistical analysis.

An alternative for the aggregate analysis would have been to rely on some of the existing time series, the most recent by Hetherington and Rudolph (2008; also Chanley, Rudolph, and Rahn 2000; Keele 2007). In the latest such study, Hetherington and Rudolph construct a quarterly measure of trust from 1976–2006. Although interested in the aggregate dynamics of trust, like I am here, the Hetherington and Rudolph indicator starts too late for my purposes. The great decline in trust already occurred by 1976. Starting the analysis with 1976, like Hetherington and Rudolph, not only reduces the aggregate variance in the trust series, but loses the era of great presidential success with Congress, the mid-1960s, when Lyndon Johnson and his large Democratic majorities enacted a large quantity of especially important legislation. Also, because the success and extremism measures are annual, it makes little sense to use quarterly trust data.[10] The analysis in this section, thus, should be view as preliminary to the individual-level analyses that follows.

Figures 7.2, 7.3, and 7.4 present scatter plots of trust with approval, success, and extremism.[11] Superimposed on the graphs is the regression line, and results of bivariate regressions also are reported. The signs of the regression coefficients and the slopes of all the regression lines are as hypothesized – as approval and success increase, so does trust, but as extremism increases, trust declines. However, only the success–trust relationship is statistically significant, with aggregate success accounting for about 20 percent of the variance in aggregate ANES trust.

Close visual inspection of the plots reveals some outliers. For instance, on the approval-trust plot (Figure 7.2), there is a data point high on the upper left

---

10 Even creating an annual measure of trust, like Hetherington and Rudolph (2008), that extends through 2012 would provide thirty-seven cases.

11 Because the ANES polls respondents during the election season, in October and November, there is little concern of endogeneity between trust and these variables, and I use the approval taken in September rather than the average of the year.

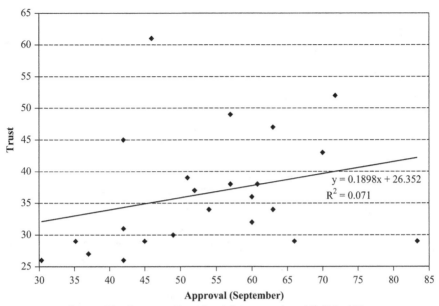

FIGURE 7.2. Scatter Plot between Presidential Approval and Political Trust, 1958–2008.
Source: Trust from ANES, 1958–2008; approval from Gallup. See text for details.

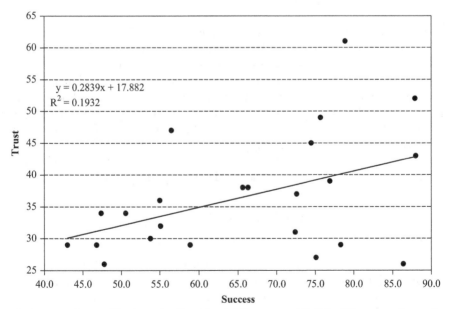

FIGURE 7.3. Scatter Plot between Presidential Success and Political Trust, 1958–2008.
Source: Trust from ANES, 1958–2008; success from CQ Annual Report, Various Years, Vote Studies, Presidential Success. See text for details.

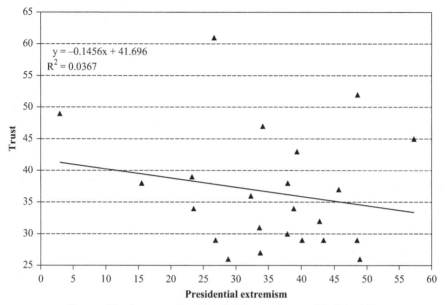

FIGURE 7.4. Scatter Plot between Presidential Extremism and Political Trust, 1958–2008.

Source: Trust from ANES, 1958–2008; extremism from the American for Democratic Action, adjusted scores. See text for details.

quadrant, 1990. Trust is quite low at 29, but presidential approval is very high, 83, a function of the First Gulf War. If we remove this outlier, the correlation between approval and trust rises from 0.27 (p = 0.11) to 0.42 (p = 0.03). In contrast, there are no apparent outliers for the success–trust relationship; however, most of the data points still fall some distance from the regression line. Finally, the regression line for the extremism–trust relationship slopes downward, as expected, but the gradient is so slight that the relationship is far from significant. At best, these results are suggestive. The small n precludes detailed and multivariate data analysis. The next section turns to the individual-level ANES data to test for the effects of presidential leadership on political trust.

SUCCESS, EXTREMISM, AND POLITICAL TRUST

An Individual-Level Analysis, 1958–2004

For the individual-level analysis, I again turn to the ANES cumulative data file, using data from 1958–2004, the period for which we have trust measured at the individual level. Because our initial concern is with the effects of success and extremism on political trust, it is important to maintain as much of the variance in those variables as possible. Thus, this analysis uses all of the years that the ANES asked respondents the trust questions, 1958 and 1964–2004.

The need to include as much temporal variation as possible has implications for the analysis, including choice of variables and estimation style. First, because success and extremism are aggregate-level, annual variables, while trust is measured at the individual level, I perform several types of estimations, including OLS and multilevel modeling. All of the analyses indicate support for the multilevel approach.

Second, I also employ several control variables, the most important being presidential approval. Citrin and Green (1986) found that presidential approval affected trust in their individual-level analysis of various ANES surveys. Since then, presidential approval has been a standard variable in individual-level studies of political trust (e.g., Citrin and Luks 2001; Keele 2005). The issue for this analysis is that ANES only began asking respondents about their approval of the president in 1972. Thus, for this initial analysis, I use the September reading from the Gallup approval series, as in the last chapter. In other words, approval is included as an aggregate variable. Including approval puts both success and extremism to a hard test because analyses reported in the previous chapter indicated that success and extremism may affect presidential approval. Success and extremism may not have any direct impact on trust with controls for approval, with their effect on trust possibly only felt indirectly through approval.

The trust literature has also found that economic performance affects trust. As the economy improves and/or voters' perceptions of the economy rise, political trust also improves (Keele 2005). As indicated earlier, I use individual-level personal economic prospections, which has been asked on all ANES studies since 1956. I also control for whether the respondent was unemployed and the Misery Index, another aggregate, annual-level measure. We expect a negative sign between economic misery and unemployment with trust and a positive sign between optimistic assessments of the economy and trust.

Although not common in trust studies, I control for whether the survey was conducted during a midterm election campaign and for the presence of divided government. Political campaign periods tend to be divisive and polarizing as the competing parties and candidates criticize their opponents. Such a climate may undermine voters' trust, assuming that they have a preference for politicians to work together (Hibbing and Theiss-Morse 1995). Because there is less political information during midterm than presidential election campaigns, we may hypothesize that trust will be higher during midterm elections. Trust too may be higher during divided than united government. The policy output of government may be less extreme during divided government, which forces the parties to compromise when making policy. Inasmuch as voters in general have a preference for middle-of-the-road rather than decidedly liberal or conservative policies, voters may prefer the policy outputs of divided government, the policy balancing hypothesis first proposed by Fiorina (1992).

The analysis also controls for co-partisanship, with the hypothesis that voters of the president's party will be more trusting than opposition party

identifiers.[12] Because black Americans have often been found to be less trusting (Avery 2006, 2009), I include a dummy for black (1 = black, 0 = non-
black). Keele (2005) also finds an association between gender and age with
trust; thus, this analysis includes them in the estimation. Further, education
is entered as a control, although research has not found education to be a
consistent influence on trust.[13] Finally, I include a control for political interest, expecting a positive sign between interest and trust. Interested individuals
may be more realistic in the expectations about government and, thus, less
disappointed or alienated by the debates and failures of Washington.

Results

Table 7.1 presents the results of several estimations, including OLS and a multilevel model. The multilevel results are preferable for several reasons. First,
the sigma u and rho values are large, indicating that the random effects for
years are picking up some of the variance. And a Hausman test comparing
the estimates of the OLS with the multilevel model finds the two to be significantly different [X^2 (14) = 1879.47, p of X^2 = 0.0000].

Turning to the key variables of interest, success and extremism, the multilevel estimation indicates that even with controls for approval, success positively affects political trust, but extremism is not a significant predictor. Nor
does extremism reach statistical significance if approval and/or divided government are removed from the estimation. The substantive effects of success
on trust are notable. A one-percentage-point increase in success is associated
with a 0.46 rise in trust. A standard deviation rise in success (13.7 percent)
corresponds with about a 6-point increase in trust on the 0 to 100 scale. Voters' trust in government will be nearly 21 points higher when the president is
most successful (88) compared to least successful (43).

Contrary to expectations, approval, measured as the average September
aggregate level, does not significantly affect trust. Only when all other variables measured at the aggregate level are removed from the estimation does
approval emerge as a significant variable. Finally, several of the control variables consistently affect trust levels. These include co-partisanship, economic
perceptions, political interest, the Misery Index, and divided government. As
hypothesized, trust is higher during divided government. None of the other
variables emerges as a significant influence on trust.

---

12 This is similar to Keele (2005), who employs a dummy variable for whether partisans are of
    the president's party or the opposition, with similar dummies for consistency of partisanship
    with control of the House and Senate.
13 Keele (2005), for instance, does not find that education has a significant effect on trust, but it
    is significant in some of Citrin and Green's (1986) estimations. Insofar as educational levels
    have increased from the 1960s to the present, education may pick up temporal as well as
    cross-sectional changes, and thus should be included in the estimation.

TABLE 7.1. *Impact of Presidential Approval, Success, and Extremism on Individual Level Political Trust, 1958–2004.*

	OLS				Multilevel Model			
	b	SE	t	p	b	SE	t	p
Economic prospections	3.36	0.22	14.97	0.000	3.23	0.22	14.73	0.000
Co-partisanship	1.15	0.07	17.27	0.000	1.18	0.07	18.05	0.000
Age	−0.03	0.01	−3.64	0.000	−0.01	0.01	−1.70	0.088
Female	−0.05	0.28	−0.18	0.857	−0.03	0.27	−0.12	0.906
Black	−0.61	0.45	−1.37	0.172	−0.29	0.44	−0.66	0.510
Education	−0.35	0.09	−4.07	0.000	0.14	0.09	1.58	0.114
Unemployed	−1.80	0.55	−3.25	0.001	−0.74	0.54	−1.36	0.174
Misery Index	−0.78	0.05	−16.87	0.000	−0.84	0.40	−2.12	0.034
Interest	0.70	0.20	3.54	0.000	0.44	0.19	2.24	0.025
Midterm	3.10	0.32	9.62	0.000	2.14	2.70	0.79	0.429
Divided	9.23	0.63	14.69	0.000	9.24	5.10	1.81	0.070
Success	0.44	0.02	23.82	0.000	0.46	0.15	2.97	0.003
Extremism	0.04	0.02	2.21	0.027	0.06	0.14	0.46	0.649
Approval	0.14	0.01	10.72	0.000	0.14	0.12	1.17	0.242
Constant	−12.84	2.39	−5.38	0.000	−15.16	18.59	−0.82	0.415
R^2	0.08				[a]			
N	26997				26997			

[a] For the multilevel model, R^2: within = 0.02, between = 0.52, overall = 0.07.
Source: American National Election Study, 1958–2004; Gallup for approval; CQ for success; ADA roll calls for extremism. See text for details.

The most important result thus far is that even with the array of controls, presidential success with Congress uplifts trust in government. But presidential policy extremism has no effect. A major limitation of this analysis was the inability use the individual-level measures of public perceptions of presidential leadership–presidential strength or collective and dyadic policy distance – as well as an individual-level measure of presidential approval. The next section presents such an analysis.

PERCEPTIONS OF PRESIDENTIAL LEADERSHIP SUCCESS AND POLITICAL TRUST

An Individual-Level Analysis, 1972–2004

The limitation of the preceding analysis was the inability to use individual-level data on voter perceptions of presidential leadership to predict trust in government. Still, the preceding analysis found that the annual level of presidential success with Congress had a large and substantively meaningful impact on trust, but extremism in presidential policy positions did not, nor did aggregate approval. The analysis in this section uses the perceptions data, as well as the individual-level measures of presidential job approval, but to do so requires that the analysis be restricted to 1972–2004, where the earlier analysis could use data from 1958–2004. The aggregate-level variables may also weaken compared to the earlier analysis due to the fewer years for the analysis.

Table 7.2 presents the results of several estimations, which provide support for the hypothesis that perceptions of presidential leadership qualities affect trust in government.[14] Model 1 contains all the leadership variables, including success and extremism, used in the previous estimation. Model 2 adds a year counter to pick up the long-term trend toward declining trust. The addition of the annual trend variable, which is significant with the hypothesized negative sign, does not affect the other variables in the model, except for minor changes in the size of coefficients. Model 3 deletes the extremism variable because it has the wrong sign (positive, instead of negative), but keeps the annual counter.

Turning first to success and strength, annual success with Congress continues to affect respondents' level of trust. Again, respondents have greater trust in government when presidents are more successful in their dealings with Congress. Using the results from Model 1 to illustrate the impact, we find that a one-percentage-point increase in presidential success leads to a 0.27 rise in trust. A one-standard-deviation shift in success, about 13.4 percent, corresponds to a swing of about 3.5 points on the trust index. Even with controls for success, public perceptions of presidential strength have a significant and measurable effect on trust. The effect is statistically significant, and the regression coefficient is sizable. A one-step increase in the 0–3 strength of leader scale lifts trust 3.7 points, for an 11-point shift in trust for the full range of the strength variable. When the president is successful with Congress and voters perceive him to be strong, voters feel more trusting toward government.

At the same time that strength and success promote trust, so does presidential representation. As noted previously, presidential extremism, the ADA roll call measure, has the incorrect sign.[15] But the two perceptual measures of representation, collective and dyadic policy distance, are significant, with collective distance appearing to be the more consequential variable. Collective distance, the policy distance of respondents on average per year with the

---

14 Ordinary least squares (OLS) is used in all cases because no difference was found between the OLS and multilevel model estimations.
15 It is not clear why the sign is incorrect. The fewer years in the analysis, combined with the correlation with success in Congress, may have something to do with the incorrect sign for extremism.

TABLE 7.2. *Impact of Presidential Leadership on Individual Level Political Trust, 1972–2004 (OLS).*

	Model 1				Model 2				Model 3			
	b	SE	t	p	b	SE	t	p	b	SE	t	p
Co-partisanship	−0.22	0.11	−2.10	0.036	−0.19	0.11	−1.83	0.068	−0.380	0.106	−3.590	0.000
Co-ideology	−0.58	0.21	−2.73	0.006	−0.64	0.21	−3.04	0.002	−0.210	0.210	−1.000	0.317
Age	0.00	0.01	0.08	0.939	0.00	0.01	0.35	0.729	0.001	0.011	0.090	0.925
Black	0.28	0.56	0.51	0.613	0.32	0.56	0.58	0.561	0.491	0.558	0.880	0.379
Female	0.22	0.35	0.63	0.529	0.22	0.35	0.62	0.535	0.173	0.356	0.490	0.627
Education	0.20	0.11	1.87	0.061	0.25	0.11	2.29	0.022	0.239	0.110	2.170	0.030
Economic retrospections	2.14	0.23	9.43	0.000	2.13	0.23	9.38	0.000	2.007	0.228	8.800	0.000
Economic prospections	1.57	0.30	5.28	0.000	1.57	0.30	5.26	0.000	1.493	0.300	4.980	0.000
Approval	5.45	0.48	11.41	0.000	5.46	0.48	11.45	0.000	4.945	0.478	10.340	0.000
Success	0.27	0.03	9.75	0.000	0.24	0.03	8.49	0.000	0.167	0.028	6.040	0.000
Extremism	0.70	0.05	13.17	0.000	0.71	0.05	13.33	0.000	—			
Misery Index	−1.04	0.07	−15.23	0.000	−1.43	0.11	−12.73	0.000	−1.152	0.111	−10.400	0.000
Strong leader	3.68	0.25	14.83	0.000	3.65	0.25	14.70	0.000	4.228	0.246	17.180	0.000
Collective distance	−25.81	1.27	−20.28	0.000	−25.36	1.28	−19.87	0.000	−16.240	1.084	−14.980	0.000
Dyadic distance	−0.76	0.28	−2.66	0.008	−0.80	0.28	−2.81	0.005	−0.499	0.286	−1.750	0.081
Divided	5.17	0.70	7.43	0.000	3.09	0.84	3.67	0.000	3.118	0.848	3.680	0.000
Midterm	9.82	0.77	12.81	0.000	9.33	0.77	12.05	0.000	1.279	0.488	2.620	0.009
Year	—				−0.25	0.06	−4.38	0.000	−0.225	0.058	−3.850	0.000
Constant	4.82	2.88	1.68	0.094	518.62	117.42	4.42	0.000	479.45	118.10	4.06	0.000
R^2	0.12				0.12				0.11			
N	14457				14457				14457			

Source: American National Election Study, 1958–2004; Gallup for approval; CQ for success; ADA roll calls for extremism. See text for details.

president, ranges nearly one unit, from about 0.38 to 1.34, with a standard deviation of 0.26. A one-standard-deviation decline in distance will produce about a 6.7-point increase in trust, but nearly 26 points when we compare the most distant from the least distant president. Clearly, the public is more trusting of government when the president is closer to voters' collective policy preferences. Additionally, dyadic distance, that between the individual and the president, also matters for trust. This variable has greater range than the collective policy distance variable, from essentially 0 to 4.3, but its coefficient is smaller, albeit healthy, at −0.76. A one-standard-deviation alteration in dyadic distance, 0.84, has but a marginal effect on trust, 0.6 points, while a full range shift will alter trust by 3.3 points. These effects, while statistically significant and correctly signed, pale when compared with collective policy distance. Overall, the results find support for the idea that both the performance of authorities (success, strength) and a sense of representation (collective and dyadic distance) affect trust in government. Notably, collective policy distance appears more important to voters' trust than dyadic representation, underscoring the value voters place on presidential representation of the nation overall.

These results hold with controls for a variety of variables – most importantly, presidential approval. Approval has a strong, positive effect on trust, with an approving respondent being about 5.4 points more trusting than a disapprover. But this effect is much less than that of the strongest leadership variables, perceptions of presidential strength and collective policy distance – another finding that suggests we need to look beyond presidential approval for understanding the importance of the presidency and voter perceptions of the presidency to American government and politics.

Several of the control variables also affected trust. Consistent with expectations, the midterm and divided government dummies are significant and positively signed: Trust is higher during midterm seasons and when government is divided. The economic variables are all significant and point in the hypothesized direction. When economic misery is higher, trust is lower, and as economic perceptions lean in an optimistic direction, respondents are more trusting of government. Of the other individual-level variables, only education is significant, but weakly. The age, race, and gender of a respondent do not affect trust.

Surprisingly, the signs on co-partisanship and co-ideology point in the wrong direction, negative, when they were hypothesized to be positive. The source of the incorrect signs appears to be multicollinearity with the presidential leadership variables. When perceptions of strength and collective and dyadic policy distance are removed from the estimation, co-partisanship and co-ideology now have properly directed signs. But removal of the presidential leadership variables also leads to a drastic reduction in the R^2, from about 0.12 to 0.04. In contrast, removal of co-partisanship and co-ideology does not affect overall model performance.

To summarize, the analysis points to the trust enhancing effects of presidential leadership, no matter if leadership is measured in presidential–congressional relations terms or as voter perceptions. When presidents are successful and viewed as strong leaders, trust rises. When presidents are viewed as collectively representative, trust also grows, although neither policy extremism nor dyadic representation seems to figure into respondents' trust in government.

PRESIDENTIAL LEADERSHIP AND CONGRESSIONAL APPROVAL

Throughout this text, I have been arguing that presidential leadership has implications for the wider political system because of the centrality of the president to voters. Voters know more about the president than any other political leader. And, much like party identification, the presidency helps voters make sense of and organize the political world; many voters view politics as a contest between the president (and his supporters) versus his antagonists and competitors. Added to this is the public demand for presidential leadership; that is, voters want a strong (successful) president who is also representative of their policy preferences. Hence, we may expect that indicators of presidential leadership along both dimensions (strength and representation) will affect public attitudes and behaviors beyond those that refer to the president directly, such as presidential approval and voting in presidential elections as found earlier. The previous section of this chapter tested this perspective on political trust, hypothesizing that trust will be higher when the president is more successful and representative and so perceived by voters. Results of that analysis demonstrated support for the linkage between presidential leadership and political trust.

There are several limitations of the political trust index, as measured in the ANES. First, it is not clear whether the index taps into general orientations toward the political system or toward incumbents in office – the Miller-Citrin debate. On one level, this debate does not have much implication for the hypothesis that presidential leadership affects trust. Assuming that the ANES questions tap attitudes toward incumbents, as Citrin argues, it is not entirely clear which incumbents come to mind when respondents answer the trust questions. The trust questions use rather vaguely worded phrases in identifying governmental authorities, such as "the government in Washington, the government, people in the government, people running the government." If the president is so central to voters, as I have been arguing, then voters may be thinking first and foremost about the president when answering the trust questions. Assuming that the trust questions are more about the president in voters' minds than anyone else, then the trust index does not give us a clean or decisive test of the spillover effects of presidential leadership.

Thus, this section turns to respondent approval of Congress as an institution and toward the voters' own representative. Since 1980, the ANES has asked respondents about approval of Congress and their representative with these questions:

- In general, do you approve or disapprove of the way [running U.S. House incumbent Representative] has been handling his or her job?
- Do you approve or disapprove of the way the U.S. Congress has been handling its job?

These questions are styled on the Gallup and ANES presidential approval questions, and it is important to point out that the representative question is only asked of respondents in districts with an incumbent running for reelection. Respondents from districts without contests are thus not included.

Influences on Congressional Approval

Research on the sources of congressional approval began in the 1970s, when scholars began to notice an apparent paradox: that voters liked their individual representative more than Congress as an institution (Cook 1979; Davidson and Parker 1972; Kimball and Patterson 1997; Parker 1977; Parker and Davidson 1979; Patterson and Magleby 1992; Patterson and Caldeira 1990; and Patterson, Ripley, and Quinlan 1992). This research stream was closely tied to the literature on the rise of the incumbency advantage in congressional elections, a phenomenon that began in the late 1960s (Cover 1977; Mayhew 1974). The ANES data used here show this same tendency of higher member than institutional approval: Where 73 percent of respondents approve of their representative, only 48 percent approve of Congress as an institution averaged across all years included in the analysis (1980–2004).

A large literature on approval of Congress as an institution now exists, much of it employing aggregate time series with the greater availability of such polls. Those studies have looked at factors such as attitudes on issues, policy congruence between voters and members, policy production, scandals, partisanship, and economic factors to explain congressional approval (Durr, Gilmour, and Wolbrecht 1997; Grant and Rudolph 2004; Jones and McDermott 2009; Lebo 2008; Patterson and Magleby 1992; Ramirez 2009, 2013; Rudolph 2002). But rarely does the president figure prominently in studies of congressional approval (but see Lebo 2008; Jones and McDermott 2009). This contrasts with the much larger literature on congressional elections, where presidential approval is a standard explanatory variable,[16] and more recently, presidential success with Congress has been used to explain congressional election outcomes (Lebo and O'Geen 2011).

But how meaningful are public evaluations of Congress as an institution? Jones and McDermott (2009), although they are not explicit on the point,

---

16 This literature is much too large to cite fully. For a review of the relevant research see Jacobson (2012).

assume that public attitudes toward Congress must be meaningful because the public at both the aggregate and individual levels can apply ideological (policy) criteria in (dis)approving of Congress as an institution. They argue, for instance, that although knowledge of Congress is not deep, voters have a reasonably accurate sense of which party controls Congress and of the ideological tendency of the institution and its policy output.

Lebo (2008) takes a less sanguine view of the meaningfulness of approval of Congress. First, the congressional approval question as posed in surveys may be ambiguous or unfocused for voters: "Does the question ask for an evaluation of the leaders of the Congress? Or is it asking about approval of the majority party, recent legislation, or the latest nomination fight in the news?" (p. 2). Thus, Lebo finds that presidential approval is positively related to congressional approval even during periods of divided government. That is, when a president of the opposition party is popular, so is Congress, and when an opposition president is unpopular, congressional popularity declines. It is hard to reconcile this finding with any notion that the public has much knowledge of Congress or even the differences between the president and Congress when under different party control.[17]

If we follow Lebo's train of thought and the theory propounded here, presidential leadership, too, should affect attitudes toward Congress. The data used here are limited, however, in testing these various perspectives. With congressional approval questions only being asked since 1980, we have only three Congresses of united government for the length of the ANES series (1980–2004). Divided government has been the norm for most of this era. Still, we can test whether presidential leadership affects approval toward Congress, comparing those leadership effects with the standard presidential approval question.

Further, we can compare the effects of presidential leadership on approval of the institution with approval of the member of Congress. Member support derives primarily from nonpartisan services that members engage in – such as case work, communications and publicity, and the like – the proverbial advantages of incumbency (Jacobson 2012). In fact, members want to redirect constituent attention away from their policy-making and partisan behaviors and toward service to the district and constituents in order to increase their electoral margins. This personal focus on members as representatives of the district, as opposed to policy makers or partisans, should help insulate members from national and political forces when constituents evaluate their representative. Thus, presidential leadership factors should have less effect on how

---

17 On the other hand, as Nicholson and colleagues (2002) argue, presidential approval may rise during divided government as blame is spread across the two branches, but during united government, the president receives the full dose of public blame. This finding can only hold if there is some public knowledge of party control and its implications.

respondents' rate their individual representative than the institution. In fact, from this perspective, it is wholly possible that presidential leadership will not prove to be a significant element in explaining member popularity. If presidential leadership *does affect* member popularity, however, then we have further evidence on the importance of presidential leadership for voters in structuring their opinions across various parts of the political system.

Results

Table 7.3 presents results of the effects of September approval, success, and extremism on representative and congressional approval. The control variables used throughout this chapter are also included in the estimation. Because the dependent variable, approval, is binary, probit is used.[18] As expected, almost none of the variables are statistically significant for representative approval. Of the control variables, only three – age, economic retrospections, and midterms – are significant. Older respondents think less highly of their representative. During midterms, representative approval is also lower, but optimistic economic attitudes are associated with approving of the representative.

Of the three variables of key interest here, only presidential approval is associated with approving of the representative. This finding extends Lebo's (2008) argument that attitudes toward Congress are less well developed than they are for presidents. Thus, he hypothesizes that approval of the president should affect approval of Congress even under divided government. Here, I find that respondents are more apt to like their representative when the president is also popular, irrespective of the representative's party. The substantive effect, however, is modest, as those approving of the president will only have a 6 percent higher probability of approving of their representative. On the other hand, with respondents already predisposed to approve of their representative, it would be hard for any variable to increase the probability of approving. But neither success nor extremism affects approving of the representative.

Matters differ when we turn to congressional approval. First, the model has a superior fit, with a pseudo-R^2 of 0.05 compared with 0.01 for representative approval, which is what we should expect given that there is more variance in the Congress than the member popularity variable. Most of the control variables also affect approval of Congress as an institution. Most important for current purposes, both success and extremism are associated with congressional approval, but presidential approval is not. As success rates rise, so does the probability of approving of Congress, while as extremism rises, the probability of approving of Congress declines.

The probability effects indicate that each one-percentage-point change in success and extremism are associated with 0.4- and 0.6-percentage-point

18 A multilevel model produced results nearly identical to the simpler probit results.

TABLE 7.3. *Impact of Presidential Approval, Success, and Extremism on Representative and Congressional Approval, 1980–2004 (Probit Results).*

	Representative Approval					Congressional Approval				
	b	SE	z	p	Effects[a]	b	SE	z	p	Effects[a]
Co-partisanship	-0.04	0.01	-6.11	0.000	-0.014	-0.06	0.01	-9.78	0.000	-0.024
Co-ideology	-0.01	0.01	-1.09	0.275	-0.004	-0.05	0.01	-4.92	0.000	-0.019
Age	0.00	0.00	4.92	0.000	0.001	-0.01	0.00	-12.81	0.000	-0.003
Black	0.04	0.04	0.91	0.364	0.012	0.03	0.03	0.80	0.426	0.010
Female	0.05	0.02	1.87	0.061	0.015	0.18	0.02	8.62	0.000	0.072
Education	-0.01	0.01	-1.57	0.117	-0.004	-0.07	0.01	-10.10	0.000	-0.026
Economic retrospections	0.04	0.02	2.36	0.019	0.012	0.07	0.01	5.36	0.000	0.029
Economic prospections	0.01	0.02	0.50	0.619	0.003	0.08	0.02	4.29	0.000	0.030
Misery Index	0.02	0.00	4.21	0.000	0.005	-0.02	0.00	-4.65	0.000	-0.006
Divided	0.09	0.05	1.79	0.074	0.029	0.36	0.04	8.47	0.000	0.139
Midterm	-0.13	0.03	-4.02	0.000	-0.042	-0.36	0.03	-13.17	0.000	-0.143
Approval	0.19	0.03	6.29	0.000	0.061	0.47	0.03	18.15	0.000	0.184
Success	0.00	0.00	0.75	0.453	0.000	0.01	0.00	6.49	0.000	0.004
Extremism	0.00	0.00	-1.47	0.140	-0.001	-0.01	0.00	-6.01	0.000	-0.006
Constant	0.38	0.21	1.85	0.065		0.30	0.18	1.72	0.085	
Pseudo-R^2	0.01					0.05				
N	12338					14933				

[a] Probability change associated with a one-unit shift in continuous independent variable or 0 to 1 for dummy variables, when all other variables are set at their mean values.

Source: American National Election Study, 1958–2004; Gallup for approval; CQ for success; ADA roll calls for extremism. See text for details.

shifts in the probability of approving of Congress, respectively. These shifts may appear tiny, but recall the great ranges for these variables. A one-standard-deviation shift in success (14.5) and extremism (5.6) corresponds to a 5.8 and 3.4 probability shift for success and extremism, respectively. Comparing the highest and lowest levels of success and extremism gives us a sense of the maximum impact of these variables on congressional approval. There is a 45 percent difference in these data between the most and least successful president, which corresponds to an 18-percentage-point probability change in congressional approval. Extremism ranges 22.2 points in these data, which can produce a 13.3-percentage-point change in the probability of congressional approval. These are substantively meaningful – in fact, quite large – effects.

But what about presidential approval – why does it not affect congressional approval? The answer to this question lies in the impact of presidential success and extremism on presidential approval. As demonstrated earlier, both success and extremism have a pronounced effect on whether respondents approve of the president. If we drop the success and extremism variables from the analysis, presidential approval emerges as a significant and potent predictor of congressional approval. A respondent who approves of the president will have an 18 percent higher likelihood of approving of Congress than a disapprover. The fact that presidential approval is not significant with controls for success and extremism furthers the point made throughout that we need to look beyond approval to understand the implications of the president on other aspects of the political system.

Table 7.4 shows results of introducing the leadership perceptions variables into the estimated models. The introduction of these variables improves model fit for member approval, but it is still modest with a pseudo-R^2 of 0.02. In addition, several more control variables become significant. But more important, now, is that all of the presidential variables are significant predictors of representative approval. Respondents are more likely to approve of their representative when they approve of the president, when the president is successful and moderate, when they view the president as a strong leader, and when collective and dyadic policy distance are small as opposed to large.

For instance, the probability that voters will approve of their representative increases by 13.5 percent when comparing the most and the least successful presidents, while it will improve by about 4.5 percent when comparing the least and the most extreme presidents. And now, respondents who approve of the president will have a 4 percent higher probability of approving of their representative. All the perceptual measures of presidential leadership also significantly affect approval of the representative. There is nearly a 7 percent change in the probability of approving when comparing respondents who highly agree that the president is strong with those who highly agree that the president is weak. Collective distance also matters – there is about a 13.5 percent higher probability of approving of the representative when collective distance is at its minimum level compared with its maximum, and the probability of

TABLE 7.4. *Impact of Presidential Leadership on Representative and Congressional Approval, 1980–2004 (Probit Results).*

	Representative Approval					Congressional Approval				
	b	SE	z	p	Effects[a]	b	SE	z	p	Effects[a]
Co-partisanship	-0.048	0.008	-6.03	0.000	-0.016	-0.068	0.007	-9.96	0.000	-0.027
Co-ideology	-0.038	0.015	-2.44	0.015	-0.012	-0.075	0.013	-5.54	0.000	-0.030
Age	0.003	0.001	4.25	0.000	0.001	-0.008	0.001	-11.68	0.000	-0.003
Black	0.011	0.042	0.26	0.794	0.004	0.004	0.036	0.12	0.904	0.002
Female	0.038	0.026	1.46	0.144	0.013	0.183	0.023	8.08	0.000	0.073
Education	-0.002	0.008	-0.26	0.793	-0.001	-0.052	0.007	-7.47	0.000	-0.021
Economic retrospections	0.019	0.017	1.12	0.262	0.006	0.064	0.015	4.42	0.000	0.026
Economic prospections	0.008	0.022	0.34	0.735	0.002	0.051	0.019	2.69	0.007	0.020
Misery Index	-0.006	0.005	-1.21	0.226	-0.002	-0.043	0.004	-9.66	0.000	-0.017
Divided	0.173	0.053	3.25	0.001	0.058	0.402	0.045	8.94	0.000	0.157
Midterm	-0.225	0.058	-3.86	0.000	-0.075	-0.255	0.050	-5.14	0.000	-0.101
Approval	0.125	0.036	3.48	0.001	0.041	0.373	0.031	12.08	0.000	0.147
Success	0.010	0.002	4.83	0.000	0.003	0.017	0.002	9.68	0.000	0.007
Extremism	-0.007	0.004	-1.66	0.049	-0.002	-0.005	0.003	-1.42	0.080	-0.002
Strong leader	0.071	0.019	3.84	0.000	0.023	0.104	0.016	6.49	0.000	0.041
Collective distance	-0.413	0.096	-4.33	0.000	-0.135	-0.682	0.082	-8.36	0.000	-0.271
Dyadic distance	-0.047	0.021	-2.26	0.012	-0.015	-0.046	0.018	-2.52	0.006	-0.018
Constant	0.651	0.218	2.98	0.003		0.428	0.185	2.31	0.021	
Pseudo-R^2	0.02					0.06				
N	10871					13183				

[a] Probability change associated with a one-unit shift in continuous independent variable or 0 to 1 for dummy variables, when all other variables are set at their mean values.

Source: American National Election Study, 1958–2004; Gallup for approval; CQ for success; ADA roll calls for extremism. See text for details.

approving increases by about 6.5 percent when comparing the minimum to maximum dyadic policy distance. For the most part, these presidential effects are substantively consequential. But, perhaps more important, they demonstrate the effects of presidential leadership, especially perceptions, on attitudes toward representatives, political leaders who voters already highly regard.[19]

The presidential leadership variables as a group also affect attitudes toward Congress as an institution. Adding the leadership perception variables slightly increases the pseudo-R^2 from 0.05 to 0.06, and they are all significant. With controls for all the leadership variables, presidential approval still affects congressional approval, with nearly a 15 percent higher probability of approving of Congress when also approving of the president. The effects of success are also notable and larger than they were before, with about a 32 percent increase in the probability of approving of Congress when the president is most successful compared with least successful. The statistical effects of presidential extremism fall. With a p-value of 0.08 in the face of the huge number of cases, this variable should not be viewed as significant.

The leadership perceptions variables are all significant predictors of congressional approval. The probability of approving of Congress increases by 12 percent when comparing the high- and low-strength ratings of presidents. Collective policy distance also strongly affects approval of Congress, with a 27 percent higher probability of approving of the legislature when collective distance is at the minimum level compared to the maximum. Finally, dyadic policy distance adds to the picture of presidential leadership effects on congressional approval. There is about a 7.7 percent higher likelihood of approving of Congress when dyadic distance is smallest compared to largest. Notably, for both representative and congressional approval, collective policy representation by the president has larger effects than dyadic representation.

CONCLUSION

This chapter has looked at the implications of presidential leadership beyond the presidency – on aspects of the larger political system, political trust, and attitudes toward Congress. The contention of this research is that the president is central to voters, that they demand leadership from presidents, and that voters define presidential leadership as strength and representation. Previous chapters found that presidential leadership affected approval of the president and voting in presidential elections. But those findings merely inform us that

---

19 The effects of most of the presidential leadership variables remain with controls for congressional approval, the number of likes/dislikes about the House incumbent (VCF0946), and the number of contacts the respondent had with the House incumbent (VCF0995). Each of these controls is strongly predictive of approval toward the incumbent. With these controls, approval, success, and collective policy distance lose their statistical significance, but extremism, strong leadership, and dyadic distance continue to be significant.

presidential leadership affects voters' attitudes and behaviors toward presidents and presidential candidates. A stronger test of the presidential leadership perspective needs to demonstrate that voters generalized their attitudes about the president's leadership beyond the presidency, to other aspects of the political system. Results in this chapter demonstrated that those perceptions affected voters' trust of government and approval of both Congress and their representative.

As to political trust, there is considerable debate over the meaning of the ANES trust index – whether it taps into general attitudes toward the functioning of the political system or whether it merely taps into assessments of incumbents in office. For the analysis here, however, the issue was whether presidential leadership has public opinion impacts beyond those that relate directly to the president, such as approval or voting in presidential elections. That analysis found that all types of presidential leadership affect trust in government, including indicators of presidential relations with Congress as well as perceptions of presidential leadership. Moreover, both of the dimensions of presidential leadership – success (strength) and representation – affected trust in government. Still, there is a certain ambiguity in interpreting these results because many respondents may be thinking primarily of the president when answering the ANES trust questions.

Thus, the second half of the chapter turned to questions that unambiguously are not presidential: approval of Congress as an institution and the respondent's own representative. Again, the results indicate that all aspects of presidential leadership, behavioral and perceptual, had implications for legislative approval. Perhaps the most important finding of all was the impact of the presidential leadership variables on approval of the respondent's representative. That literature has emphasized the personal, incumbency, and constituency-service basis of representative popularity. In their early study comparing the popularity of representatives with Congress, Parker and Davidson (1979) say this about why voters love their member of Congress so much more than Congress:

"[F]ew voters voice specific policy concerns-indeed, few voice policy concerns of any kind-in evaluating members' performance. For Congress as an institution, in contrast, citizens enunciate the task of resolving national problems." (p. 59)

This has been the underlying foundation for all studies on the topic since, a perspective so accepted that research on the sources of representative approval has virtually vanished from the scholarly agenda.

A second point emerges from this analysis: There is more to public orientations toward the president than job approval. Even with controls for approval, perceptions of presidential leadership had separate, independent, and statistically significant effects on trust in government and congressional/representative approval. As argued earlier, it is possible for voters to approve of a president but view him as weak and/or not representative. Carter is a case in point, where many Democrats approved of him, presumably because he was a Democratic and had policy views closer to them than a Republican president would. But Democratic voters also thought Carter was a weak president. Reagan provides another example, this time with Democrats disapproving of his job performance but still viewing him as a strong president. Public attitudes toward presidents are richer than just job approval. And public attitudes about the president spill beyond the president and the office of the presidency to affect other aspects of the political system.

8

Presidential Leadership, Public Opinion, and American Democracy

There is probably no more common refrain among voters than the call for *presidential leadership*. For many, perhaps most voters, the president stands in the center of their political world. They view politics and policy making in terms of the president (and his allies) versus the president's competitors, rivals, opponents, etc. Not only do many voters organize these often confusing and complex political events with this presidential schema, they also rely on the president for psychological assurance in an often dangerous and threatening world (Greenstein 1974). Moreover, the unitary nature of the office *personalizes* the presidency to many voters. The news media reinforces the personalization of the office by the way it reports on the presidency. Thus, it is little wonder that voters seek leadership from their presidents. But what do voters mean when they say they want presidential leadership?

There is a considerable and well-established literature that suggests voters' expectations of presidents are idealized and contradictory (Cronin 1980; Cronin and Genovese 1998; Simon 2009). But there is another literature that looks at voter evaluation of incumbent presidents, a performance standard – most notably in the vast literature on presidential approval. This book extends the performance standard from approval to voters' perceptions of presidential leadership.

Despite their lofty and unrealistic idealized expectations for presidential leadership, voters desire that a sitting president be strong and representative. Presidential strength is an elusive and fuzzy concept, but as I have argued in this book, how often a president "wins" or "loses," especially in his dealings with Congress, will have a large impact on whether voters view that president as strong or weak. This does not deny that there are many other arenas where voters can look to see if the president has won or lost, but, as argued here, perhaps the most important is the congressional arena. Accounting for success or failure in the congressional arena is straightforward: Was the president on the winning side of a congressional roll call? Did Congress enact a presidential proposal? The news media aid voters in learning how often the president wins or loses in Congress. Such news is common, and journalists, too, equate presidential victory or defeat on a roll call as success or failure for the president. A representative president is one whose policy positioning is not too distant from the preferences of voters as individuals and not too far from what the nation on average prefers. Again, the positions that presidents take on roll calls before Congress also inform voters as to the president's policy location and how near or far his position is from theirs. In addition, news media reporting helps inform voters about this aspect of presidential behavior vis á vis the legislature.

If voters value success and policy representation from presidents, we would then expect presidents in their dealings with Congress to take positions that have a high prospect for winning and, at the same time, are located where most voters are located – that is, near the center. But as argued, it is not always possible, in fact, it is highly unlikely, for presidents to be both successful and moderate in the congressional arena. The factors that promote presidential success in Congress – most particularly, party control – also lead presidents to take extreme policy positions, that is, to act more as a representative of their party than the nation. Thus, there is a trade-off between presidential success and representation.

The next section of this concluding chapter briefly revisits the argument and findings presented in this book. Then I discuss lingering questions and directions for future research. The final section discusses the importance of presidential leadership as understood here for the functioning of the American political system.

SUMMARY OF THE ARGUMENT AND FINDINGS

The argument of this book proceeded in several steps. First and maybe most importantly, we had to clarify the central concept employed in this book – *presidential leadership*. Despite the number of studies on presidential leadership, and leadership in general, there is no agreed-upon conceptual definition for what constitutes presidential leadership. The lack of such a definition, in part, reflects the complexity and multidimensional nature of leadership and presidential leadership. In developing a definition for this research, my aim was not to argue that my definition was superior and that others should follow my lead. Instead, my aim was to be as explicit as possible in my use of the concept of presidential leadership so that readers would understand how I use the concept and so that I could develop testable hypotheses.

At its most basic level (Goertz 2006), my definition of presidential leadership distinguishes between behavioral and perceptual dimensions of leadership. The *behavioral dimension* involves presidential actions to alter the behaviors and/or opinions of others. This has been, in one guise or another, the dominant perspective in studies of presidential leadership. The major message of empirical studies in this vein is the difficulty presidents have in changing the behaviors and opinions of others (Edwards 1989, 2003, 2009a).

In contrast, the *perceptual dimension* refers to followers' opinions about the leadership that the president provides. This is the focus of research reported in this book – in particular, voters' perceptions of presidential leadership. But what do voters mean when they say a president is a good leader? The argument here is that voters have two ideas in mind: the president is strong and the president is representative. But how do voters decide whether a president is strong and representative? As argued, there are many factors that influence voter perceptions, including information about the president's background and experiences, as well as voters' projection of leadership qualities onto the president based upon their political predispositions, such as partisanship. But in this study, I focused on how presidential behavior, especially with regard to interactions with Congress, influences voters' perceptions of presidential leadership.

Chapter Two asked whether voters desire strength and representation from presidents. A review of numerous surveys asking voters about desired characteristics in presidents found support for the idea that voters want presidents to be strong and representative. The second step in the argument looked at how presidential interactions with Congress affect the two key dimensions of leadership – strength and representation – that voters use to assess presidents. Chapter Three offered a theory that argued that party control and the degree of party polarization in Congress will affect both the president's success in the legislature and the policy positions that presidents take – that is, whether the executive will take moderate or extreme positions. Ideally, voters want a president to be successful and moderate on policy. Success with Congress reflects on presidential strength, while moderation improves policy representation.

Thus, we might think that presidents would try to do both at the same time with regard to issues before Congress. But the key factor that leads to success, presidential party control, also leads presidents to take more extreme positions. Presidents, it appears, can be successful and extreme or less successful and moderate; the worst of all possible worlds is for minority party presidents during periods of high polarization – they will be unsuccessful and extreme. Chapter Three also tested the theory and found support for it. But for voters to use presidential interactions with Congress for assessing the president's strength and representation, they must have some knowledge of the president's congressional success levels and policy positions. The news media are critical in this regard. There has to be sufficient news about these aspects of presidential–congressional relations for voters to use in assessing presidential performance. Chapter Three also presented evidence on news coverage and found a considerable volume of news on the legislative presidency. However, that analysis was limited because we lacked any data on actual voter knowledge of presidential success and policy positions with Congress or that voters actually pay much attention to and learn from news reporting on presidential relations with Congress. These are questions for future research.

Chapter Four looked at the factors that affect whether voters view a president as strong or weak, testing the key hypothesis that presidential success in Congress conditions those perceptions. Two types of data were employed in the analyses in the chapter. First was a newly constructed time series of all questions that asked voters to rate the strength of particular presidents, which allowed aggregate time-series analysis. The American National Election Studies has often been asking voters whether they thought the president was strong or weak in most of its biennial surveys since 1972, providing individual-level data for analysis. Both the aggregate- and individual-level data analyses found that success in Congress influenced whether voters rated a president as strong or not. As hypothesized, when presidents win with some frequency in the congressional arena, voters are likely to view them as strong. To a large degree, voters equate strength and success.

Chapter Five turned to the second dimension of presidential leadership, representation. Presidential representation is conceptualized in policy terms: How close are the policy positions of the president and voters? The closer the president's and voters' policy preferences, the better job a president is doing at policy representation. But do voters prefer that the president represent them individually or the nation as a whole? The president is the only leader elected from a national constituency, and, in many ways, the president acts as the nation's representative – for instance, when he is negotiating with foreign leaders and/or making other decisions concerning U.S. foreign policy. The president may also represent the nation, but more symbolically – for instance, when he gives a speech as a national ceremony, especially after a tragedy, such as President Obama's national address in Newtown, Connecticut, after the mass shootings at the Sandy Hook elementary school there.

Voters may also desire a president to combat narrow and partisan interests in policy debates. More than a century ago, Woodrow Wilson argued that parochial, narrow, sectional, and local forces had a stranglehold on Congress, resulting in policies that served those special interests at the expense of the national interest. To Wilson, only the president could redress the balance in policy making toward the nation's interest. Thus, there is a tension in the presidential representation dimension: whether voters more highly regard national (collective) or personal (dyadic) representation from the president.

Unlike strength perceptions, there are no good survey questions asking voters how good of a job they think the president is doing at representing them. Thus, the analysis in Chapter Five asked whether actual policy representation, measured in both collective and dyadic terms, affected job approval ratings. The analyses, using both aggregate- and individual-level job approval data, found that both collective and dyadic policy distance affected presidents' job approval ratings. Furthermore, when added into this analysis, strength perceptions also affected job approval ratings. The findings thus far reviewed unearthed support for some major ideas in this book – that voters assess actual presidential leadership along two dimensions, strength (success) and representation, and that presidential relations with Congress strongly affect voters' perceptions of presidential leadership. Contrary to the studies of voter expectations for the ideal president, when it comes to assessing leadership from presidents in office, voters appear to be holding presidents to reasonable and realistic standards.

Another theme advanced in this study is that voters' perceptions of presidential leadership have consequences throughout the political system. For instance, analysis found that success, strength, and policy representation affect voters' approval of the president, attitudes toward candidates for the presidency, and the vote decision in presidential elections. But, perhaps most surprising, when the presidential leadership variables were entered into the voting models, presidential approval no longer had such strong effects on voting behavior, either weakening considerably or failing to maintain its statistical significance. This finding is reminiscent of Lebo and O'Geen (2011), who found that when presidential success was added to their model of congressional election results, presidential approval also fell and became statistical insignificant.

The final empirical chapter, Chapter Seven, looked at the impact of presidential leadership beyond the presidency to its effects on political trust and evaluations of Congress and its members. As argued here, public perceptions of the president have widespread effects that reach far beyond just the president and the executive branch. All aspects of presidential leadership – success in Congress, perceptions of strength, and policy representation – appear to affect voters' trust in government. When voters feel good about the leadership of the incumbent president, they also tend to feel good about their government.

Almost the same thing can be said about Congress. The more positive voters' assessments of presidential leadership, the more highly they will regard Congress. There is logic to this connection between presidential leadership and approval of Congress as an institution, even when different parties control the executive and legislative branches. Success in Congress leads to positive assessments of presidential strength. Although success in Congress may be primarily a function of presidential resources, like party control, to voters it signifies that the two branches are working together to produce policy and that Congress is accepting presidential leadership in the production of policy. As to this last point, voters may be mistaken about the leadership efforts of presidents. Presidents can boost their success levels by taking positions on policies destined for passage because of their broad-based popularity in Congress. As Bond and Fleisher so cogently argued, there is a difference between success and influence (Bond and Fleisher 1990, p. 54). Presidents can be successful without being influential. Yet this distinction may not matter much to voters. Due to the centrality of the president to voters, when presidents take a stand and win, even if they merely jumped onto the congressional bandwagon, voters credit them with enactment of the policy. But there is a downside for presidents—when they take a stand and lose, voters may blame them.[1]

Finally, Chapter Seven also showed that voter approval of individual members rises when presidents are successful in Congress, are thought of as strong, and are representative. Again, this was an unexpected finding. Research on the popularity of members of Congress has found that voters invariably like their representative, even if they appear to invariably dislike the institution. After a spate of studies on the topic in the 1970s and 1980s, there has been little, if any, scholarly attention to the question of the sources of member approval among voters. The consistently high support that voters gave their representative in Congress left little to explain. And the consistently high level of voter approval of their own representative erects a considerable hurdle to finding presidential leadership effects. Yet, the analysis in Chapter Seven finds evidence of presidential leadership effects on public attitudes toward their own representative, which underscores the importance of presidential leadership perceptions across the political system.

LINGERING QUESTIONS AND DIRECTIONS FOR FUTURE RESEARCH

Despite the wealth of findings reported in this book, there are a number of unanswered questions. First, in several places in the book, assumptions were made that could stand supporting empirical evidence. This is especially the case in Chapter Three, concerning the legislative presidency in the news. The analysis used data from the Policy Agendas Project (PAP) to track the amount of news on the legislative presidency; however, these data were of limited value to this project. Ideally, we would have liked more detailed information about the stage of the legislative process covered in the news story and especially news on whether the president won or lost in Congress. The PAP only coded for whether the president and Congress were identified in a news story, using the index of *The New York Times* as the database.

Although the PAP provides some of the best data yet on news coverage, needs for the research presented in this book differed from the goals of the PAP. Future research may be able to extract information from news that hand-coding projects, like PAP, cannot easily do. In particular, hosting of media, like *The New York Times*, in machine readable form, plus "smart" content analysis programs may enable future scholars to retrieve the kind of data called for in this study, as well as other types, perhaps only limited by our imagination (e.g., Grimmer and Stewart 2013). With more refined data collection of news, we may also be able to address questions like these: How often do roll call outcomes where the president took a side get reported in the press?

---

[1] Recognizing the costs of position taking, Cohen (2012) argues that when submitting legislative proposals to Congress, presidents will limit how many such proposals they submit when the odds of enactment are poor.

Once reported, how much news coverage do they receive? Does the president receive credit for the victory or blame for the defeat? What factors account for the volume and attributes of such news?

A second limitation of data noted in Chapter Three on the legislative presidency also had to do with public opinion. Once we have the preceding types of news data, we can begin to address the question of whether this type of news coverage affects public opinion. For instance, does reporting on the success or defeat of the president affect job approval ratings? That we now have daily readings of the president's job approval ratings from several organizations (e.g., Gallup, Rasmussen) stretching back about a decade, allows us to investigate the short-term, as well as longer-term, impact of presidential relations with Congress on public opinion.

Among the messages of this book is that there is a lot more to public opinion regarding the president than job approval ratings. The attempt in Chapter Four to build a time-series indicator of voter assessment of presidential strength provides one example, as does the complete lack of measures of whether voters think the president is doing a good job at representing them and the nation. Collecting data on news coverage of the president in the legislative arena, while important, will only go a short way to understanding the effect of such news on public opinion other than job approval because of the lack of nonapproval data. We can begin to collect such data, but it will be a long time before there are enough administrations of various nonapproval job questions (outside of the ANES biennial studies) for analysis. In the shorter term, experiments may tell us how voters process news about presidents.

An experiment can be designed that alters the content of news (or merely information) on the president – for instance, giving the president credit (or blame) for a legislative victory or not. We can then see the reaction of voters to different types of news. There are number of issues with regard to survey experiments to determine the effect of certain types of stimuli when it comes to the presidency. Voters, for example, know a lot about presidents, and they often have well-established images of the current (and past) president in their minds. Survey experiments on the presidency will need to be realistic in design, and given how much the current state of affairs (history) affects voters opinions about presidents, we may have to replicate the same experiment several times under varying conditions to get a sense of the stability and magnitude of the survey-induced effects (Barabas and Jerit 2010; Gaines, Kuklinski, and Quirk 2007; Mutz 2011).

This study employed a conventional definition of success – how often the president wins or loses in Congress. Albeit an important form of presidential success, legislative victories and defeats do not exhaust the forms of presidential success nor the types of success that may affect public perceptions of presidential leadership. The advantages of using legislative success are many. It reflects on an important aspect of the job of modern presidents, and whether the president wins or loses on a roll call is easily understood and measured.

In addition, it is easily quantified and somewhat objective. We can analogize winning on a roll call to winning a baseball game (or most any other sport); thus, voters will also have an easy time understanding legislative success.

Although I have discussed and used roll calls as a clear and unproblematic measure of presidential success, not everyone will agree. As argued here, a minority president will have to compromise with the opposition party that controls Congress if he is to secure a legislative win, and even majority presidents have to compromise with Congress on policy. A president who compromises with Congress over the substance of legislation obviously does not receive as much policy benefit as one who receives all that he asks for. How much must a president compromise away from his most preferred policy outcome before we can no longer say that the president won what he was seeking? Is it enough that a president claims to be on the winning side of a roll call for us and voters to view the president as successful and strong, much like Senator George Aiken's (R-VT) recommendation during the Vietnam War that the United States should declare that it won the war and then leave (Eder 1966)?[2] Do voters view a president as successful if the president had to compromise?

Finally, presidents win and lose outside of the congressional arena. They deal with and negotiate with bureaucrats, journalists, interest group representatives, leaders of foreign nations, and even federal courts. The news media also reports on many of these interactions, often framing them into contests between the president and the adversary and discussing the incident in terms of whether the president won or lost. It is quite likely that these types of interactions may also affect voters' assessments of presidential success and strength, as well as the policy stances of presidents. Certainly, they are more difficult to identify and to measure as a success or defeat than a congressional roll call, but content analysis of media reporting on such events may be one way to do so. Extending from the congressional arena to the entirety of the president's public activities is necessary in order to gain a fuller understanding of how presidential actions affect public perceptions of presidential leadership.

THE PERENNIAL DILEMMA OF PRESIDENTIAL LEADERSHIP

Citizens in democracies are often disenchanted with their government. In the United States, there is the oft-noted decline in political trust in government, discussed in Chapter Seven. But disaffection with government is not isolated to the United States (Dalton 2005). For instance, using the combined European Values Survey and the World Values Survey, in 2008, only 37 percent

---

2 Peterson (1990) is the most extensive analysis that measures presidential success along a continuum from winning all that the president asked for, compromising a little and winning, compromising a lot and winning, and losing. His analysis suggests that presidents, indeed, compromise frequently with Congress and that minority presidents compromise more than majority ones.

of respondents said they had a great deal or some confidence in their government with 63 percent saying that they had little or no confidence in their government. Obviously, timing has something to do with the global level of confidence in government; the Great Recession began that year. But even in "gentler" times, these surveys report low levels of confidence in government around the world. In 1990, the distribution of confidence is similar, with 40 percent saying they have some or a great deal of confidence compared with 60 percent with little or no confidence. Many factors have been identified to explain the low level of trust in government, from corruption to increasing demands being made on government to political polarization, globalization, and economic and social change.[3]

Citizen expectations of government – and the inability of government to meet those expectations – may also account for this disenchantment. In other words, government performance and the gap between expectations and performance probably have much to do with citizen disaffection from government. In addition, chief executives often feel the brunt of citizen demands, being the most visible political leaders and the most responsible for the implementation of government policies.

Two connected sets of attitudes among voters, it is argued, lead to eventual disillusionment with the incumbent president: expectations for an ideal president and a personalized perspective of the office. As noted throughout this book, public expectations for presidents are high and contradictory (Cronin 1980; Cronin and Genovese 1998; Simon 2009). No individual president can live up to these expectations, known as the expectations gap thesis (Jenkins-Smith et al. 2005; Stimson 1976; Waterman et al. 1999). Yet, the public also believes that changing the incumbent in office with a new personality, better suited to the challenges of the presidency, is the solution to the problems of government, known as the personalized, heroic presidency perspective (Bailey 2002; Lowi 1985). To some degree, presidents may feed both the idealized and heroic and personalized perspectives of the presidency with their rhetoric about how they view and define leadership (Carpenter 2007).

In this book, I have argued that voters also have a more realistic, less idealistic way of evaluating presidential leadership: Voters want a president who is strong (i.e., successful, a winner) and who represents the nation and their individual policy preferences. From the analysis presented in this book, voters do a pretty good job of estimating these desired attributes of presidential leadership. When presidents are successful in Congress, voters perceive the president as strong. Voters can also accurately place the president in an ideological, left–right, policy space. The implications of positive assessments of presidential leadership are wide-ranging, too. Voters feel better about other branches of government, such as Congress, and government in general, when they perceive the president as being strong and representative.

---

3 For a good review, see Dalton (2005).

This seemingly provides a magic formula for good government, for restoring and maintaining public confidence and trust in government and the incumbents in office. A president should only take positions on policies that Congress will enact, and those positions should be close as possible to voters' preferences. A president, to be viewed as an effective leader, thus, does not have to be out in front of the public on issues, to be transformative, influential, persuasive, heroic, etc. Instead, he can be successful, and thus, be viewed as strong by following George Edwards' (2003, 2009a) prescription of being a facilitator, of exploiting the opportunities presented to him, with the caveat that he still cannot take policy positions very distant from those of voters.

This would appear to be a simple formula for leadership success. But the factors that lead to success with Congress also push the president away from the public's preferred policies. The most important factor with implications for success is party control. Presidents will win more often when their party controls Congress. But pressures from their party will also lead presidents to take relatively extreme policy positions, positions close to their party's preferences and distant from voters. When their party controls Congress, presidents become representatives of their party more than representatives of the nation, of voters. On the other hand, presidents are more likely to be faithful representatives of the nation when their party does not control Congress. That situation forces presidents to compromise in order to realize any policy victories. And while minority presidents can increase their victory rate with Congress by compromising with the opposition party, even when polarization between the parties is not too great, minority party presidents can rarely, if ever, approximate the victory level of a majority party president.

The best that presidents can hope for then is to be viewed as successful and strong but not representative or as a good representative but not necessarily strong. Changing the person in office will not resolve this leadership dilemma for presidents. It is baked into the structure of policy making as well as public definitions of effective leadership (Rockman 1984). Presidents – probably all chief executives – will perennially face this dilemma between being strong and representative at the same time. There is probably no solution to this dilemma. Thus, American voters will probably always be somewhat dissatisfied with their presidents.

Sources

Aberbach, Joel D., and Gillian Peele, eds. 2011. *Crisis of Conservatism?: The Republican Party, the Conservative Movement, and American Politics After Bush*. New York: Oxford University Press.

Abramowitz, Alan I. 2010. *The Disappearing Center: Engaged Citizens, Polarization, and American Democracy*. New Haven, CT: Yale University Press.

Achen, Christopher H. 1978. "Measuring Representation." *American Journal of Political Science* 22 (August): 475–510.

Ahlquist, John S., and Margaret Levi. 2011. "Leadership: What It Means, What It Does, and What We Want to Know About It." *Annual Review of Political Science* 14: 1–24.

Aldrich, John H. 1995. *Why Parties? The Origin and Transformation of Political Parties in America*. Chicago: University of Chicago Press.

Aldrich John H., and David W. Rohde. 2001. "The Logic of Conditional Party Government: Revisiting the Electoral Connection." In Lawrence C. Dodd and Bruce I. Oppenheimer, eds. *Congress Reconsidered*. Washington, DC: CQ Press, 7th ed., pp. 269–92.

Almond, Gabriel A. and Sidney Verba. 1963. *The Civic Culture: Political Attitudes and Democracy in Five Nations*. Princeton, NJ: Princeton University Press.

Althaus, Scott L. 2003. *Collective Preferences in Democratic Politics: Opinion Surveys and the Will of the People*. New York: Cambridge University Press.

Anderson, Sarah, and Philip Habel. 2009. "Revisiting Adjusted ADA Scores for the U.S. Congress, 1947–2007." *Political Analysis* 17 (1): 83–8.

Ansolabehere, Stephen, and Philip Edward Jones. 2011. "Dyadic Representation." In Eric Shickler and Francis E. Lee, eds. *Oxford Handbook of the American Congress*. New York: Oxford University Press, pp. 293–314.

Ansolabehere, Stephen, Jonathan Rodden, and James M. Snyder. 2006. "Purple America." *Journal of Economic Perspectives* 20 (Spring): 97–118.

Appelbaum, Binyamin. "Price of Gas Matters to Voters, but Doesn't Seem to Sway Votes." *The New York Times*, Saturday, March 17, 2012, p. A1, accessed at http://www.nytimes.com/2012/03/17/us/politics/gas-prices-matter-to-voters-but-they-matter-little-to-votes.html?_r=1&hp on March 17, 2012.

Avery, James M. 2006. "The Sources and Consequences of Political Mistrust among African Americans." *American Politics Research* 34 (September): 653–82.

Avery, James M. 2009. "Political Mistrust among African Americans and Support for the Political System." *Political Research Quarterly* 62 (March): 132–45.

Baer, Kenneth S. 2000. *Reinventing Democrats: The Politics of Liberalism from Reagan to Clinton*. Lawrence, KS: University Press of Kansas.

Bafumi, Joseph, and Michael C. Herron. 2010. "Leapfrog Representation and Extremism: A Study of American Voters and Their Members in Congress." *American Political Science Review* 104 (August): 519–42.

Bailey, Michael E. 2002. "The Heroic Presidency in the Era of Divided Government." *Perspectives on Political Science* 31 (Winter): 35–45.

Balestra, Pietro, and Jayalakshmi Varadharajan-Krishnakumar. 1987. "Full Information Estimations of a System of Simultaneous Equations with Error Component Structure." *Econometric Theory* 3 (April): 223–46.

Balutis, Alan P. 1977. "The Presidency and the Press: The Expanding Public Image." *Presidential Studies Quarterly* 7 (Fall): 244–51.

Bankert, Alexa, and Helmut Norpoth. 2013. "Guns 'N Jobs: The FDR Legacy." *Electoral Studies* 32 (September): 551–56.

Barabas, Jason, and Jennifer Jerit. 2010. "Are Survey Experiments Externally Valid?" *American Political Science Review* 104 (May): 226–42.

Barber, James David. 1972. *The Presidential Character: Predicting Performance in the White House.* Englewood Cliffs, NJ: Prentice-Hall.

Barker, David C., and Christopher Jan Carman. 2010. "Yes WE Can or Yes HE Can? Citizen Preferences Regarding Styles of Representation and Presidential Voting Behavior." *Presidential Studies Quarterly* 40 (September): 431–48.

Barker, David C., and Christopher Jan Carman. 2012. *Representing Red and Blue: How the Culture Wars Change the Way Citizens Speak and Politicians Listen.* New York: Oxford University Press.

Barrett, Andrew W., and Matthew Eshbaugh-Soha. 2007. "Presidential Success on the Substance of Legislation." *Political Research Quarterly* 60 (March): 100–12.

Bartels, Brandon L., Janet M. Box-Steffensmeier, Corwin D. Smidt, and Renée M. Smith. 2011. "The Dynamic Properties of Individual-level Party Identification in the United States." *Electoral Studies* 30 (March): 210–22.

Bass, Bernard M., and Ruth Bass, ed. 2008. *The Bass Handbook of Leadership: Theory, Research, and Management Applications,* 4th ed. New York: Free Press.

Baum, Matthew A. 2003. *Soft News Goes to War: Public Opinion and American Foreign Policy in the New Media Age.* Princeton, NJ: Princeton University Press.

Baum, Matthew A., and Samuel Kernell. 1999. "Has Cable Television Ended the Golden Age of Presidential Television?" *American Political Science Review* 93 (March): 99–114.

Baum, Matthew A., and Samuel Kernell. 2001. "Economic Class and Popular Support for Franklin Roosevelt in War and Peace." *Public Opinion Quarterly* 65 (June): 198–229.

Baum, Matthew A., and Samuel Kernell. 2007. "Has Cable Television Ended the Golden Age of Presidential Television: From 1969 to 2006." *The Principles and Practice of American Politics,* 3rd ed. Kernell Samuel and Smith Steven S., eds. Washington, DC: CQ Press, pp. 311–15.

Beckmann, Matthew N. 2010. *Pushing the Agenda: Presidential Leadership in U.S. Lawmaking, 1953–2004.* New York: Cambridge University Press.

Berry, William, Matt Golder, and Daniel Milton. 2012. "Improving Tests of Theories Positing Interaction." *Journal of Politics* 74 (July): 653–71.

Beyle, Thad, Richard G. Niemi, and Lee Sigelman. 2002. "Gubernatorial, Senatorial, and State-level Presidential Job Approval: The US Officials Job Approval Ratings (JAR) Collection." *State Politics & Policy Quarterly* 2 (September): 215–29.

Bond, Jon R., and Richard Fleisher. 1980. "The Limits of Presidential Popularity as a Source of Influence in the U.S. House." *Legislative Studies Quarterly* 5 (February): 69–78.

Bond, Jon R., and Richard Fleisher. 1984. "Presidential Popularity and Congressional Voting: A Reexamination of Public Opinion as a Source of Influence in Congress." *Western Political Quarterly* 37 (June): 291–306.

Bond, Jon R., and Richard Fleisher. 1990. *The President in the Legislative Arena.* Chicago: University of Chicago Press.

Bond, Jon R., and Richard Fleisher. 2001. "The Polls: Partisanship and Presidential Performance Evaluations." *Presidential Studies Quarterly* 31 (September): 529–40.

Bond, Jon R., Richard Fleisher, and Michael Northrup. 1988. "Public Opinion and Presidential Support." *Annals of the American Academy of Political and Social Science* 499 (September):47–63.

Bond, Jon R., Richard Fleisher, and B. Dan Wood. 2003. "The Marginal and Time Varying Effects of Presidential Approval on Success in Congress." *Journal of Politics* 65 (February): 92–110.

Borrelli, Stephen A., and Grace L. Simmons. 1993. "Congressional Responsiveness to Presidential Popularity: The Electoral Context." *Political Behavior* 15 (June): 93–112.

Brace, Paul, and Barbara Hinckley. 1992. *Follow the Leader: Opinion Polls and Modern Presidents.* New York: Basic Books.

Brambor, Thomas, William Roberts Clark, and Matt Golder. 2006. "Understanding Interaction Models: Improving Empirical Analyses." *Political Analysis* 14 (Winter): 63–82.

Brody, Richard. 1991. *Assessing the President: The Media, Elite Opinion, and Public Support.* Stanford, CA: Stanford University Press.

Brown, Adam R. 2010. "Are Governors Responsible for the State Economy? Partisanship, Blame, and Divided Federalism." *Journal of Politics* 72 (July): 605–15.

Calder, James D. 1982. "Presidents and Crime Control: Kennedy, Johnson and Nixon and the Influences of Ideology." *Presidential Studies Quarterly* 12 (Fall): 574–89.

Callaghan, Karen J., and Simo Virtanen. 1993. "Revised Models of the "Rally Phenomenon": The Case of the Carter Presidency." *Journal of Politics* 55 (August): 756–64.

Campbell, Colin, and Jamie Gillies. 2009. "Personalization of Leadership and the US Presidency." Paper prepared for the American Political Science Association Annual Conference, September 2–5, 2009, Toronto, Ontario.

Campbell, James E., Bryan J. Dettrey, and Hongxing Yin. 2010. "The Theory of Conditional Retrospective Voting: Does the Presidential Record Matter Less in Open-Seat Elections?" *Journal of Politics* 72 (October): 1083–1095.

Canes-Wrone, Brandice. 2006. *Who Leads Whom? Presidents, Policy, and the Public.* Chicago: University of Chicago Press.

Canes-Wrone, Brandice, David W. Brady, and John F. Cogan. 2002. "Out of Step, Out of Office: Electoral Accountability and House Members' Voting." *American Political Science Review* 96 (March): 127–40.

Canes-Wrone, Brandice, and Scott De Marchi. 2002. "Presidential Approval and Legislative Success." *Journal of Politics* 64 (May): 491–509.

Canes-Wrone, Brandice, and Kenneth W. Schotts. 2004. "The Conditional Nature of Presidential Responsiveness to Public Opinion." *American Journal of Political Science* 48 (October): 690–706.

Caplan, Bryan. 2007. *The Myth of the Rational Voter: Why Democracies Choose Bad Policies.* Princeton, NJ: Princeton University Press.

Carman, Christopher. 2007. "Assessing Preferences for Political Representation in the U.S.," *Journal of Elections, Public Opinion and Parties* 17 (No. 1): 1–19.

Carman, Christopher, and David Barker. 2009. "Political Geography, Church Attendance and Mass Preferences regarding Democratic Representation," Journal of Elections, Public Opinion and Parties, 19 (No. 1): 125–145.

Carmines, Edward G., and James Woods. 2002. "The Role of Party Activists in the Evolution of the Abortion Issue." *Political Behavior* 24 (December): 361–77.

Carpenter, Dick M. 2007. "Presidents of the United States on Leadership." *Leadership* 3 (August): 251–80.

Carson, Jamie L., Gregory Koger, Matthew J. Lebo, and Everett Young. 2010. "The Electoral Costs of Party Loyalty in Congress." *American Journal of Political Science* 54 (July): 598–616.

Cavari, Amnon. 2013. "The Short-Term Effect of Going Public." *Political Research Quarterly.* 66 (June): 336–51.

Chanley, Virginia A., Thomas J. Rudolph, Wendy M. Rahn. 2000. "The Origins and Consequences of Public Trust in Government: A Time Series Analysis." *Public Opinion Quarterly* 64 (November): 239–56.

Chong, Dennis, and James N. Druckman. 2013. "Public-Elite Interactions: Puzzles in Search of Researchers." In Shapiro Robert Y. and Jacobs Lawrence R., eds. *The Oxford Handbook of American Public Opinion and the Media.* New York: Oxford University Press, pp. 170–88.

Citrin, Jack. 1974. "Comment: The Political Relevance of Trust in Government." *American Political Science Review* 68 (September): 973–88.

Citrin, Jack, and Donald Philip Green. 1986. "Presidential Leadership and the Resurgence of Trust in Government." *British Journal of Political Science* 16 (October): 431–53.

Citrin, Jack, and Smantha Luks. 2001. "Political Trust Revisited: Déjà Vu All Over Again?" in John R. Hibbing, Elizabeth Theiss-Morse, eds. *What Is It about Government That Americans Dislike?* New York: Cambridge University Press, pp. 9–27.

Clarke, Harold D., Marianne C. Stewart, Mike Ault, and Euel Elliott. 2005. "Men, Women and the Dynamics of Presidential Approval." *British Journal of Political Science* 35 (January): 31–51.

Cohen, Jeffrey E. 1997. *Presidential Responsiveness and Public Policy-Making: The Public and the Policies That Presidents Choose.* Ann Arbor, MI: University of Michigan Press.

Cohen, Jeffrey E. 1999a. "The Polls: Favorability Ratings of Presidents." *Presidential Studies Quarterly* 29 (September): 690–96.

Cohen, Jeffrey E. 1999b. "The Polls: The Dynamics of Presidential Favorability, 1991–1998." *Presidential Studies Quarterly* 29 (December): 896–902.

Cohen, Jeffrey E. 2000. "The Polls: The Components of Presidential Favorability." *Presidential Studies Quarterly* 30 (March): 169–78.

Cohen, Jeffrey E. 2002a. "The Polls: Policy-Specific Presidential Approval, Part 1." Presidential Studies Quarterly 32 (September): 600–9.

Cohen, Jeffrey E. 2002b. "The Polls: Policy-Specific Presidential Approval, Part 2." *Presidential Studies Quarterly* 32 (December): 779–88.

Cohen, Jeffrey E. 2008. *The Presidency in an Era of 24 Hours News.* Princeton, NJ: Princeton University Press.

Cohen, Jeffrey E. 2009. "The Presidency and the Mass Media." In George C. Edwards III and William G. Howell, eds. *The Oxford Handbook of the American Presidency.* New York: Oxford University Press, pp. 254–85.

Cohen, Jeffrey E. 2010a. *Going Local: Presidential Leadership in the Post-Broadcast Age.* New York: Cambridge University Press.

Cohen, Jeffrey E. 2010b. "Public Demand for Representation from American Presidents." Paper prepared for delivery at Conference on Political Representation, Political Science Department, Texas A&M University, College Station, TX, November 12–13, 2010.

Cohen, Jeffrey E. 2011a. "Presidents, Polarization, and Divided Government." *Presidential Studies Quarterly* 41 (September): 504–20.

Cohen, Jeffrey E. 2011b. "Whose Approval Matters? Reelection, Constituency Approval, and Senate Support for President George W. Bush." *Congress & the Presidency* 38 (September–December): 253–70.

Cohen, Jeffrey E. 2012. *The President's Legislative Policy Agenda, 1789–2002*. New York: Cambridge University Press.

Cohen, Jeffrey E. 2013. "Everyone Loves a Winner: On the Mutual Causality of Presidential Approval and Success in Congress." *Congress & the Presidency* 40 (September): 285–307.

Cohen, Jeffrey E., Jon R. Bond, and Richard Fleisher. 2013. "Placing Presidential-Congressional Relations in Context: A Comparison of Barack Obama and His Predecessors." *Polity* 54 (January): 105–26.

Cohen, Jeffrey E., Jon R. Bond, Richard Fleisher, and John A. Hamman. 2000. "State-Level Presidential Approval and Senatorial Support." *Legislative Studies Quarterly* 25(November): 577–90.

Cohen, Jeffrey E., and John A. Hamman. 2003. "The Polls: Can Presidential Rhetoric Affect the Public's Economic Perceptions." *Presidential Studies Quarterly* 33 (June): 408–22.

Cohen, Jeffrey E., and John A. Hamman. 2005. "Presidential Ideology and the Public Mood." In Diane Heith and Lori Cox Han, eds. *The Public Domain: Presidents and the Challenge of Public Leadership*. Albany, NY: SUNY Press, pp. 141–62.

Cohen, Marty, David Karol, Hans Noel, and John Zaller. 2008. *The Party Decides: Presidential Nominations before and after Reform*. Chicago: University of Chicago Press.

Collier, Kenneth. 1994. "Eisenhower and Congress: The Autopilot Presidency". *Presidential Studies Quarterly* 24 (Spring): 309–25.

Collier, Kenneth, and Terry Sullivan. 1995. "New Evidence Undercutting the Linkage of Approval with Presidential Support and Influence." *Journal of Politics* 57 (February): 197–209.

Comstock, George, and Erica Scharrer. 2005. *The Psychology of Media and Politics*. Burlington, MA: Elsevier.

Conley, Richard S. 2002. *The Presidency, Congress, and Divided Government: A Postwar Assessment*. College Station, TX: Texas A&M University Press.

Conover, Pamela Johnston, and Lee Sigelman. 1982. "Presidential Influence and Public Opinion: The Case of the Iran Hostage Crisis." *Social Science Quarterly* 63 (June): 249–64.

Cook, Timothy. 1979. "Legislature vs. Legislator: A Note on the Paradox of Congressional Support." *Legislative Studies Quarterly* 4 (February): 43–52.

Cook, Timothy E. 1986. "House Members as Newsmakers: The Effects of Televising Congress." *Legislative Studies Quarterly* 11 (May): 203–26.

Cook, Timothy E. 1989. *Making Laws and Making News: Media Strategies in the U.S. House of Representatives*. Washington, DC: Brookings Institution.

Cook, Timothy E. and Paul Gronke. 2005. "The Skeptical American: Revisiting the Meanings of Trust in Government and Confidence in Institutions." *Journal of Politics* 67 (August): 784–803.

Cornwell, Elmer E., Jr. 1959. "Presidential News: The Expanding Public Image." *Journalism Quarterly* 36 (Summer): 275–83.

Cover, Albert D. 1977. "One Good Term Deserves Another: The Advantage of Incumbency in Congressional Elections." *American Journal of Political Science* 3 (August): 523–41.

Craig, Stephen C. 1993. *The Malevolent Leaders: Popular Discontent in America*. Boulder, CO: Westview.

Cronin, Thomas E. 1980. *The State of the Presidency*. 2nd ed. Boston: Little Brown.

Cronin, Thomas E. and Michael Genovese. 1998. *Paradoxes of the American Presidency*. New York: Oxford University Press.

Dalton, Russell J. 2005. "The Social Transformation of Trust in Government." *International Review of Sociology* 15 (March): 133–54.

Davidson, Roger H., and Glenn R. Parker. 1972. "Positive Support for Political Institutions: The Case of Congress." *Western Political Quarterly* 25 (December): 600–12.

Delli Carpini, Michael X., and Scott Keeter. 1996. *What Americans Know about Politics and Why It Matters*. New Haven, CT: Yale University Press.

Dionne, E. J., Jr. 1991. *Why Americans Hate Politics*. New York: Simon & Schuster.

Donley, Richard E., and David G. Winter. 1970. "Measuring the Motives of Public Officials at a Distance: An Exploratory Study of American Presidents." *Behavioral Science* 15 (May): 227–36.

Dowd, Maureen. 2013. "No Bully in the Pulpit." *The New York Times, Sunday Review*, April 20, 2013, accessed online at http://www.nytimes.com/2013/04/21/opinion/sunday/dowd-president-obama-is-no-bully-in-the-pulpit.html?_r=0.

Druckman, James N., and Justin W. Holmes. 2004. "Does Presidential Rhetoric Matter? Priming and Presidential Approval." *Presidential Studies Quarterly* 34 (December): 755–78.

Druckman, James N., and Lawrence R. Jacobs. 2009. "Presidential Responsiveness to Public Opinion." In George C. Edwards III and William G. Howell, eds. *The Oxford Handbook of the American Presidency*. New York: Oxford University Press, pp. 160–81.

Durr, Robert H., John B. Gilmour, and Christina Wolbrecht. 1997. "Explaining Congressional Approval." *American Journal of Political Science* 41 (January): 175–207.

Easton David. 1965. *A Systems Analysis of Political Life*. New York: Wiley.

Edelman, Murray J. 1964. *The Symbolic Uses of Politics*. Champaign, IL: University of Illinois Press.

Edelman, Murray J. 1974. "The Politics of Persuasion." In James David Barber, ed. *Choosing the President*. Englewood Cliffs, N.J: Prentice-Hall, pp. 149–73.

Eder, Richard. 1966. "Aiken Suggests U.S. Say It Has Won the War." *The New York Times*. October 20, 1966, pp. 1, 16.

Edwards, George C. III. 1976. "Presidential Influence in the House: Presidential Prestige as a Source of Presidential Power." *American Political Science Review* 70 (March): 101–13.

Edwards, George C. III. 1980. *Presidential Influence in Congress*. San Francisco: W. H. Freeman.

Edwards, George C. III. 1983. *The Public Presidency: The Pursuit of Popular Support.* New York: St. Martin's.

Edwards, George C. III. 1985. "Measuring Presidential Success in Congress: Alternative Approaches." *Journal of Politics* 47 (May): 667–85.

Edwards, George C. III. 1989. *At the Margins: Presidential Leadership of Congress.* New Haven, CT: Yale University Press.

Edwards, George C. III. 1997. *"Aligning Tests with Theory: Presidential Approval as a Source of Influence in Congress."* *Congress & the Presidency* 24 (Autumn): 113–30.

Edwards, George C. III. 2003. *On Deaf Ears: The Limits of the Bully Pulpit.* New Haven, CT: Yale University Press.

Edwards, George C. III. 2009a. *The Strategic President: Persuasion and Opportunity in Presidential Leadership.* Princeton, NJ: Princeton University Press.

Edwards, George C. III. 2009b. "Presidential Approval as a Source of Influence in Congress." In George C. Edwards III and William G. Howell, eds. *The Oxford Handbook of the American Presidency.* New York: Oxford University Press, pp. 339–61.

Edwards, George C. III. 2012. *Overreach: Leadership in the Obama Presidency.* Princeton, NJ: Princeton University Press.

Ellis, Christopher. 2012. "Public Ideology and Political Dynamics in the United States." *American Politics Research* 40 (March): 327–54.

Ellis, Christopher, and James A. Stimson. 2012. *Ideology in American.* New York: Cambridge University Press.

Erikson, Robert S. 2004. "Macro vs. Micro-Level Perspectives on Economic Voting: Is the Micro-Level Evidence Endogenously Induced?" Prepared for the 2004 Political Methodology Meetings, July 29–31, 2004. Stanford University.

Erikson, Robert S., Michael MacKuen, and James A. Stimson. 2002. *The Macro Polity.* New York: Cambridge University Press.

Eshbaugh-Soha, Matthew, and Brandon Rottinghaus. 2013. "Presidential Position Taking and the Puzzle of Representation." *Presidential Studies Quarterly* 43 (March): 1–15.

Evans, Rowland, and Robert D. Novak. 1972. *Nixon in the White House: The Frustration of Power.* New York: Vintage Books.

Farnsworth, Stephen J., and S. Robert Lichter. 2006. *The Mediated Presidency: Television News and Presidential Government.* Lanham, MD: Rowman and Littlefield.

Fiorina, Morris P. 1992. *Divided Government.* New York: MacMillan.

Fiorina Morris P., with Samuel J. Abrams and Jeremy C. Pope. 2005. *Culture War? The Myth of a Polarized America.* New York: Pearson Longman.

Fleisher, Richard, Jon R. Bond, and B. Dan Wood. 2008. "Which Presidents Are Uncommonly Successful in Congress?" In Bert A. Rockman and Richard W. Waterman, eds. *Presidential Leadership: The Vortex of Power.* New York: Oxford University Press, pp. 191–214.

Fox, Gerald T. 2012. "Macroeconomic Time Consistency and Wartime Presidential Approval." *Journal of Macroeconomics* 34 (September): 891–902.

Free, Lloyd A., and Hadley Cantril. 1967. *The Political Beliefs of Americans: A Study of Public Opinion.* New Brunswick, NJ: Rutgers University Press.

Friedrich, Robert J. 1982. "In Defense of Multiplicative Terms in Multiple Regression Equations." *American Journal of Political Science* 26 (November): 797–833.

Gaines, Brian J., James H. Kuklinski, and Paul J. Quirk. 2007. "The Logic of the Survey Experiment Reexamined." *Political Analysis* 15 (No. 1): 1–15.

Geer, John G. 2006. *In Defense of Negativity: Attack Ads in Presidential Campaigns.* Chicago: University of Chicago Press.

Gerring, John. 1998. *Party Ideologies in America: 1828–1996.* Cambridge: Cambridge University Press.

Gilens, Martin. 1988. "Gender and Support for Reagan: A Comprehensive Model of Presidential Approval." *American Journal of Political Science* 32 (February): 19–49.

Gleiber, Dennis W., Steven A. Shull, and Colleen A. Waligora. 1998. "Measuring the President's Professional Reputation." *American Politics Research* 26 (July): 366–85.

Goertz, Gary. 2006. *Social Science Concepts: A User's Guide.* Princeton, NJ: Princeton University Press.

Goidel, Robert K., Todd G. Shields, and Mark Peffley. 1997. "Priming Theory and RAS Models: Toward an Integrated Perspective on Media Influence." *American Politics Quarterly* 25 (July): 287–318.

Goldenberg, J. Eddie and Michael W. Traugott. 1984. *Campaigning for Congress.* Washington, DC: Congressional Quarterly Press.

Gomez, Brad T., and J. Matthew Wilson. 2001. "Political Sophistication and Economic Voting in the American Electorate: A Theory of Heterogeneous Attribution." *American Journal of Political Science* 45 (October): 899–914.

Goren, Paul. 2002. "Character Weakness, Partisan Bias, and Presidential Evaluation." *American Journal of Political Science* 46 (July): 627–41.

Goren, Paul. 2007. "Character Weakness, Partisan Bias, and Presidential Evaluation: Modifications and Extensions." *Political Behavior* 29 (September): 305–25.

Grant, Tobin J., and Thomas J. Rudolph. 2004. "The Job of Representation in Congress: Public Expectations and Representative Approval." *Legislative Studies Quarterly* 24 (August): 431–45.

Green, Donald P., Alan S. Gerber, and Suzanna L. de Boef. 1999. "Tracking Opinion Over Time: A Method for Reducing Sampling Error." *Public Opinion Quarterly* 63 (Summer): 178–92.

Greene, Steven. 2001. "The Role of Character Assessments in Presidential Approval." *American Politics Research* 29 (March): 196–210.

Greenstein, Fred I. 1974. "What the President Means to Americans: Presidential 'Choice' Between Elections." In James David Barber, ed. *Choosing the President.* Englewood Cliffs, NJ: Prentice-Hall.

Greenstein, Fred I. 2012. *The Presidential Difference: Leadership Style from FDR to Barack Obama.* 3rd ed. Princeton, NJ: Princeton University Press.

Grimmer, Justin, and Brandon M. Stewart. 2013. "Text as Data: The Promise and Pitfalls of Automatic Content Analysis Methods for Political Texts." *Political Analysis* 3 (Summer): 267–297.

Grint, Keith. 2010. *Leadership: A Very Short Introduction.* New York: Oxford University Press.

Groeling, Tim. 2010. *When Politicians Attack: Party Cohesion in the Media.* New York: Cambridge University Press.

Gronke, Paul. 1999. "Policies, Prototypes, and Presidential Approval." Paper presented at the American Political Science Association Meeting.

Gronke, Paul, and John Brehm. 2002. "History, Heterogeneity, and Presidential Approval: A Modified ARCH Approach." *Electoral Studies* 21 (September): 425–52.

Gronke, Paul, and Brian Newman. 2003. "FDR to Clinton, Mueller to ? A Field Essay on Presidential Approval." *Political Research Quarterly* 56 (December) 501–12.

Gronke, Paul, and Brian Newman. 2009. "Public Evaluations of Presidents." In George C. Edwards III and William G. Howell, eds. *The Oxford Handbook of the American Presidency*. New York: Oxford University Press, pp. 232–53.

Groseclose, Tim, Steven D. Levitt, and James M. Snyder. 1999. "Comparing Interest Group Scores across Time and Chambers: Adjusted ADA Scores for the U.S. Congress." *American Political Science Review* 93 (March): 33–50.

Groseclose, Tim, and Nolan McCarty. 2001. "The Politics of Blame: Bargaining before an Audience." *American Journal of Political Science* 45 (January): 100–19.

Grossman, Michael Baruch, and Martha Joynt Kumar. 1981. *Portraying the President: The White House and the News Media*. Baltimore: Johns Hopkins University Press.

Grunwald, Michael. 2012. *The New New Deal: The Hidden Story of Change in the Obama Era*. New York: Simon and Schuster.

Hantz, Charles A. 1996. "Ideology, Pragmatism, and Ronald Reagan's World View: Full of Sound and Fury, Signifying...?" *Presidential Studies Quarterly* 26 (Fall): 942–49.

Harmel, Robert M., ed. 1984. *Presidents and Their Parties: Leadership or Neglect?* New York: Praeger.

Hayes, Danny. 2005. "Candidate Qualities through a Partisan Lens: A Theory of Trait Ownership." *American Journal of Political Science* 49 (October): 908–23.

Hayes, Danny. 2009. "Has Television Personalized Voting Behavior?" *Political Behavior* 31 (June): 231–60.

Hetherington, Marc J. 2001. "Resurgent Mass Partisanship: The Role of Elite Polarization." *American Political Science Review* 95 (September): 619–31.

Hetherington, Marc J. 2004. *Why Trust Matters: Declining Political Trust and the Demise of American Liberalism*. Princeton, NJ: Princeton University Press.

Hetherington, Marc J., and Thomas J. Rudolph. 2008. "Priming, Performance, and the Dynamics of Political Trust." *Journal of Politics* 70 (April): 498–512.

Hibbing, John R., and Elizabeth Theiss-Morse. 1995. *Congress as Public Enemy: Public Attitudes toward Political Institutions*. New York: Cambridge University Press.

Hibbing, John R., and James T. Smith. 2004. "Is it the Middle that is Frustrated? Americans' Ideological Positions and Governmental Trust." *American Politics Research* 32 (November): 652–78.

Hicks, Alexander. 1984. "Elections, Keynes, Bureaucracy, and Class: Explaining United States Budget Deficits, 1961–1978." *American Sociological Review* 49 (April): 165–82.

Highton, Benjamin. 2009. "Revisiting the Relationship between Educational Attainment and Political Sophistication." *Journal of Politics* 71 (October): 1564–76.

Hill, Kim Quaile. 1998. "The Policy Agendas of the President and the Mass Public: A Research Validation and Extension." *American Journal of Political Science* 42 (October): 1328–34.

Holbrook, Thomas M. 2010. "Forecasting US Presidential Elections." In Jan E. Leighley, ed. *The Oxford Handbook of American Elections and Political Behavior*. New York: Oxford University Press, pp. 346–71.

Holbrook, Thomas M., and Jay A. DeSart. 1999. "Using State Polls to Forecast Presidential Election Outcomes in the American States." *International Journal of Forecasting* 15 (April): 137–42.

Howell, William G. 2003. *Power without Persuasion: The Politics of Direct Presidential Action*. Princeton, NJ: Princeton University Press.

Hurley, Patricia A. 1982. "Collective Representation Reappraised." *Legislative Studies Quarterly* 7 (February): 119–36.

Jacobs, Lawrence R., and Robert Y. Shapiro. 2000. *Politicians Don't Pander: Political Manipulation and the Loss of Democratic Responsiveness*. Chicago: University of Chicago Press.

Jacobson, Gary C. 2000. "Party Polarization in National Politics: The Electoral Connection." In Jon R. Bond and Richard Fleisher, eds. *Polarized Politics: Congress and the President in a Partisan Era*. Washington, DC: CQ Press, pp. 9–30.

Jacobson, Gary C. 2012. *The Politics of Congressional Elections*. 8th ed. New York: Pearson.

Jacoby, William G. 2002. "Liberal-Conservative Thinking in the American Electorate." *Research in Micropolitics: Political Decision Making, Participation, and Deliberation* 6 (No. 1): 97–147.

James, Scott C. 2006. *Presidents, Parties, and the State: A Party System Perspective on Democratic Regulatory Choice, 1884–1936*. New York: Cambridge University Press.

Jenkins-Smith, Hank C., Carol L. Silva, and Richard W. Waterman. 2005. "Micro- and Macrolevel Models of the Presidential Expectations Gap." *Journal of Politics* 67 (August) 690–715.

Jennings, M. Kent. 1992. "Ideological Thinking Among Mass Publics and Political Elites." *Public Opinion Quarterly* 56 (Winter): 419–41.

Jerit, Jennifer, Jason Barabas, and Toby Bolsen. 2006. "Citizens, Knowledge, and the Information Environment." *American Journal of Political Science* 50 (April): 266–82.

Jones, Bryan D., and Frank R. Baumgartner. 2004. "Representation and Agenda Setting." *Policy Studies Journal* 32 (February): 1–24.

Jones, Charles O. 2005. *The Presidency in a Separated System*. 2nd ed. Washington, DC: Brookings Institution Press.

Jones, David R., and Monika L. McDermott. 2009. *Americans, Congress, and Democratic Representation: Public Evaluations of Congress and Electoral Consequences*. Ann Arbor, MI: University of Michigan Press.

Karol, David. 2009. *Party Position Change in American Politics: Coalition Management*. New York: Cambridge University Press.

Keele, Luke. 2005. "The Authorities Really Do Matter: Party Control and Trust in Government." *Journal of Politics* 67 (August): 873–86.

Keele, Luke. 2007. "Social Capital and the Dynamics of Trust in Government." *American Journal of Political Science* 51 (April): 241–54.

Kernell, Samuel. 2007. *Going Public: New Strategies of Presidential Leadership*. 3rd ed. Washington, DC: CQ Press.

Kernell, Samuel, and Gary C. Jacobson. 1987. "Congress and the Presidency as News in the Nineteenth Century." *Journal of Politics* 49 (November): 1016–35.

Kernell, Samuel and Laurie L. Rice. 2011. "Cable and the Partisan Polarization of the President's Audience." *Presidential Studies Quarterly* 41 (December): 693–711.

Kimball, David C., and Samuel C. Patterson. 1997. "Living Up to Expectations: Public Attitudes toward Congress." *Journal of Politics* 59 (August): 701–28.

Kinder, Donald R., Mark D. Peters, Robert P. Abelson and Susan T. Fiske. 1980. "Presidential Prototypes." *Political Behavior* 2 (No. 4): 315–37.

King, Anthony, ed. 2002. *Leaders' Personalities and the Outcomes of Democratic Elections*. New York: Oxford University Press.

King, David C. 1997. "The Polarization of American Parties and Mistrust of Government." In Joseph S. Nye, Philip D. Zelikow, and David C. King, eds. *Why People Don't Trust Government*. Cambridge, MA: Harvard University Press, pp. 155–78.

King, David C. 2003. "Congress, Polarization, and Fidelity to the Median Voter." Working Paper, Kennedy John F. School of Government, Harvard University.

King, Gary. 1986. "The Significance of Roll Calls in Voting Bodies: A Model and Statistical Estimation." *Social Science Research* 15 (June): 135–52.

King, Gary, James Honaker, Anne Joseph, and Kenneth Scheve. 2001. "Analyzing Incomplete Political Science Data: An Alternative Algorithm for Multiple Imputation." *American Political Science Review* 95 (March): 49–70.

Kiousis, Spiro. 2003. "Job Approval and Favorability: The Impact of Media Attention to the Monica Lewinsky Scandal on Public Opinion of President Bill Clinton." *Mass Communication and Society* 6 (No. 4): 435–41.

Klarner, Carl. 2010. "Forecasting the 2010 State Legislative Elections." *PS: Political Science & Politics* 43 (October): 643–48.

Knight, Kathleen. 2006. "Transformations of the Concept of Ideology in the Twentieth Century." *American Political Science Review* 100 (November): 619–26.

Kramer, Gerald H. 1983. "The Ecological Fallacy Revisited: Aggregate- versus Individual-level Findings on Economics and Elections, and Sociotropic Voting." *American Political Science Review* 77 (March): 92–111.

Krause, George A., and Anne M. Joseph O'Connell. 2011. "Cycles of Increasing Effectiveness in Presidential Appointments: Experiential Learning and the Selection of Bureaucratic Leaders in US Federal Government Agencies." Paper prepared for delivery at the 2011 annual meeting of the American Political Science Association, Seattle, Washington, August 31–September 3, 2011.

Krehbiel, Keith. 1998. *Pivotal Politics: A Theory of US Lawmaking*. Chicago: University of Chicago Press.

Kriner, Douglas, and Eric Schickler. 2014. "Investigating the President: Committee Probes and Presidential Approval, 1953–2006." *Journal of Politics* 76 (April): 521–34.

Krosnick, Jon A., and Laura A. Brannon. 1993a. "The Impact of the Gulf War on the Ingredients of Presidential Evaluations: Multidimensional Effects of Political Involvement." *American Political Science Review* 87 (December): 963–75.

Krosnick, Jon A., and Laura A. Brannon. 1993b. "The Media and the Foundations of Presidential Support: George Bush and the Persian Gulf Conflict." *Journal of Social Issues* 49 (Winter): 167–82.

Krosnick, Jon A., and Donald R. Kinder. 1990. "Altering the Foundations of Support for the President through Priming." *American Political Science Review* 84 (June): 497–512.

Kuklinski, James H., and Paul J. Quirk. 2000. "Reconsidering the Rational Public: Cognition, Heuristics, and Mass Opinion." In Arthur Lupia, Mathew D. McCubbins, and Samuel L. Popkin, eds. *Elements of Reason: Cognition, Choice, and the Bounds of Rationality*. New York: Cambridge University Press, pp. 153–82.

Kuklinski, James H., and Lee Sigelman. 1992. "When Objectivity is Not Objective: Network Television News Coverage of U.S. Senators and the "Paradox of Objectivity." *Journal of Politics* 54 (August): 810–33.

Ladd, Jonathan M. 2007. "Predispositions and Public Support for the President During the War on Terrorism." *Public Opinion Quarterly* 71 (Winter): 511–38.

Ladd, Jonathan M. 2011. *Why Americans Hate the Media and How It Matters.* Princeton, NJ: Princeton University Press.

Langston, Thomas S. 1992. *Ideologues and Presidents: From the New Deal to the Reagan Revolution.* Baltimore, MD: Johns Hopkins University Press.

Langston, Thomas S. 2012. "Ideology and Ideologues in the Modern Presidency." *Presidential Studies Quarterly* 42 (December): 730–53.

Larson, Stephanie Greco. 1988. "The President and Congress in the Media." *Annals of the American Academy of Political and Social Science* 499 (September): 64–74.

Lau, Richard R., David J. Anderson, and David P. Redlawsk. 2008. "An Exploration of Correct Voting in Recent U.S. Presidential Elections." *American Journal of Political Science* 52 (April): 395–411.

Lau, Richard R., and David P. Redlawsk. 2001. "Advantages and Disadvantages of Cognitive Heuristics in Political Decision Making." *American Journal of Political Science* 45 (October): 951–71.

Layman, Geoffrey C., Thomas M. Carsey, and Juliana Menasce Horowitz. 2006. "Party Polarization in American Politics: Characteristics, Causes, and Consequences." *Annual Review of Political Science* 9 (No. 1): 83–110.

Layman, Geoffrey C., Thomas M. Carsey, John C. Green, Richard Herrera, and Rosalyn Cooperman. 2010. "Activists and Conflict Extension in American Party Politics." *American Political Science Review* 104 (May): 324–46.

Lebo, Matthew J. 2008. "Divided Government, United Approval: The Dynamics of Congressional and Presidential Approval." *Congress & the Presidency* 35 (Autumn): 1–16.

Lebo, Matthew J., and Daniel Cassino. 2007. "The Aggregated Consequences of Motivated Reasoning and the Dynamics of Partisan Presidential Approval." *Political Psychology* 28 (December): 719–46.

Lebo, Matthew J., and Andrew J. O'Geen. 2011. "The President's Role in the Partisan Congressional Arena." *Journal of Politics* 73 (July): 1–17.

Lee, Frances E. 2009. *Beyond Ideology: Politics, Principles, and Partisanship in U.S. the Senate.* Chicago: University of Chicago Press.

Lee, Han Soo. 2012. "Learning Presidents: Do Presidents Learn from the Public's Reactions to Their Behavior?" *The Forum* 10 (No. 2): online publication, http://www.degruyter.com/view/j/for.2012.10.issue-2/1540-8884.1472/1540-8884.1472.xml?format=INT.

Lenz, Gabriel S. 2013. *Follow the Leader? How Voters Respond to Politicians' Policies and Performance.* Chicago: University of Chicago Press.

Levendusky, Matthew S., Jeremy C. Pope, and Simon D. Jackman. 2008. "Measuring District-Level Partisanship with Implications for the Analysis of US Elections." *Journal of Politics* 70 (July): 736–53.

Levi, Margaret, and Laura Stoker. 2000. "Political Trust and Trustworthiness." *Annual Review of Political Science* 3: 475–507.

Levy, Dena, and Peverill Squire. 2000. "Television Markets and the Competitiveness of U.S. House Elections." *Legislative Studies Quarterly* 25 (May): 313–25.

Lewis-Beck, Michael S. 1988. *Economics and Elections.* Ann Arbor: University of Michigan Press.

Lewis-Beck, Michael S., William G. Jacoby, Helmut Norpoth, and Herbert F. Weisberg. 2009. *The American Voter Revisited.* Ann Arbor, MI: University of Michigan Press.

Lewis-Beck, Michael S., Nicholas F. Martini, D. Roderick Kiewiet. 2013. "The Nature of Economic Perceptions in Mass Publics." *Electoral Studies* 32 (September) 524–28.

Light, Paul C. 1982. *The President's Agenda: Domestic Policy Choice from Kennedy to Carter.* Baltimore, MD: Johns Hopkins University Press.

Light, Paul C. 1999. *The President's Agenda: Domestic Policy Choice from Kennedy to Clinton,* 3rd ed. Baltimore, MD: Johns Hopkins University Press.

Lockerbie, Brad, and Stephen A. Borrelli. 1989. "Getting inside the Beltway: Perceptions of Presidential Skill and Success in Congress." *British Journal of Political Science* 19 (January): 97–106.

Lockerbie, Brad, Stephen A. Borrelli, and Scott Hedger. 1998. "An Integrative Approach to Modeling Presidential Success in Congress." *Political Research Quarterly* 51 (March): 155–72.

Lowi, Theodore J. 1985. *The Personal President: Power Invested, Promise Unfulfilled.* Ithaca, NY: Cornell University Press.

Luskin, Robert C., and John G. Bullock. 2011. "'Don't Know' Means 'Don't Know': DK Responses and the Public's Level of Political Knowledge." *Journal of Politics* 73 (April): 547–57.

Manza, Jeff, and Fay Lomax Cook. 2002a. "A Democratic Polity? Three Views of Policy Responsiveness to Public Opinion in the United States." *American Politics Research* 30 (November): 630–67.

Manza, Jeff, and Fay Lomax Cook. 2002b. "The Impact of Public Opinion on Public Policy: The State of the Debate." In Jeff Manza, Fay Lomax Cook, and Benjamin I. Page, eds. *Navigating Public Opinion: Polls, Policy, and the Future of American Democracy.* New York: Oxford University Press, pp. 17–32.

Marshall, Bryan W., and Brandon C. Prins. 2007. "Strategic Position Taking and Presidential Influence in Congress." *Legislative Studies Quarterly* 32 (May): 257–84.

Masket, Seth. 2007. "It Takes an Outsider: Extra-legislative Organization And Partisanship in the California Assembly, 1849–2006." *American Journal of Political Science* 51 (July): 482–97.

Mattei, Franco, and Herbert F. Weisberg. 1994. "Presidential Succession Effects in Voting." *British Journal of Political Science* 24.4 (October): 495–516.

Matusow, Allen J. 1998. *Nixon's Economy: Booms, Busts, Dollars, and Votes.* Lawrence, KS: University Press of Kansas.

Mayer, Kenneth R. 2002. *With the Stroke of a Pen: Executive Orders and Presidential Power.* Princeton, NJ: Princeton University Press.

Mayhew, David R. 1974. "Congressional Elections: The Case of the Vanishing Marginals." *Polity* 6 (Spring): 295–317.

McAvoy, Gregory E. 2006. "Stability and Change: The Time Varying Impact of Economic and Foreign Policy Evaluations on Presidential Approval." *Political Research Quarterly* 59 (March): 71–83.

McAvoy, Gregory E. 2008. "Substance versus Style: Distinguishing Presidential Job Performance from Favorability." *Presidential Studies Quarterly* 38 (June): 284–99.

McClosky, Herbert, Paul J. Hoffman, and Rosemary O'Hara. 1960. "Issue Conflict and Consensus among Party Leaders and Followers." *American Political Science Review* 54 (June): 406–27.

McKay, David H. 1989. *Domestic Policy and Ideology: Presidents and the American State, 1964–1987.* New York: Cambridge University Press.

Memmott, Mark. 2012. "Love Blog: Romney Takes Aim at Obama's 'Appalling Lack of Leadership,'" National Public Radio, April 4, 2012, accessed on April 24, 2012, at http://www.npr.org/blogs/thetwo-way/2012/04/04/149992232/coming-up-romney-talks-to-news-editors.

Milkis, Sidney M. 1994. *The President and the Parties: The Transformation of the American Party System Since the New Deal.* New York: Oxford University Press.

Miller, Arthur H. 1974. "Political Issues and Trust in Government, 1964–1970." *American Political Science Review* 68 (September): 951–72.

Miller, Gary, and Norman Schofield. 2003. "Activists and Partisan Realignment in the United States." *American Political Science Review* 97 (May): 245–60.

Miller, Joanne M., and Jon A. Krosnick. 2000. "News Media Impact on the Ingredients of Presidential Evaluation: Politically Knowledgeable Citizens Are Guided by a Trusted Source." *American Journal of Political Science* 44 (April): 295–309.

Miller, Susan H. 1977. "News Coverage of Congress: The Search for the Ultimate Spokesman." *Journalism Quarterly* 54 (No. 3): 459–65.

Miller, Susan H. 1978. *Reporters and Congressmen: Living in Symbiosis.* Lexington, KY and Minneapolis, MN: Association for Education in Journalism.

Miller, Warren E., M. Kent Jennings, and Barbara G. Farah. 1986. *Parties in Transition: A Longitudinal Study of Party Elites and Party Followers.* New York: Russell Sage Foundation.

Mondak, Jeffrey J. 1993. "Source Cues and Public Approval: The Cognitive Dynamics of Public Support for the Reagan Administration." *American Journal of Political Science* 37 (February): 186–212.

Mondak, Jeffrey J. 2001. "Developing Valid Knowledge Scales." *American Journal of Political Science* 45 (January): 224–238.

Mondak, Jeffery J., Christopher J. Lewis, Jason C. Sides, Joohyun Kang, and J. Olyn Long. 2004. "Presidential Source Cues and Policy Appraisals, 1981–2000." *American Politics Research* 32 (March): 219–35.

Moore, David W. 1995. *The Superpollsters.* New York: Four Walls Eight Windows.

Murray, Shoon Kathleen. 2006. "Private Polls as Presidential Policymaking: Reagan as Facilitator of Change." *Public Opinion Quarterly* 70 (Winter): 477–98.

Mutz, Diana C. 1992. "Mass Media and the Depoliticization of Personal Experiences." *American Journal of Political Science* 36 (May): 483–508.

Mutz, Diana C. 1994. "Contextualizing Personal Experience: The Role of the Mass Media." *Journal of Politics* 56 (August): 689–714.

Mutz, Diana C. 2011. *Population-Based Survey Experiments.* Princeton, NJ: Princeton University Press.

Neustadt, Richard E. 1960. *Presidential Power: The Politics of Leadership.* New York: Wiley.

Neustadt, Richard E. 1991. *Presidential Power and the Modern Presidents: The Politics of Leadership from Roosevelt to Reagan.* New York: Simon and Schuster.

Newman, Brian. 2002. "Bill Clinton's Approval Ratings: The More Things Change, the More They Stay the Same." *Political Research Quarterly* 55 (December): 781–804.

Newman, Brian. 2003. "Integrity and Presidential Approval, 1980–2000." *Public Opinion Quarterly* 67 (Fall): 335–67.

Newman, Brian. 2004. "The Polls: Presidential Traits and Job Approval: Some Aggregate-Level Evidence." *Presidential Studies Quarterly* 34 (June): 437–48.

Newman, Brian, and Emerson Siegle. 2010. "Polls and Elections: The Polarized Presidency: Depth and Breadth of Public Partisanship." *Presidential Studies Quarterly* 40 (June): 342–63.

Newman, Brian, and Andrew Forcehimes. 2010. "'Rally Round the Flag' Events for Presidential Approval Research." *Electoral Studies* 29 (March): 144–54.

Newman, Brian, and Kevin Lammert. 2012. "Polls and Elections: Divided Government and Foreign Relations Approval." *Presidential Studies Quarterly* 41 (June): 375–92.

Nickelsburg, Michael, and Helmut Norpoth. 2000. "Commander-in-Chief or Chief Economist? The President in the Eye of the Public." *Electoral Studies* 19 (June): 313–32.

Nicholson, Stephen P., Gary M. Segura, and Nathan D. Woods. 2002. "Presidential Approval and the Mixed Blessing of Divided Government." *Journal of Politics* 64 (August): 701–20.

Niven, David, and Jeremy Zilber. 1998. "What's Newt Doing in People Magazine?" The Changing Effect of National Prominence in Congressional Elections." *Political Behavior* 20 (No. 3): 213–24.

Ostrom, Charles W., Jr., and Dennis M. Simon. 1985 "Promise and Performance: A Dynamic Model of Presidential Popularity." *American Political Science Review* 79 (June): 334–58.

Page, Benjamin I., and Robert Y. Shapiro. 1984. "Presidents as Opinion Leaders: Some New Evidence." *Policy Studies Journal* 12 (June): 649–61.

Page, Benjamin I., and Robert Y. Shapiro. 1992. *The Rational Public: Fifty Years of Trends in Americans' Policy Preferences.* Chicago: University of Chicago Press.

Page, Benjamin I., Robert Y. Shapiro, and Glenn R. Dempsey. 1987. "What Moves Public Opinion?" *American Political Science Review* 81 (March): 23–44.

Parker, Glenn R. 1977. "Some Themes in Congressional Unpopularity." *American Journal of Political Science* 21 (February): 93–109.

Parker, Glenn R., and Roger H. Davidson. 1979. "Why Do Americans Love Their Congressmen So Much More Than Their Congress." *Legislative Studies Quarterly* 4 (February): 53–61.

Patterson, Kelly D., and David B. Magleby. 1992. "Poll Trends: Public Support for Congress." *Public Opinion Quarterly* 56 (Winter): 539–51.

Patterson, Samuel C., and Gregory A. Caldeira. 1990. "Standing Up for Congress: Variations in Public Esteem since the 1960s." *Legislative Studies Quarterly* 15 (February): 25–47.

Patterson, Samuel C., Randall B. Ripley, and Stephen V. Quinlan. 1992. "Citizens' Orientations toward Legislatures: Congress and the State Legislature." *Western Political Quarterly* 45 (June): 315–38.

Patterson, Thomas E. 2000. "Doing Well and Doing Good: How Soft News and Critical Journalism are Shrinking the News Audience and Weakening Democracy—And What News Outlets Can Do About It." Joan Shorenstein Center for Press, Politics, and Public Policy, John F. Kennedy School of Government, Harvard University.

Pessen, Edward. 1984. *The Log Cabin Myth: The Social Backgrounds of the Presidents.* New Haven, CT: Yale University Press.

Peterson, Mark A. 1990. *Legislating Together: The White House and Capitol Hill from Eisenhower to Reagan.* Cambridge, MA: Harvard University Press.

Pickup, Mark Alexander, and Christopher Wlezien. 2009. "On Filtering Longitudinal Public Opinion Data: Issues in Identification and Representation of True Change." *Electoral Studies* 28 (September): 354–67.

Poole, Keith T., and Howard Rosenthal. 1997. *Congress: A Politico-Economic History of Roll Call Voting*. New York: Oxford University Press.

Powell, G. Bingham, Jr., and Guy D. Whitten. 1993. "A Cross-National Analysis of Economic Voting: Taking Account of the Political Context." *American Journal of Political Science* 37 (May): 391–414.

Ragsdale, Lyn. 1991. "Strong Feelings: Emotional Responses to Presidents." *Political Behavior* 13 (No. 1): 33–65.

Ragsdale, Lyn. 2009. *Vital Statistics on the Presidency*. 3rd ed. Washington, DC: CQ Press.

Ramirez, Mark D. 2009. "The Dynamics of Partisan Conflict on Congressional Approval." *American Journal of Political Science* 53 (July): 681–94.

Ramirez, Mark D. 2013. "The Policy Origins of Congressional Approval." *Journal of Politics* 75 (January): 198–209.

Rivers, Douglas, and Nancy L. Rose. 1985. "Passing the President's Program: Public Opinion and Presidential Influence in Congress." *American Journal of Political Science* 29 (May): 183–96.

Roberts, Scott L., and Brandon M. Butler. 2012. "Idealizing and Localizing the Presidency: The President's Place in State History Textbooks." In Heather Hickman and Brad J. Porfilio, eds. *The New Politics of the Textbook Critical Analysis in the Core Content Areas*. Rotterdam, The Netherlands: SensePublishers.

Robinson, Michael J., and Kevin R. Appel. 1979. "Network News Coverage of Congress." *Political Science Quarterly* 94 (Autumn): 407–18.

Rockman, Bert A. 1984. *The Leadership Question: The Presidency and the American System*. New York: Praeger.

Rosen, Corey M. 1973. "A Test of Presidential Leadership of Public Opinion: The Split-Ballot Technique." *Polity* 6 (Winter): 282–90.

Rottinghaus, Brandon. 2010. *The Provisional Pulpit: Modern Presidential Leadership of Public Opinion*. College Station, TX: Texas A & M University Press.

Rozell, Mark J. 1996. *In Contempt of Congress: Postwar Press Coverage on Capitol Hill*. Westport, CT: Greenwood.

Rudolph, Thomas J. 2002. "The Economic Sources of Congressional Approval." *Legislative Studies Quarterly* 27 (November): 577–99.

Sanchez, J. M. 1996. "Old Habits Die Hard: The Textbook Presidency is Alive and Well." *PS: Political Science and Politics*. 29 (March): 63–66.

Saunders, Kyle L., and Alan I. Abramowitz. 2004. "Ideological Realignment and Active Partisans in the American Electorate." *American Politics Research* 32 (No. 3): 285–309.

Schaffner, Brian F., and Patrick Sellers. 2003. "The Structural Determinants of Local Congressional News Coverage." *Political Communication* 20 (No. 1): 41–57.

Scheele, Paul E. 1978. "President Carter and the Water Projects: A Case Study in Presidential and Congressional Decision-Making." *Presidential Studies Quarterly* 8 (Fall): 348–64.

Schoen, Douglas E., and Jessica Tarlov. 2012. "A Mandate for Moderation: Voters Didn't Validate Obama Wholesale." *New York Daily News*, Thursday, November 29, 2012, accessed online at http://www.nydailynews.com/opinion/mandate-moderation-article-1.1209717, June 6, 2013.

Sellers, Patrick. 2010. *Cycles of Spin: Strategic Communication in the U.S. Congress.* New York: Cambridge University Press.

Shafer Byron E. 2003. *The Two Majorities and the Puzzle of Modern American Politics.* Lawrence, KS: University Press of Kansas.

Shaffer, William R. 1980. "A Discriminant Function Analysis of Position-Taking: Carter vs. Kennedy." *Presidential Studies Quarterly* 10 (Summer): 451–68.

Shapiro, Robert Y. 2011. "Public Opinion and American Democracy." *Public Opinion Quarterly* 75 (No. 5): 982–1017.

Shields, Todd, and Robert K. Goidel. 1996. "The President and Congress as Sources in Television News Coverage of the National Debt." *Polity* 28 (Spring): 401–10.

Shull, Steven A., and James M. Vanderleeuw. 1987. "What Do Key Votes Measure?" *Legislative Studies Quarterly* 12 (November): 573–82.

Sidman, Andrew H., Maxwell Mak, and Matthew J. Lebo. 2008. "Forecasting Nonincumbent Presidential Elections: Lessons Learned from the 2000 Election." *International Journal of Forecasting* 24 (April–June): 237–58.

Sidman, Andrew H., and Helmut Norpoth. 2012. "Fighting to Win: Wartime Morale in the American Public." *Electoral Studies* 31 (June): 330–41.

Sigelman, Lee. 1979. "Presidential Popularity and Presidential Elections." *Public Opinion Quarterly* 43 (Winter): 532–34.

Sigelman, Lee. 1980. "Gauging the Public Response to Presidential Leadership." *Presidential Studies Quarterly* 10 (Summer): 427–33.

Sigelman, Lee, and Pamela Johnston Conover. 1981. "The Dynamics of Presidential Support during International Conflict Situations: The Iranian Hostage Crisis." *Political Behavior* 3 (No. 4): 303–18.

Simon, Dennis M. 2009. "Public Expectations of the President." In George C. Edwards III and William G. Howell, eds. *The Oxford Handbook of the American Presidency.* New York: Oxford University Press, pp. 135–59.

Sinclair, Barbara. 1992. "The Emergence of Strong Leadership in the 1980s House of Representatives." *Journal of Politics* 54 (August): 657–84.

Skowronek, Stephen S. 1993. *The Politics Presidents Make: Leadership from Jon Adams to George Bush.* Cambridge, MA: Harvard University Press.

Smith, Hedrick. 1978. "For President a Vital Victory." *The New York Times*, March 17, 1978, p. A12.

Song, Anna V., and Dean Keith Simonton. 2007. "Personality Assessment at a Distance." In Richard W. Robins, R. Chris Fraley, and Robert F. Krueger, eds. *Handbook of Research Methods in Personality Psychology.* New York: Guilford Press, pp. 308–21.

Soumbatiants, Souren, Henry W. Chappell, Jr., and Eric Johnson. 2006. "Using State Polls to Forecast US Presidential Election Outcomes." *Public Choice* 127 (April): 207–23.

Sovey, Allison J., and Donald P. Green. 2011. "Instrumental Variables Estimation in Political Science: A Readers' Guide." *American Journal of Political Science* 55 (January): 188–200.

Squire, Peverill. 1988. "Who Gets National News Coverage in the US Senate?" *American Politics Research* 16 (April): 139–56.

Stanley, Timothy Randolph. 2009. "'Sailing against the Wind': A Reappraisal of Edward Kennedy's Campaign for the 1980 Democratic Party Presidential Nomination." *Journal of American Studies* 43 (August): 231–53.

Stern, Mark. 1992. *Calculating Visions: Kennedy, Johnson, and Civil Rights.* New Brunswick, NJ: Rutgers University Press.

Stevenson, Randolph T., and Raymond Duch. 2013. "The Meaning and Use of Subjective Perceptions in Studies of Economic Voting." *Electoral Studies* 32 (June) 305–20.

Stimson, James A. 1976. "Public Support for American Presidents A Cyclical Model." *Public Opinion Quarterly* 40 (Spring): 1–21.

Stimson, James A. 1999. *Public Opinion in America: Moods, Cycles, and Swings.* 2nd ed. Boulder, CO: Westview Press.

Stock, James H., and Mark W. Watson. 2007. *Introduction to Econometrics: International Edition.* 2nd ed. Upper Saddle River, NJ: Prentice Hall.

Tedin, Kent. 1986. "Change and Stability in Presidential Popularity at the Individual Level." *Journal of Politics* 40 (Winter): 1–21.

Tedin, Kent, Brandon Rottinghaus, and Harrell Rodgers. 2011. "When the President Goes Public: The Consequences of Communication Mode for Opinion Change across Issue Types and Groups." *Political Research Quarterly* 64 (September): 506–19.

Thomas, Dan, and Lee Sigleman. 1984. "Presidential Identification and Policy Leadership: Experimental Evidence on the Reagan Case." *Policy Studies Journal* 12 (No. 4): 663–75.

Tidmarch, Charles M. and John J. Pitney, Jr. 1985. "Covering Congress." *Polity* 17 (Spring): 463–83.

Valentino, Nicholas. 1999. "Crime News and the Priming of Racial Attitudes During Evaluations of the President." *Public Opinion Quarterly* 63 (Autumn): 293–320.

Vermeer, Jan Pons. 1987. *Campaigns in the Media: Mass Media and Congressional Elections.* Westport, CT: Greenwood Press.

Vinson, Danielle. 2003. *Local Media Coverage of Congress and its Members: Through Local Eyes.* Cresskill, NJ: Hampton Press.

Waterman, Richard W., Hank C. Jenkins-Smith and Carol L. Silva. 1999. "The Expectations Gap Thesis: Public Attitudes toward an Incumbent President." *Journal of Politics* 61 (November): 944–66.

Waterman, Richard W., Gilbert St. Clair, and Robert Wright. 1999. *The Image-Is-Everything Presidency: Dilemmas in American Leadership.* Boulder, CO: Westview Press.

Waterman, Richard W., and Bert A. Rockman. 2008. "What is Presidential Leadership?" in Bert A. Rockman and Richard W. Waterman, eds. *Presidential Leadership: The Vortex of Power.* New York: Oxford University Press, pp. 1–17.

Wattenberg, Martin P. 1991. *The Rise of Candidate-centered Politics: Presidential Elections of the 1980s.* Cambridge, MA: Harvard University Press.

Wayne, Stephen J. 1982. "Expectations of the President." In Doris Graber, ed. *The President and the Public.* Philadelphia, PA: Institute for the Study of Human Affairs, pp. 17–38.

Weisberg, Herbert F. 2002. "Partisanship and Incumbency in Presidential Elections." *Political Behavior* 24 (December): 339–60.

Weissberg, Robert. 1978. "Collective vs. Dyadic Representation in Congress." *American Political Science Review* 72 (June): 535–47.

West, Darrell M. 1991. "Television and Presidential Popularity in America." *British Journal of Political Science* 21 (April): 199–214.

Wilson, Woodrow. 1885 (reprinted 1958). *Congressional Government.* Boston: Houghton Mifflin (1885); New York: Meridian Books (1958).

Wilson, Woodrow. 1908 (reprinted 1961). *Constitutional Government in the United States.* New York: Columbia University Press.

Winter, David G. 2002. "Motivation and Political Leadership." In Linda O. Valenty and Ofer Feldman, eds. *Political Leadership for the New Century: Personality and Behavior among American Leaders.* Westport, CT: Praeger, pp. 25–47.

Winter, David G. 2005. "Things I've Learned About Personality From Studying Political Leaders at a Distance." *Journal of Personality* 73 (June): 557–84.

Wlezien, Christopher and Christopher Carman. 2001. "Ideological Placements and Political Judgments of Government Institutions." *Public Opinion Quarterly* 65 (Winter): 550–61.

Wlezien, Christopher and Stuart Soroka. 2007. "Public Opinion and Public Policy." In Russell J. Dalton and Hans-Dieter Klingemann, eds. *The Oxford Handbook of Political Behavior.* New York: Oxford University Press, pp. 799–817.

Wood, B. Dan. 2007. *The Politics of Economic Leadership: The Causes and Consequences of Presidential Rhetoric.* Princeton, NJ: Princeton University Press.

Wood, B. Dan. 2009. *The Myth of Presidential Representation.* New York: Cambridge University Press.

Wood, B. Dan. 2012. *Presidential Saber Rattling: Causes and Consequences.* New York: Cambridge University Press.

Wood, B. Dan, and Han Soo Lee. 2009. "Explaining the President's Issue Based Liberalism: Pandering, Partisanship, or Pragmatism." *Journal of Politics* 71 (October): 1577–92.

Zaller, John. 1992. *The Nature and Origins of Mass Opinion.* New York: Cambridge University Press.

Zaller, John R. 1998. "Monica Lewinsky's Contribution to Political Science." *PS: Political Science and Politics* 31 (June): 182–89.

Zilber, Jeremy, and David Niven. 2000. *Racialized Coverage of Congress: The News in Black and White.* Westport, CT: Greenwood Publishing Group.

Index

HARVARD UNIVERSITY

http://lib.harvard.edu

**If the item is recalled, the borrower will
be notified of the need for an earlier return.**

Thank you for helping us to preserve our collection!